Trevor's Travels

Trevor's Travels

in Southern California

Trevor Summons

TREVOR'S TRAVELS
IN SOUTHERN CALIFORNIA

iUniverse books may be ordered through booksellers or by contacting:

iUniverse
1663 Liberty Drive
Bloomington, IN 47403
www.iuniverse.com
1-800-Authors (1-800-288-4677)

ISBN: 978-1-4917-8582-9 (sc)
ISBN: 978-1-4917-8583-6 (e)

Library of Congress Control Number: 2015921136

Print information available on the last page.

iUniverse rev. date: 01/11/2016

CONTENTS

THIS BOOK IS the result of 15 years of a weekly Sunday column, called Trevor's Travels, published in The San Bernardino Sun and other publications in the Los Angeles Newspaper Group.

I'm proud to say that in that time I have only missed about a dozen issues through scheduling difficulties, but mostly it's there each Sunday morning for the readers.

The catchment area of Southern California is quite large, and to begin with I tried hard to keep my wanderings to the county of San Bernardino, which is the largest county in the USA.

However my editors have been kind enough to allow me to travel outside the area and on occasions even capitalize on my trips abroad. These columns have not been included, but they will make up the contents of another volume to be published soon.

Each of the 150 weekly columns is about 700 words long and often contains photographs to help with the story. Some of these photos are included here.

The general idea of the Trevor's Travels column is to persuade people to forgo the couch, and even the Sunday football game to get out and explore the many places of interest in our area. That too is the object of this book, which might also be used as a reference for enjoyment and curiosity.

From art galleries to minor league baseball, I've tried to cover most places that might entice a visitor.

Due to the extended time period, some of the references to past events may no longer be relevant, but I have avoided dating the items as they should stand alone. However as these columns stretch back a decade and a half I recommend checking the Web sites in case opening times have changed. I have deliberately left off pricing as this is often changing. Once again the Web sites will provide details.

From the Museum of Death to the wonders of the Getty Museum, there's a lot out there to explore; so get out and enjoy this bounty of treasures in Southern California. At least you don't have to worry about the weather!

FIRE LOOKOUTS

NESTLING IN A cluster of microwave and repeater station antennas stands the most eastern of the Mountaintop San Bernardino fire lookouts, Strawberry Peak. It is from this point and its two sister stations that the watch is kept for the suddenness of fire in the region.

As we enter the period of maximum dryness and the approaching Santa Ana winds to fan the flames, sharp eyes are constantly scanning the mountains for any symptoms of fire; that most devastating and dangerous phenomenon. From Strawberry Peak, such eyes belong to one of the many volunteers in the Fire Lookout Host program, Marge Gardner. She has been doing this work on a part time basis for three years.

A native of Oregon, but having lived for many years in Atlanta, she came to Southern California because she "was attracted to the wonderful blue skies." Now a resident of Lake Arrowhead, she drives to and from the lookouts in the Mountaintop Region, to look for fires and also to greet the many visitors that come to her lofty towers.

Keller Peak Fire Lookout

The three lookouts are great points of interest for visitors from all over the world, as the visitor books will attest. Recently a group of Chinese tourists unloaded to take in the views, as they had heard glowing reports about the towers. And the sites are fairly easy to reach. Strawberry Peak is perhaps the easiest. It is just outside Rim Forest on Highway 18. You take Bear Springs Road, which is well-paved with the lookout post at the end of a two miles stretch. The tower was built in 1933 and is 6,153 feet above sea level. A short climb up to the top will provide you with wonderful views of the San Bernardino Valley, Pomona Valley and out across Bloomington, Rialto and Fontana. To the north you can see into the desert and out across Lake Arrowhead.

All three posts are continuously manned from Memorial Day to the first snow, and being within some thirty miles of each other, are a great opportunity to see some of the best views in the whole of the State. And you can be sure of a welcome by all of the volunteers. Each day two of them climb the stairs to their posts; one in the morning and one in the afternoon. Here they scan the mountains for any telltale signs of smoke. If storm clouds gather and lightening is seen, then they have to clear their cabins of visitors and concentrate on the strikes, noting where each lands. Marge Gardner points to the furniture in her room, which has glass insulators at the ends of all of the legs.

The bed, chairs, and stools are all so insulated in the event of a direct strike. Her duties are to look through the Osborne Fire Finder, which is the center of her operations, mark the strike and radio the fire crews, who are waiting for instructions.

The same procedure is carried out at Keller Peak, which is the oldest lookout, built in 1926. Here, hosts Charles Hennessey and Ellen Baum, show off the specifics of their building. It is a wooden cabin of 14' by 14' perched on the top of a granite hill with views of Snow Summit, Sugarloaf Mountain, and the San Gabriel Mountains. It survived the Bear Fire of 1970, and also served as the almost permanent home of Wilma "Billie" Murphy, a fire-watcher from 1939 to 1965. Here she lived with her dog, with only the radio for company.

On display are also some remnants of the tragic Airforce crash that took place on December 30, 1941. A B26 took off from Edward's base and due to some adverse conditions in the Cajon Pass came through the mountains. Its wing just hit the ground below Keller Peak and the plane crashed, killing all nine of its occupants. A plaque is on the rock below the lookout.

Keller Peak is located 1 mile east of Running Springs on Highway 18. It is a five-mile drive on a twisting well-paved road just east of Deerlick Fire Station, through some spectacular country. The view from Butler Peak is the last and perhaps the best of all three, as it is at 8,535 feet. However the drive does offer some challenges. It is located west of Fawnskin along 3N14, and then onto 2N13. It is important to watch for 2N13C, which is a sharp left turn at about three miles out of Fawnskin. The road is unpaved, but quite easy to traverse, and the effort is well worth it.

The tower was built in 1936 and commands views out across the desert, Big Bear Lake and to the south, the San Bernardino Valley. You do need good walking shoes to climb the last few rocks to the steps into the tower, where once again, you will be met by an enthusiastic host for the day.

Due to the atmosphere, the views are best experienced from all three towers earlier rather than later. Smog can build up in the Valleys, and also mists begin to gather after lunch. It the Santa Anas are blowing then all the mists disappear, but in normal conditions, it is best to get there as soon after opening as possible.

You can visit all three towers easily in a day, and entrance is free, although a small donation is much appreciated. More information can be obtained from the Forest Service or at any Ranger Station. The lookouts are open from 9.00am to 5.00pm every day in the season.

PIONEERTOWN

Pioneertown's Church on Mane Street

FORTY MILES OF good road separate the two valley townships of Lucerne and Yucca. Route 247 is a two-lane highway running through clean desert views, with the San Bernardino Mountains off to one side and desert floor off to the other. With a 65 mph speed limit, one can make the journey in close to half an hour and pass near to the small town of Landers, scene of the earthquake that occurred ten years ago this June. Just beyond the curiously named Flamingo Heights - one wonders if the Floridian bird has ever been seen in these parts - there is a turning to Pipes Canyon, and a seven-mile link to Pioneertown road.

Straight across this road is a one-mile unpaved road leading to the Pipes Canyon Nature Preserve, which is a privately funded area bought by the Wildlands Conservancy Group for the benefit of all those interested in wildlife and its surroundings

The preserve is a silent oasis of some of the best scenery in the desert, and it is very quiet. Apart from the gentle breezes rustling through the grasses and the occasional birdsong from one of the windswept trees, it is a place to escape the sounds of humanity, and enjoy the trails that have been marked out. Every so often a quail will run through the undergrowth waving its jaunty headdress, and the odd rabbit will race around as well. But mostly you have to look carefully to see the large eco-system living here although well-marked notices along the trail will inform you of its proximity.

Rattlesnakes live in this area and it is as well to be aware of them. They are not normally dangerous unless they are disturbed or cornered, as they don't like us any more than we like them. Also black bear are often seen in the hills round about, as well as cougars, coyotes, foxes and weasels. There are two principal trails for ramblers, one of 5.6-mile, and a longer one of seven miles, which climbs up 1500 feet. From here you can look down on the many birds that visit the various waterholes in the park.

Once your appetite for wildlife is filled then perhaps you should re-enter the human arena with a gentle introduction via the simple delights of Pioneertown, which is just two miles down the road from the Preserve.

Originally built for movies and somewhere for the crew to stay, then adapted to regular life by Roy Rogers and a bunch of his friends, this is a real small town. It looks older than it is, as it was thought of mainly as a movie set, when it was erected in 1946. It still has an unfinished look as if old developers were waiting for some nineteenth century planning permission to come through, but that only adds to its charm.

A sound studio is up for sale here giving the place a link with its entertainment past, and one wonders what sort of music would be recorded there these days. But with a dusty Mane (sic) Street and an old fashioned six-lane bowling alley, where Roy Rogers bowled the first ball - naturally it was a strike - this is a place that reeks of yesteryear. A walking tour will lead you past a score of numbered sites. Number four is the Photo Shop, with a fine saguaro cactus right outside that must be one of the best and most photographed around.

Pioneertown is closed during the week, and begins to come to life Thursday afternoons. On Sundays there are gunfights in the center of town, and live music at Pappy and Harriet's Place at the end of town. Three Dog Night, Eric Burden, and Donovan have all performed here. The Place also serves good food from the bar. It's a real family business going back a couple of generations.

Pioneertown was named after The Sons of the Pioneers, who were the original investors. Many of them stayed at the motel, which has 19 rooms if you should decide to stay over. You can be assured that many famous stars of the old western days have stayed there before you. Russell Hayden, Bud Abbott and Gene Autry were all keen on the place as well as the famous Roy Rogers. Here they made such famous films as The Cisco Kid, Judge Roy Bean and Hopalong Cassidy. Louella Parsons would also come along to critique their lives and report accordingly. But good times have always been the order of things here, and the same is true today.

LAKE GREGORY

WATER ALWAYS TENDS to draw people, and the lake that gives Lake Gregory its name is certainly a crowd magnet. It was filled in 1938 and it is three miles around totaling 86 acres. Superintendent Bart Ryder oversees the smooth running of the water facilities and he has witnessed a steady increase in visitors over recent years.

Lake Gregory is a township that is larger than at first appears. It has some 12,000 residents, who have chosen this little piece of alpine heaven as their permanent home. The number swells on the weekends with people escaping from the lower area's heat, traffic and smog. The combed and manicured sands around the lake are one of the reasons the visitors come.

On the water itself, there are many activities to enjoy. Kayaks, windsurfers, canoes and pedal craft are for hire, and trained lifeguards monitor the swim beach. There is a twin-flumed water slide, and in fact everything you would want for a day at the beach, without the surf.

For those with a desire to pit their wits against the local fish, there is plenty of year round lake access, outside the swim beach. The website for Lake Gregory Regional Park is sbcounty.gov/parks.

Lake Gregory falls within the Crestline area for commercial activities, and a spokesperson for the Chamber of Commerce reports that equal federal funds have been promised for an overall face-lift for the main street of the town. Currently there is an assortment of local business catering to residents and visitors alike. Small restaurants compete for eating dollars and there are several souvenir and antique shops in the town.

Lake Gregory is proud of having its own bowling alley. It was built in the early sixties and its 16 lanes host many local leagues, as well as the increasingly popular "Cosmic" bowling. Here the lights are mostly turned off, except for the "black" lights that show up the effects and heighten the music sounds. It's becoming quite a local scene.

Many of the residents chose the town as being that little bit lower in elevation to the top of the mountain. Its level is 4,700 feet, which means it escapes the heavier snows and ice at Running Springs and Big Bear. But it does not lose any of the mountain feeling, while allowing visitors to arrive sooner than if they were on the longer drive. It is hoped that the upcoming improvements will not remove the small town feel and the friendly atmosphere.

For those wishing to try something different, make the turn off Route 30 for the three miles of Lake Gregory Drive, and see what a true beach resort in the mountains can do for you. For more information, visit the Crestline website at crestlinechamber.net, or call (909) 338-2706.

SEVEN OAKS

AS YOU MAKE your way up Route 38 to the Big Bear Area, you may admire the new black top surface and bright yellow lines that separate the traffic lanes, and allow the motorists to speed safely and easily to their designations. But imagine what it must have been like before the days of concrete and tarmac. Even before there was a Route 38 to travel over. It was not long ago.

In order to reach Big Bear in the mid-nineteenth century the preferred way was Clarke's Grade, which twisted and turned up a sharp incline from the bottom of the Santa Ana River to the crest of the hills above. It was done mostly by oxcart and the journey could take days. Therefore it was not surprising that travelers would like to break the arduous journey, and in 1845 one Charles Mathew Lewis did just that.

He chose a spot that he named Seven Oaks after his beloved English hometown of Sevenoaks, in Kent. It was a place just five miles below the source of the Santa Ana River and is just four miles off Route 38 along Glass Road. It is now, as it was then, full of leafy tress with plenty of shade. It became a sheep ranch and then with the opening of Big Bear Lake, it developed into a resort.

The current owner, Earl Fink, discovered Seven Oaks in 1977, and decided that it would be an ideal future for his family. "It took me a couple of years to get the place right," he says. "It badly needed plumbing and electrical work." His hard work paid off and now it is a favorite stop for visitors to the region and it has a lot to offer. It is in fact the oldest resort in Southern California.

The river bubbles through with fish to delight an angler's heart. Trout and German Browns are among the favorites. You can camp out beside the river and sleep to the gentle sound of the river. There is a duck pond, and a bar and lounge. The original Lodge dates back to 1876 and is now Earl's home with a well stocked gift shop on the ground floor.

The restaurant is open on the weekends. Fink says: "We specialize in good American food, and we have a games room next door to keep the children happy." The store is open seven days a week and stocks most things a passing traveler or visitor might need. RV hook-ups are also available.

There is a charge for day use but that entitles a visitor to the use of the swimming pool - different from the duck pond! Hiking trails spread out to Barton Flats and other mountain designations. And you can easily see the old Clarke's Grade from many places along the way.

The Porsche Company is planning to assist in re-opening the grade with local authorities. This is in order to promote off road activity in which their cars can take part. It will no doubt stir the air above tranquil Seven Oaks, but the river will still meander and the fish will still jump as they have done now for some hundred and twenty-five years.

For directions and reservations call (909) 794-2917.

LAKE SILVERWOOD

THE LAKES IN the San Bernardino Mountains this past summer have all been suffering from the drought and dropping levels. Big Bear Lake is down thirteen feet and although much deeper, Lake Arrowhead is down too. Lake Gregory is suffering as well. However at a little lower elevation, Lake Silverwood is as full as ever and we have the California Aqueduct to thank for that, as well as the mostly underground Mojave River.

The water for the lake flows 700 miles from Lake Orville to the north, and when Silverwood was created thirty years ago, it meant the flooding of a small town. Today, this little community is left to its silent watery grave out where boaters enjoy their leisure time. The lake is the highest in the California State Water Project and a tribute to some very dramatic engineering.

There is no charge to launch your boat, although there is a $3.00 parking fee. Ranger Bobbie Scissel reports, however, "We're not just for boats though. We have two swimming areas and thirteen miles of shoreline." It is also acknowledged to be a wonderful place for nature lovers. "We have over 130 species of birds here," she explains. "And in the winter months, we have free bald eagle tours on the weekends." Bears, mountain lions, bobcats and coyotes also share the space with their human friends, although you have to be on the alert to ever see them.

There are four parks located along the Mojave River and three of these are run by the San Bernardino County Parks Department. Each one is unique and Silverwood is the only one where boats can go. The others are mostly for fishing, horseback riding and of course, communing with nature.

With the San Bernardino Mountains on three of its sides however, Lake Silverwood has an atmosphere of being in the hills, but being very accessible from Interstate 15, and then Highways 173 and 138, it is ideal for a short day trip. BBQ areas and picnic tables make it an easy and fun place for the whole family even if you don't have a boat. But if you do, remember there is a 35 mph speed limit on the water, but that seems plenty fast enough for most people. For more information contact the park at (760) 389-2303. Information is also available on all the county parks at www.sbcounty.gov/parks.

Just six miles down the road there is the Mojave River Forks Park, which used to be under private ownership, but is now run by the California State Parks Department. Here there are over 100 camp sites within 600 acres, and it is truly a peaceful place to spend your time. Hiking is the great favorite here and also there are many trails for horses to cover. No off road vehicles are permitted and this helps in creating the sense of solitude that reigns. With plenty of organized areas it is a fine place for groups to gather for picnics and BBQ's.

Mojave River Forks Park is located on Highway 138.

CALICO 1

THE GHOST TOWN of Calico, and the hills surrounding it, has a romantic sound to the name. It was christened Calico by a bunch of old men sitting around one quiet evening over 100 years ago. At that time one of them said that the place was as pretty as a young girl's calico skirt; and the name stuck. So says Steve Nelson, who has been the town's marketing director and film coordinator for the last six years. "It is a pretty place," he says. "And Hollywood has recognized that, since they have made a number of memorable films here. The latest being Broken Arrow with John Travolta."

Even in the height of summer, the atmosphere of this old town remains calm and bearable in the heat of the day. "The reason is because there's always a nice breeze coming through, and that attracts people." Nelson adds, and to prove it another busload of tourists joins the strolling visitors to snap away with their cameras. "They're here just in time to see one of the gunfights that go on throughout the day." Sure enough, an argument breaks out and Marshall Dallas Shelby is called to quiet things down. The protagonist proves difficult and Marshall Dallas is forced to draw his antique Colt and shoot the fellow right there, in the center of the main street. Fortunately, the Marshall's bullets are as blank as the actor's eyes as he hits the dirt. He jumps up again, the tourists applaud and business resumes once more.

Marshall Dallas is regularly joined by several volunteers to look after things. Many of them come from the Mojave Muleskinners. Gunfighter Cliff Whitehorse says: "We've even got our own website." Which rather brings them into present days, although they seem the genuine article as most of Calico does. It has 23 shops and businesses, where interesting and unique items are sold. Many of the sites are original, like the 1000-foot deep mine. Vendors' stalls are around the town at convenient locations for a quick snack or a beverage. It's not quite the same as the original 20 bars that the town supported in its hey day, but they are attractive and, above all, safe from the violence of the past.

Unfortunately a fire started last year in the candle shop, and destroyed six of the buildings, but things are back to normal now, and the town is eagerly awaiting Calico Days. This has been a tradition for the last 36 years and from October 11th to the 13th every kind of Western celebration can be enjoyed. Among a packed event itinerary there will be a two-day gunfight championship, during which no doubt the Muleskinners will give a good account of themselves. A burro run will charge through the streets and 5 nations will hold displays of Native American dances and culture. On opening night, after the re-dedication of the town, which officially opens the town following the fire there will be a steak fry and dance. On Saturday night the Riders of the Purple Sage give a "starlight cowboy concert," starting at 7.00pm. The event finishes with a Trailride from Camp, which starts at 9.00am on Sunday, and also the finals of the Miners' Triathlon

Calico had a population of 5,000 people in its prime around 1902, and it was the largest silver boomtown in all of California. It is said that Wyatt Earp came here, although it has not been proven. However, his lofty ideals might have been the reason that fatal shootings were kept down to a minimal one, which was very low for the times. Nelson says: "They were so busy digging for silver and then spending all their time in the bars, there was little time for killing."

Mr. Knott of Knott's Berry Farm visited here, and said that if he made his fortune, he would want to come back and buy the place, he was so taken with it. He made that fortune, and in the nineteen-forties returned with checkbook in hand. It was under the control of the Knott's family until 1966, when it was donated to San Bernardino Parks, who have looked after it ever since. In 1972 it was awarded landmark status, and today it is a self-funding operation with over 500,000 visitors last year. It accepts no tax dollars from the state.

Sadly for Calico's original life, the silver began to run out and prices began to drop, so it rapidly ended its boom years. Today there are still occasional mine markers in place from private miners, who search for nuggets of the ore, but it is now a place of memories. The heavy traffic along route 15 from Las Vegas might forget the place as it roars along, but it is well worth the time to take the turn off to Calico Ghost Town. It is just a few miles from Barstow, and here you can wander along the tree-lined streets and recall times gone past. You will almost certainly find Marshall Dallas upholding the law, as there always seems to be a regular line of characters from the past that need his persuasion to behave in front of visitors.

CALICO 2

ONCE AGAIN FOR the tenth year, the Ghost town of Calico will rumble with the sound of troops' gunfire, as they reenact the battles of the Civil War. The weekend of February 14, 15 and 16 will draw spectators and combatants alike in a great show of force.

"We want to provide people with a real sense of the Civil War by allowing them to enter an occupied town that would have been under attack," said Ken Guinn, President of the American Civil War Society. Guinn will be presenting all the reenactments at the site.

"Calico is unique in being able to offer an entire town for troop occupation," Guinn continued. "Nowhere else on the West Coast can the public enter an historic town, interact with the troops and experience life during the Great War. There is a great sense of history here."

The weekend will offer two one-hour battles each day. They will occur on Saturday and Sunday at 11:45 a.m. and 2:30 p.m. and on Monday at 11:30 a.m. and 2 p.m. Ten thousand rounds of ammunition will be fired during these battles and the sound of cannon will resound over the area, presenting a spectacle not often seen in California.

Under normal conditions, Calico is a peaceful place. It received its name over 100 years ago from a bunch of old men sitting out under the evening skies. They thought the place was a pretty as a young girl's calico skirt, and so the place was named.

On weekends, there are regular gunfights in the town. Many of them come from the Mojave Muleskinners. Gunfighter Cliff Whitehorse says: "We've even got our own Web site." Which rather brings them into the present days, although they seem the genuine article as most of Calico does. It has 23 shops and businesses, where interesting and unique items are sold. Many of the sites are original, like the 1000-foot deep mine. Vendors' stalls are around the town at convenient locations for a quick snack or a beverage.

Calico used to be a magnet for the early silver miners. At one time its population was 5,000 and there are rumors that the famous Wyatt Earp came here, although it's never been proved. Nonetheless it was a fairly peaceful place with a low incidence of violence. "Maybe they were all so busy digging for silver and drinking in the bars," an employee remarked.

Sadly for Calico's original life, the silver began to run out and prices began to drop, so it rapidly ended its boom years. Today there are still occasional mine markers in place from private miners, who search for nuggets of the ore, but it is now principally a place of memories.

Town manager, Ernie Escajeda reported a new event coming up. "We will have the Death Valley Museum here on March 1st." he reported. "It's been traveling around the world and you need to be on the waiting list to have it. It will be here for three months." The exhibit will be a walk in display of items from the famous region.

Gunfighters in Calico

On the weekend of President's Day however, visitors to Calico will have their minds on one of the great defining moments of this country's history, where the Blue and the Gray will again fight it out in one of the most historical settings in the state.

Where: Calico Ghost Town
Ghost Town Road, and I-15
Just 10 minutes north of Barstow

Hours: 9 a.m. to 5 p.m. daily

For more information call 1 (800)-TO-CALICO or visit the Web site www.calicotown.com

LYTLE CREEK

AS AN EXAMPLE of the huge difference in Southern California's environment, you only have to drive the short distance from Fontana's burgeoning housing estates up into the hills around Lytle Creek. Sierra Avenue changes to Lytle Creek Road when it goes under Interstate 15, and suddenly one is out in wild country with the mountains and nature all around.

Like most places in the San Bernardino Mountains, some restrictions are in operation to protect us from the dangers of fire. It has been one of the driest periods on record, and it only needs a spark to start a firestorm. The authorities have wisely chosen to keep the greatest risk at bay by keeping humans out. However, the rangers and staff at Lytle creek, who man the station from 8.00am to 4.30pm will continue to make your trip to the area interesting and enjoyable.

Chaeli Judd, who is a Public Information Technician at the Ranger Station, says: "We get lots of people here from the local cities. They come up on the weekends to picnic with their families." There are several picnic areas within a short distance of the road. "We also have several trails and other outdoor activities that are still open."

Seven miles along the road from the Ranger Station up into the hills, there is a Target Shooting Range, which is open from Thursday through Monday. There is an $8.00 fee for shooters and a $1.00 fee for spectators. And although the creek levels are down, there is still some fishing to be had.

One of Chaeli's great interests is the introduction of this nature spot to youngsters. "I'd like to do more outreach programs if possible," she says. Regularly, schools visit her and her colleagues to learn more about the exciting world that surrounds each and every one of us. "There are many animals that live out here," she continues. "Coyotes, mountain lions, and snakes all live close to us. And we have a very interesting little animal called the desert wood rat. People call them pack rats as they will steal items from people and take them back to their own homes."

Although restrictions are in force for many of the trails, there are still plenty of places to get away from it all and maybe just sit and relax. It is hard to realize that the city is so close. The ranger station itself is well stocked with items for your visit - maps, books T-shirts and a staff of very helpful, knowledgeable people to help you with any inquiries you might have.

There has been station here since the 1800's, as the area has always been of interest to people wanting to experience something of nature. Although not very high up at 2,700 feet, rising to 3,300 feet, one feels very much in the mountains without the need to drive a long distance. An Adventure Pass is necessary for any exploring you might want to do, but it's good value for all the sights you will see before you have to get back to true civilization, just ten miles away.

Ranger Station phone number: (909) 887-2576
Target Shooing Range number: (909) 782-7438

HISTORICAL MARKERS

MOSTLY WE ARE in a tremendous hurry in Southern California as we rush to and fro to get to the next errand or project. It's the price we pay to stay in touch and competitive. One of the casualties of our hurry is that we rarely, if ever, stop to look at the places where historical markers are signposted on the highways. "Historical Marker 100 Feet" is one of those mostly taken for granted sights we ignore, as we travel through the traffic as fast as we can.

But at weekends, when maybe you've washed the car and perhaps even polished it, you will need to drive it. Cleaning a car always improves its performance, as everyone knows from the very first clunker we own. But finding a drive that will show off this transformation, and maybe incorporate a day out for the family is often a problem. If you've even applied polish and chrome cleaner, it will necessitate a decent distance, and not just round the block.

There are many historical markers in the State – in fact about 1100 of them. www.landmarkquest.com will get you into this informative site. But for a short day out here are four places that will slow your pace down, and let you learn a little of what went on before your time. So pack a cold lunch, and head on out for a 100 mile round trip to learn a little history

Some thirty-five miles south of Victorville, on Route 15, you will come to the small township of Devore. Not a lot goes on here nowadays, but it was a regular passage for earlier peoples on their way through the area. The Glen Helen Parkway leads directly to the Glen Helen Park and in the East End of this park is the site of the Renaissance Fair, now since finished for the season. Sycamore Grove is sited just inside gate number three, and is the sight for our first Historical Marker.

It marks the place where the Mormon Colony stopped for four months in 1851. Here they negotiated Rancho San Bernardino from the Luga family before passing on their way. The stone explains it all. Just along the way is Joe's Country Café, where you may like to stop for some late breakfast or early lunch. But leave those sandwiches alone as there is a better spot for a picnic. If something more in the line of an adult beverage is on your list, you may want to visit The Screaming Chicken, a no-frills bikers' bar located in a disused filling station at the junction of the 15 and the 215.

Back towards the desert in Hesperia, and on Lake Arrowhead Lane, is the Hesperia Fishing Lake. A positive oasis in the hot season, it welcomes campers, travelers and fishermen with its cool water, shady trees and of course, an Historical Marker.

12,000 years ago the Anasazi Peoples used this as a trading route to the sea. In 1776, Padre Francisco Garces came through, and later still, Kit Carson. More recently, a fractured pipe in 1917 created the lake from the spring beneath. All this information is on the monument located just inside the entrance, where a $7.00 fee is charged for adults and $3.00 for children. It is an ideal spot to open up that cold box, relax and watch the various geese, egrets and cormorants. If you want to try your hand with a line, everything is available at the shop and you might bring home a catfish for your supper.

Returning once again to Arrowhead Lane to the north, you will find yet another marker on the left by the golf course. It marks the Holcomb Valley Road, which was laid down by the citizens of Belleville at a cost of $1500. Jed Van Duzen, a local blacksmith, handled the work.

The name of Bill Holcomb is well known in the area of the high desert and the local mountains. He made a big gold strike in Big Bear, and gave his name to many places. If you travel along the Bear Valley Cut-off and join route 18, you will come to Lucerne Valley. It was along this route in January 1867 that Holcomb, and a group of settlers, rode to finish a fight with local Indians, who had been causing trouble.

Four miles outside Lucerne stand two monuments to this final battle in California. One of the stones has a sighting tube that will show you Chimney Rock, where the Indians camped before it all ended forever. The trouble had started with the killing of some boys at a sawmill in

Big Bear. Later on a Spanish man was ambushed and killed in the Cajon Pass. Hostilities had reached a point where the settlers were deeply troubled and forced to make a stand.

Traffic now roars along Route 18, mostly unaware that two cultures were to finish their grievances here in the only way they knew - with force; desperate people and desperate times, not so long ago.

Unfortunately, by the time you return, your earlier washed car might need a dusting from the miles, and almost certainly, the performance you noticed as soon as you took it out in the morning, will have diminished. Could it be just in the mind? But behind you there is now some knowledge and you'll always remember what those signposts meant when they told you of an Historical Marker ahead.

LAKE ARROWHEAD

IT'S ONLY TWENTY miles from San Bernardino, and yet the community of Lake Arrowhead is a completely different atmosphere to visit. Not as high as Big Bear, which is 6,750 feet above sea level as against Lake Arrowhead's more modest 5,100, it is nonetheless an unmistakable mountain resort. The lake is not as large as Big Bear's, although it is far deeper, and it has one other main distinction, it is privately owned.

Due to its closeness to the main cities of Southern California, it suffered from early development, much of it by the famous film stars of the day. This means that lake access is confined to just the part called The Village, but the views from that area are extensive and the shopping makes up for any lack of lakeside strolls one might care to take.

Well known manufacturers such as Coach, Geoffrey Beane, Bass and Izod rub shoulders alongside specialty shops offering home furnishings, cookware, and food stores. As might be expected there are plenty of good eating establishments as well to cater to every taste.

Spokesperson for the Chamber of Commerce, Leslie McLellan, reports that ownership of The Village recently changed hands. "The new management are doing lots to make things even better here," she says. "From the infrastructure of the parking lot to the overall facilities available, we are intent on making Lake Arrowhead a premier destination for all of Southern California. It's a real family place with lots to do."

For a start, there is a now a chance to ice skate at the new facility beside the lake. This has been a request from many people, both visitors and locals alike. Since the collapse of the Blue Jay Ice Castle two years ago, when the roof fell in, there has been a definite need to provide skating. The new rink opened around Thanksgiving this year and is attracting both young and old to its glistening surface. A 45-minute session costs $7.00 for adults and $5.00 for children and skate rental is just $3.00. There is enough room for 100 skaters.

Due to its depth, the lake does not appear too low, and the rain dance that was held a little earlier in the season did have some effect in that some two inches fell on the area. None of which seems to bother the elegant Arrowhead Queen, which sails daily from the beach area behind the shops. Tickets for the vessel are available locally and sailing times are prominently posted.

Through New Year's The Village is in full festive spirits, with strolling musicians and street entertainers. Over at the Children's Museum there is a bounce house and face painting is available for the little ones, whose parents might just need to spend a little time in the glamorous shops, while they are occupied. There are horse and carriage rides every Saturday and Sunday and there's even a new go-cart dirt racetrack for thrill seekers age seven and up.

"In fact," says McLelland, "We have everything to get everyone into the holiday spirit." With plenty of free parking, Lake Arrowhead makes an ideal place to spend a day in the run up before Christmas, and the months that follow. In the surrounding areas there are places to hike, ski and just enjoy the mountains that are so close. With a shorter journey time and perhaps a little more sophistication, the citizens of this community will be pleased to see you.

For more information call (909) 337-2533, or visit the website on lakearrowheadvillage.com.

LINCOLN SHRINE

Lincoln Shrine in Redlands

THE HOLIDAY SEASON can be a grueling period of time. Not only are we over Thanksgiving, but the Christmas period bears down upon us, and in between there's the shopping. And of course lurking in the rear of it all is New Year's Eve. It's a tough and long road to travel each year. Fortunately, San Bernardino County has a number of areas where one can escape the mad dash of it all and possibly seek solace from the crowds.

Undoubtedly, such an oasis for the weary shopper was far from the mind of Robert Watchorn, when he conceived the Lincoln Shrine in Redlands. In fact as he toiled away in the dark and dank coal mines of Derbyshire, England, thoughts of the great opportunities in America could only have been mere phantasms as he tore at the face of black earth under the hills.

He came to the United States in 1880, and eventually made his fortune in oil while at the same time developing a serious interest in President Abraham Lincoln. He was fascinated by the tall and lanky leader, who had succeeded against difficult odds and made his way from a log cabin to the White House.

One of the posts that Robert Watchorn was appointed to was that of the governor of Ellis Island. In 1905, he oversaw the immigration of the many people who had fled from Europe and other lands to seek freedom here. Watchorn also began to visit California and take an interest in Redlands in particular. Coupled with his interest in Lincoln, he worked on an idea to bring to the area a shrine to celebrate the life and times of his hero.

It was in 1932 that he and his wife, Alma, opened the building. As well as the former President, it was also dedicated to his son, Emory Ewart, who had died of injuries as an aviator in the First World War.

Looking around the Shrine, it is difficult to imagine how a man with no formal education, and who from the age of eleven only earned 27 cents a day, could produce such a fortune and such a striking memorial to a man who was not even one of his countrymen. If asked about the object of his admiration, Watchorn could go on for a very long time, but when rendered down it was the fact that Lincoln had "…turned the currents of freedom into the souls of millions of fellow men," that had inspired him so much.

Today the Shrine has increased a little from its original size, and reflects more truly the wishes of its original patron, who died in 1944. Inside there are many artifacts and mementos from Lincoln's life and the times he lived through, and was in many ways responsible for. Two annual events take place each February with Lincoln's birthday on the 12th, and also on the Sunday before this, the Shrine holds its yearly

Open House, which allows the staff to showcase newly acquired pieces for the exhibition.

The Lincoln Shrine is located directly behind the Smiley Museum, which has itself undergone a facelift for the end of year holidays. The address is 125 West Vine Street, Redlands, CA 92373. Telephone number (909) 798-7632. Opening hours are Tuesday through Sunday 1.00pm to 5.00pm. Closed Mondays and Holidays. So, if you need to escape the mall's traffic jams both human and motorized, The Lincoln Shrine is a fine place to spend some quality time.

DISCOVERY CENTER

TEARING DOWN THE well-groomed slopes in pursuit of speed doesn't motivate every one of the thousands of visitors to the local mountains. There is also a growing number of other visitors who just enjoy the blue skies and the peacefulness of snow lying on the varied terrain. And one of the best ways to get the most out of the need to commune with nature is to visit the Big Bear Discovery Center.

According to Jim McGowan, the volunteer organizer, the Center, which was opened in 1998, has received over 750,000 visitors. "We handle all the inquiries regarding the local forest for visitors to the area. These includes Eagle Tours, Nature Walks, and evening activities like our Star Nights," he says.

"Our naturalist, Rob Whipple, has put together some very interesting events planned around our native bald eagles, and they're very well attended." The Moonridge Animal Park also brings over one of its eagles to help in explaining this majestic animal to the onlookers. These are eagles that have become too damaged to be able to look out for themselves in the wild.

"Currently we have counted three pairs up here, which is just about the regular amount," McGowan reports. "Including of course, our famous local pair, George and Gracy, who have been returning now for years. They're very popular with everyone who is lucky enough to spot them.

A number of areas are sealed off around the lake to help the birds in their breeding, but it's only until April when the gates are once again unlocked. On a trip round the lake you may well see an eagle lifting off with its huge wings over the icy water, or even standing sentinel on a frozen base looking out for its next meal.

The Discovery Center's Eagle Tour takes in a ride around the lake to spot the quarry, and also keeps a good look out for coyotes, and other animals native to the area. Costs are $5.00 for adults and $3.00 for children. Times and days vary so contact the Center on (909) 866-3437 or on its web site at bigbeardiscoverycenter.com.

In order to take advantage of the extremely clear air on the mountain, the Center has organized a number of Star Parties with the local astronomical society. The next event will be on January 31, 2003, and it will include an explanation of the many constellations turning slowly over us. "Of course, the telescopes provided are slightly different from the ones we use for the eagles," McGowan mentions. "But everything is provided to ensure all the visitors have a good time, and learn something."

The Discovery Center is located on the north shore of Big Bear Lake, on route 38 just to the east of Fawnskin. It is managed jointly by the San Bernardino Forest and the San Bernardino Forest Association. Many of the tours and information programs are free, but as always, donations are very much appreciated.

ASISTENCIA

Asistencia

SAN BERNARDINO COUNTY'S Asistencia is more correctly called The Estancia. But as co-site manager, Kim Turpin says: "It's a wonderful old all-wood adobe and plaster building from the 1800's." And as she and her husband, Mark, oversee the operations there every week, she is intimately aware of all the many facets of the single story buildings located a couple of miles from the busy I-10 to the north.

The Asistencia was an outpost of the Mission San Gabriel's Rancho San Bernardino, and was originally built in 1819, but has undergone an additional four distinct periods in its life. Originally it functioned as an outpost for cattle grazing over the lands that were a part of the Rancho. The overseer of the time began construction for the worship of those working and living in the area, but the site was then about one mile from its current location,

The present buildings' reconstruction began in 1925, when it was taken over from the then owners, the Barton family, who had owned it for some seventy prior years. Unfortunately, during that time, many of the materials had been taken away and used in other projects - an oft-repeated act by those who came before, and who seemed sometimes to have little interest in much earlier history.

The famous Horace P. Hinkley directed the building project, and it was he who decided the finished site needed a raison d' être. Weddings became that reason and today the Asistencia has hosted countless couples, who have chosen the romantic surroundings to start their lives journey together.

"Since 9/11, some of the bookings fell off a little," Kim Turpin says. "Maybe it was the general drop in the economy. But it seems to be getting back to normal now." She points out that the facility can handle not only large groups of 100 guests, but because of the intimate nature of the rooms, a small gathering doesn't become lost. And of course, there is always the outdoors with the green lawns, old whitewashed walls and red tiles to offset the bougainvillea and other lush plants. Husband Mark is a registered minister and officiates in the ceremonies.

The permanent museum at the Asistencia is open Wednesday through Saturday from 10.00am to 4.00pm, and on Sundays from 1.00pm to 4.00pm, and provided no wedding is taking place, Kim recommends seeing the chapel. "It's really beautiful, and the statue on the altar is a must." She says. "We get lots of children's tours here from the local school district, and often the place is full of young voices." But at other times there is a silence over the area, and one can imagine how it must have been a fine place of rest for hard working people toiling to turn the land into a fruitful place.

Whether you call it the Estancia or the Asistencia, the Turpins will be sure to show you the history of the small sub-mission and explain how its existence has been a recording of the life of earlier times in our county.

As with many of the local historic sites, admission is free, but donations are always welcome. The San Bernardino Rancho "Asistencia" is located at 26930 Barton Road, Redlands, CA 92373. (Between Nevada Street and Alabama Street.) Telephone number is (909) 793-5402. It is closed Mondays and Tuesdays, New Year's Day, Thanksgiving and Christmas. It is listed as California State Historical Landmark #42.

FIRE MUSEUM

THERE ARE A lot of memories at the Victorville Fire Department Museum. Hats, old uniforms, and photos adorn the walls, and one can feel much of the atmosphere of the old days. "I've met a number of the old fellows," says Greg Coon, the curator, and a hazard materials specialist himself with the fire department. "I've been with the department for 16 years, but that's nothing compared to one of our old vets."

He is referring to Ernie Kraft, who was with the station from 1932 to 1975. "He's still alive at 103," Coon says. "I've met him and he's still very sharp, although he lives away from the area up in Union City these days." It seems that Ernie was literally walking through Victorville in 1932 looking for work, when he found out the fire department needed men, so he volunteered.

The building that houses the museum has not been a fire station since 1988, and before that its use changed somewhat over the years, but today it houses a neat and well-displayed collection of memorabilia. This includes a couple of old fire engines that have been lovingly restored. The pride of the collection is undoubtedly the 1930 Ahrens-Fox Model V. This stands at the entrance as it did when used to fight the local fires that would spring up in the town. Its shining condition is a tribute to the care and dedication of the volunteers who look after this old station.

The white hat and well-worn uniform of one time Fire Chief Pete Weise hangs alongside others who made their life's work serving the people of Victorville. His photos show a dedicated man in the old style; tough and resolute.

At the back of the building stands the old tower with its siren aloft. Coon takes obvious delight in starting up the motor, and the noise is quite deafening. Originally, the siren was installed to warn residents of a potential flood if the Arrowhead dam should break. Subsequently, its wailing would alert the mostly volunteer firemen to their duties.

The siren continued to be used for this purpose until the FCC granted a radio license to the department in 1963. "For quite some time afterwards, though, if we ran the siren, firefighters would turn up, looking for directions to the fire." Coon explains. "The system here had always been that the two houses at the rear of the station were given to firemen and their families on one important condition.

"One of the houses had to be occupied at all times, in order to handle any emergency. Then someone would stand outside the station holding up the directions on a board as to where the fire was located. But after the radios came in 1963 all that changed."

The museum's mission is to educate the public about the importance of fire and life safety and the history of the fire service. It is open on Saturdays from 10.00am to 2.00pm and tours are by arrangement. The telephone number is (760) 955-5229. The museum is located at 15620 Eighth Street, Victorville, CA 92392. Entrance to the museum is free, but donations are always welcome.

COLTON MUSEUM

Colton Museum

FOR MOST PEOPLE, Colton only lasts a few moments as they rush along Interstate 10 on their way to Los Angeles or points east. However, the small city was not always bypassed by motorists, as it was once considered an important place for the area. "We used to be called Hub City." Said Larry Sheffield, the president of the Colton Area Museum

Association. "It was a phrase coined by the local newspaper of the day, and it stuck for a long time."

Information on Colton is available for everyone to see at an impressive building located on La Cadena Drive. "Originally it was Colton's public Library and the funds necessary for its construction were donated by Andrew Carnegie." Sheffield said. "It was built in 1908 and served the community until 1982, when it moved to a new location." The building then was unused until it reopened as a museum in 1992.

The association and its band of enthusiastic volunteers keep the exhibits and records in good condition in this elegant building. It has much of the high quality of the era with attractive pillars framing the steps up to the interior.

Volunteer Schuyler Donnel has been involved with the association for six years. "We have lots of stuff from the old days here," he said. "In this cabinet there are prizes and pictures from the time Colton won the Little League championship." Donnel has volunteered his time at the museum for some four years now, and obviously enjoys the work. The ground floor is packed with glass cases and displays of the time when Colton was a provider of three essential services to the Southland. Sheffield explained: "We were a center for the citrus, railroad, and cement industries. All of which were very important for the area."

One corner of the museum is dedicated to the growing and picking of citrus fruits, which declined in the 1930's. But before then the orchards stretched out to where people are living today. It was a booming place and many of the current houses are on the historical list protecting them.

"We have close to 40 houses protected." Volunteer Gretchen Hart-Von Keller, said. "But we expect there will be more soon." Hart-Von Keller has only just become a full time volunteer with the museum but shares the same interest in the goals of the establishment. Its motto is Preserving the past for future generations. And the effort involved is a continuing work in progress.

There are plans afoot to place more of the exhibits in theme areas to help capture what life was like in the old days. One set of exhibits is devoted to the Earp family. Many people may not know that Virgil Earp, the brother of Wyatt Earp, was Colton's first Marshall. Also the

Colton Police and Fire departments are well represented, as well as Indian artifacts, and early clothing and paintings of the time.

Currently, Colton may have a look of a small quiet city with the sound of traffic rushing by on the interstate, but it is a fairly good bet that as the Inland Empire continues to expand and fill with people, Colton could once again come into its own. When that happens, the volunteers of the museum will be on hand to explain how life has altered for the area, and to help keep alive the spirit of those times.

The Colton Area Museum is located at 380 North La Cadena Drive, Colton, CA 92324. Telephone number is (909) 824-8814. Hours of opening are Fridays 1.00pm to 4.00pm and also on the fourth Sunday of every month. There is no admission fee, however donations are gladly accepted. There is also an active campaign to recruit membership in the association to continue to administer the museum.

WILDHAVEN RANCH

THE MOTTO OF Wildhaven Ranch is: Preserving wildlife helps heal the human spirit. And this has proved to be factual for director Diane Dragotto Willams. "I was an only child and as such I was rather lonely," she said from her comfortable living room in the heart of the ranch. "I was born in Los Angeles and my parents used to bring me up here to the forests. I was always drawn to the wild animals. And this was at a time when there were a lot more of them visible."

Evidence of her love of animals is all around her and she has enjoyed considerable success as a wildlife artist; the paintings looking down attest to this. But her life is now caring for the various animals in her charge at Wildhaven, and her staff of ten and the over 100 volunteers she relies upon work hard to make this a sanctuary for all creatures with problems.

"Basically, we divide the animals into two categories: those who are here for rehabilitation and those for educational purposes." She explained. It is the last category that the public is allowed to see on the open days each Saturday between 1.00pm and 3.00pm. Visitors must call first to arrange for directions as the ranch is buried within the forest at Cedar Glen near Lake Arrowhead.

Currently there is a great deal of interest in the latest arrivals; two little brown bear cubs called Quincy and Woodie. These were brought here within days of their birth, as they had been found by people, who mistook them for abandoned puppies. Once the mistake was realized, the California Department of Fish and Game brought them to Wildhaven for care. "The cubs couldn't be taken back to their mother by then as it would have been too dangerous." Dragotto Williams explained.

Returning them would have meant insuring that they were with the real mother, and then covering the mother's nose with petroleum jelly to make sure she did not smell humans on them. This would have required anaesthetizing her as well. Just returning the cubs to their shallow burrow would have meant that they could have been taken by other wild creatures. Currently they enjoy the warmth and safety of the director's home in a playpen. The have to be fed every three hours.

Ed Auer, the foreman of the ranch has been there for 18 months. "My particular favorites are the eagles," he said. There are several eagles, that are convalescing from broken wings and other ailments, that he watches over. "This is a wonderful place and the work is very important." A golden eagle looked down at him as he made the flying area neat and tidy.

Volunteer Kathy Costa returned from a visit to a local school with a raccoon. "She's been on her best behavior all morning," she said. "So now she's decided to be difficult." The black-eyed creature hung on to the fence as Costa gently removed the long fingers. The raccoon has become one of the residents here and seemed to enjoy the trip to meet children. This is a regular part of the educational side of the ranch's work.

Incorporated in 1994, the current premises were dedicated in October 2000, and in full operation since August 2001, so it is still quite a new venture for the area. However there seems to be an unending supply of animals that need our assistance, and from the appearance of all the helpers, the motto of helping the human spirit seems to be very true.

For an appointment call (909) 337-7389.
Wildhaven Ranch PO Box 1782, Lake Arrowhead, CA 92352
Visiting days Saturdays from 1.00pm to 3.00pm.

MOUNTAIN SKIES ASTRONOMY

"MAKING THE COMPLEX more understandable," should possibly be the motto of the Mountain Skies Astronomical Society (MSAS), as that seems to be the goal of their enthusiastic staff, who work up at the Rim of the World in Lake Arrowhead. "We have lots of visitors here, and we always hope they go away with information that they understand," said Mark Traver, an instructor with the Society for the last two years, and who assists with the many programs put on.

The facility, which is perched high above the hills in the Lake Arrowhead and Crestline area, is right next to the high school, although they are not involved with each other. On a clear day the view goes right over the San Bernardino area, and at nights the sky is mostly clear and bright.

Director and Board Secretary, Dorothy Allmon, said "We largely run this place with volunteers, and some of them put in many hours to help us keep the standard so high." Three buildings make up the facility with the domed Robert Brownlee Observatory having pride of place. It houses the main 16-inch custom optic telescope, which allows excellent viewing into deep space.

"By far the most visitors here are from the public, and not academia," Allmon continued. "So we make it our business to try and lighten up the subject and demystify it. In fact our President, Dr. Lorann Parker is wonderful at explaining many of the mysteries of space and astronomy." Enthusiasts fill the chairs at the lectures that Dr. Parker gives to understand more fully the complexities of the worlds beyond ours.

A library is connected to the complex and the small museum is full of artifacts from the world of this science. There is even some lunar material on loan from the National Aeronautical and Space Administration (NASA) that can be examined under the electron microscope that is on permanent show. A bright golden key that was taken into space is also exhibited in one of many display cases. It is the key that opened the facility on May 15, 1999, at the Grand Opening.

NASA is a very important part of the MSAS world as it is currently focused on the building of the International Space Station. A lecture is planned with a guest speaker from The Boeing Company, who will outline progress and answer questions on this enormous project. It is one of several subjects planned for the rest of the year to help people come to turns with what is going on in space.

"We know that the more people there are, who understand about these things the more support will be out there." Allmon explained. "We believe it is very important that we explore our universe at the same time as trying to solve the many problems back home. The two must go on hand in hand. Also the benefits that we bring back from our space travels help enormously with life here on Earth." It is a difficult task, but one that is more easily understood after a visit to the Rim of the World.

There is a very comprehensive website available and the facility is open from 10.00am to 4.00pm every day. Evening viewing of space is weather dependent, but one can find out the situation by Internet or phone.

MSAS Astronomy Village
2001 Observatory Way, off Hwy 18
West of Rim of the World High School
Lake Arrowhead, CA 92352
(909) 336-1699
Open Daily from 10.00am to 4.00pm.

Website: mountain-skies.org

GREEN VALLEY LAKE

Green Valley Lake

"WE'RE VERY LUCKY, the lake belongs to all the homeowners, but the public can use it too." Said Judy Green a resident of Green Valley Lake for the last 23 years. "All of us are shareholders of the lake, but we let the public enjoy it as well." She continued, talking about the small eleven-acre lake community, which boasts it is the highest in the San Bernardino Mountains. At 7,200 feet above sea level, it actually overlooks Lake Arrowhead by almost 2,000 feet, but is often forgotten by people visiting the local mountain resorts.

"We are just four miles off Highway 18 a few miles east of Running Springs," said Diane Rozgay, another resident of the area. "We used to be the main road into the Big Bear Valley many years ago, but we're no longer a through route." That is probably why Green Valley Lake is a quiet spot for residents and visitors alike. Rozgay pointed out: "When the toll road closed, most people on Highway 18 just kept on going and left us alone, but we rather like it like that." For people who have discovered this small place however, it is a haven of peace and quiet and for fisherfolk, it is a great place to catch their limits.

Rod Peacock who is the operations manager for the Green Valley Mutual Water Company, oversees what happens on the small dammed lake. "Right now we have plenty of water." He said. "We collect run-off from all the surrounding hills and currently, it is at maximum." Which puts it in a very enviable position compared to Big Bear Lake, which is still down some thirteen feet.

"We rent out row-boats, pedal boats, canoes, kayaks - both single and double, and we have a beach area with all the usual amusements like volleyball and swings," Peacock explained. "To get out on the water, rent a row-boat, but no motors are allowed on the lake, which makes it very peaceful."

There are close to 900 homeowners in the small town, which has the lake as it center. The lake was dammed in the early 30's and set up for everyone who owned a house to also own a share. It is open from May 1st to November 1st or as weather permits. The fish are regularly stocked and the daily cost is modest. A valid California Fish and Game license is also needed. The limit is five fish. "And this is an easy lake to catch them," Peacock added. "You have to do this in the daytime however, as no night fishing is allowed as the lake closes at 8.00pm."

Visitors are often reminded of the early days of Big Bear, when they first come to Green Valley. It is the lack of development that gives it its earlier feel. Small rustic cabins look down on the calm waters and the few soft ripples produced by a passing canoe. An air of peace prevails over the scene and the few shops on Main Street are able to provide all that is necessary for a day's refreshment for body and soul.

All visitors are made welcome, although the web site asks that you "Keep it a secret!"

Green Valley Lake,
3 1/2 miles off Highway18,
east of Running Springs and Arrowbear.
Information (909) 867-2000
Website green-valley-lake.com

HIGH DESERT CENTER
FOR THE ARTS

THE BUILDING AT the corner of 8th and 'C' in Old Town Victorville could be said to have come full circle. It used to be a USO facility in World War II, for the Victorville Army Base. As such it put on lots of different forms of entertainment for the troops, and then for many years it filled several uses, but now it is home to the high Desert Center for the Arts. Also it is a building of historical importance.

Formed in June 2001, the Center now hosts several plays each year, and, as well as a permanent art museum, it arranges several functions for the growing citizenry of the area. "I remember back in the fifties when this whole desert area only had about 30,000 people in it." Recalled T.R. Marino, the facilities director at the Center. "But we've got close to a quarter million here now."

Due to the large number of retirees in the area as well, there are plenty of volunteers to help manage the Center. "We have between 75 and 100 available to help us," said Jane Niez, the Volunteer Director. "Everyone's very keen to help," she added.

When it came to modifying the building volunteers helped in that too. "We had to raise over $100,000 just to put it right," Dick Dorwald the Executive Director said. He referred to the 170-seat theater at the rear of the building. "It used to be a basketball court, but now it hosts really good plays each month to packed houses. One of the most recent was a play called The Kosher Grocer. It was a drama/comedy and commentary on racial issues. It caused tears and laughs. The cast was terrific,"

47

The plays are very popular with the local residents and some have had to be extended. "We have our most popular attraction next January, the Burlesque." Marino added. "It's the third one we're doing and we have made plans to put on more performances, as it's so well received."

The attractions at the Center are, to use a well-used phrase, eclectic. Ballet classes are run by Master Teacher Victor Moreno, and are very popular with dancers and spectators alike. The art shows that the Center organizes contain works by 75 local artists, and usually 40 works are on display all the time. Large cabinets show off various ceramic and other works of art, much relating to the immediate area.

But it is the plays that keep people coming back again and again. The next feature is called Murder Room. "It's a goofy mixed up mystery." Dorwald reported. "I've watched some of the rehearsals, and it's a great play. I know that our audiences will love it." Marino agreed. He is also the president of the Theater Arts Guild and admits to having high standards.

The volunteers that make up this vibrant group all have a high energy and enthusiasm for being the center for culture in the High Desert. But no job is too small to miss the attentive eye of any of them. Marino picked up his shears and went back to trimming the hedge outside - even the gardening needs some help.

High Desert Center for the Arts,
Corner 8th and "C'
Old Town Victorville
Information: (760) 243-7493
Open Tuesday through Sunday.
Tues - Fri 10am to 4pm
Sat 10am to 4pm, Sat night 6pm to closing.

GUBLER ORCHIDS

WHEN THE BIG earthquake hit Landers eleven years ago, it was not just the human population that suffered from the temblor, some half-a-million exotic orchids at the Gubler Orchid Farm were severely effected too. "The shaking caused the greenhouses to tilt and the ground to ripple, and much of our traditional growing area was broken." So said Chris Gubler, the president of the firm that was begun by his father in the fifties. "The result of the damage was that we had to change a lot of our growing beds, and of course we took the opportunity to improve them." Today in the 50,000 square foot premises in Landers, huge planting trays are on rollers and allow the growing process to take place in less space than before the 'quake.

Growing orchids is not for the faint hearted nor the impatient. "It takes up to five years before a plant can be sold," Gubler explained. "Some can be picked after three but it takes a long time to see any return on investment. Also disease can really effect the plants." In the summer months disease is most prevalent and a small area of the nursery is set aside for plants in intensive care to see if a recovery can be undertaken. Gubler inspected one with a brown area on its otherwise pristine leaves. "I'm afraid this one is destined for orchid Heaven," he remarked.

Landers was chosen as a new location by his parents after they decided to move away from the original site in Temple City near San Gabriel. Orchids need sun, good air and a high sugar content in the water. "This area was perfect," continued Gubler. "It had been a hydroponic tomato farm where the plants were grown in water, so it was ideal for us." Today it grows around 500,000 different plants and tours of the facility are taken very seriously by the staff. "We like to encourage an interest in the plants. Most people don't realize that orchids are the largest flowering species in the plant kingdom with over 30,000 different varieties.

"In October we hold a huge orchid festival along with the local Rotary, and last year we had over 2,000 visitors. It is one of the biggest fairs around here." Gubler enthused. He estimated his facility is the fourth largest orchid business in the state, with branches in Hawaii, Florida and also Lucerne Valley.

A visitor's tour begins at the very start of the process with seeding in small glass tubes. These then are tended carefully for up to two years before they are separated and placed into pots. All the while his staff watch over them like the small babies they are. Everything about the environment is measured from the humidity to the temperature and the amount of sunshine they receive. It's a labor-intensive business, and accounts in some part for the perceived high price of the flowers. Blooms start at about $10 and can rise up into the hundreds for the real enthusiast. "But you can get more than one flowering out of a plant if you treat them well," Gubler explained.

Gubler did not realize he was destined for the family business, as his interest lay in electronics, but when he was at college he took a course in biology, "and meeting all the people in this field I became hooked. It made my father very pleased." He said with a smile.

Parties of ten or more should call for a time to visit; smaller groups can come anytime. The farm is located a couple of miles off Route 147 (Old Woman Spring Road,) then a left turn along Belfield Road in Landers. Closed on Sundays. Ample parking

Gubler Orchid Farm
2200 Belfield Road
Landers, CA

For more information: (760) 364-2282 or
Web site: gublerorchids.com

JENKS LAKE

FISH FARMS SEEM to be a comparatively recent idea, although Beavers have been at it all their lives, but it may come as a shock to realize that one, Lorin Shaw Jenks began one in the San Bernardino Mountains in the 1870's.

Cap' Jenks as he was known by all, not only decided that fish farming was the way to go, but he had to dig a ditch one-an-a-half miles from the South Fork of the Santa Ana River to reach the spot he had chosen for his venture. The rumor he put about was that he dug it himself.

After damming the end of a small canyon with earth and rocks, he filled the lake with trout and began to sell the results of his labor down in San Bernardino. This continued until the state, for some reason, outlawed the practice of commercially selling fish from lakes and streams in the area. As a result Cap' Jenks retired to live out his years telling tall tales to anyone who would listen. However, he left behind one of those small bright jewels in the mountains that now provide a great leisure spot and also of course, some fish.

Jenks Lake is a short diversion off Highway 38, known as the 'back way' to those visiting the Big Bear Valley region. It is about three miles into the forest area and the drive takes one through some very pretty woodland glades. Chuck Webb is the host of the facility and he constantly enjoys the serenity by which he is surrounded. "My wife wanted somewhere quiet to carry on with her painting, and this is ideal," he said. For sometime they have both looked after a site in San Gorgonio. "But this is a lot different," Webb said.

Although the immediate area is wooded, it is something of a shock to find this small beautiful lake in its surroundings. Somehow the area seems too dry to support this clear water. But Cap' Jenks obviously knew what he was about. And the number of fishermen, both young and old who stand, either on the ready made pier, or along the water's edge are testament to the fish who live there. The Fish and Game Agency are currently attempting to breed large mouth bass and bluegill sunfish as the trout become fished out within days of stocking.

Visiting fisherman, Bill Sutton, said: "I've been coming here for about five years." With his grandson, Brandon Sutton, he had been fishing since 8 a.m. But by lunchtime they hadn't had a bite. "Sometimes it's good here and sometimes bad." Brandon agreed, but didn't seem to mind the lack of result from the clear green water.

At the far end of the lake a number of canoes are often seen skimming along, but they belong to the Barton Flats Association and are not for hire. If you want to get out on the lake itself you have to bring you own vessel. And only non-motorized craft are allowed. No engines go out on Jenks Lake to spoil the peace and quiet. Things seem pretty much as they have for the last hundred and thirty years. No doubt the Cap' would approve.

Where: Jenks Lake
Jenks Lake Road
Barton Flats, off Highway 38.

For more information call
The Mill Creek Ranger Station
(909) 794-1123

Hours: Open from 6 a.m. to sunset.
No night fishing.

OLD VICTORVILLE

MOST PEOPLE THINK of Victorville as one of those places that has grown beyond recognition and straddles the busy Interstate 15 route between Las Angeles, and Las Vegas. With its big signs promising wonderful goods and services at all the local malls and suppliers, it is hard to imagine that there once was a Victorville that existed long ago. Yet such a place existed, and is still available for those who are prepared to make a small detour.

"A lot of people in the area have no idea how much they are supported by tourism," said Bill Caldenhead, who is a volunteer at the Route 66 Museum in Old Victorville. "In fact, 20% of our visitors come from Europe. We get so many tourists here, who are making the run to and from Las Vegas. Just a little while ago this morning we had a man in here from Denmark."

The Old Town is a collection of small shops gathered around an area that roughly stands between the freeway and Eleventh Street, and the river and Forest Avenue. It has received a facelift in recent years. Its merchant association is active in promoting the work of the local vendors and is intent on attracting more visitors to the scene of the old Route 66.

"There used to be 23 filling stations along this short stretch of road," said Penny Edmiston, at the Santa Fe Trading Post on 7th Street. "We're now in one of them, but most have completely disappeared." She and partner Steve Blech run the home furnishing store, and also look after the affairs of the merchants association. "We have a separate association as we have slightly different needs to the Chamber of Commerce. For instance, most of our members run the businesses themselves and can't get away for lunches and other functions during the day."

Edmiston also promotes a nature walk in the local area. "People have no idea how much nature is all around us here. For instance, when I first arrived, I didn't know there was a river running just a couple of blocks away." She referred to the Mojave River, which is just the other side of the railway tracks. It is here that she escorts a regular nature Old Town walking tour on the last Saturday of every month. "We even have our own natural statue to look at. We call him Chief Mojave, and he is a natural 20 feet formation in the rock face." New Hampshire's Old Man of the Mountains recently had a serious fall, but it seems that Victorville's answer, The Chief, is still standing. You have to know the angle from which to look though.

Old Victorville boasts not only a unique collection of boutiques and craft shops, but also a fine museum dedicated to the early days of fire fighting in the area. The Victorville Fire Department Museum is located on Eighth Street and houses a collection of memorabilia from the early part of the last century. Its pride and joy is a fully restored Ahrens-Fox Model V fire engine in all it's sparkling glory. But no visit to the old part of town can be complete without looking in on the California Route 66 Museum and Visitors Center. Here the premises are stuffed with memories of America's Mother Road, recollections of Steinbeck, and Nat 'King' Cole's emotive voice will all come flooding back. It also comes with free admission, which is a real trip down memory lane.

California Route 66 Museum
D Street between 5th and 6th
P.O. Box 2151
Victorville, CA 92393
(760) 951-0436
Web site www.califrt66museum.org
Open Thursday – Monday 10 a.m. to 4 p.m.

Santa Fe Trading Co
15464 7th Street
Victorville, CA 92392
(760) 962-1290

Victorville Fire Museum
15620 Eighth Street
Victorville, CA 92392
(760) 955-5229
Open Saturdays only 10 a.m. to 2 p.m.

SHOOTING

LOVE THEM OR hate them, guns are an integral part of American life. No matter how many regulations are voted in, there are a lot of guns out there, and a lot of gun owners who like to shoot them. Collectors and enthusiasts as well as just regular owners need somewhere safe to shoot their weapons and talk about their hobby.

One such place is the Big Bear Valley Sportsman's Club, which although deep in the hills on the north side of Big Bear Lake, enjoys great views of the lake and surrounding scenery. That is once you look away from the target areas, as those are located in the hill itself.

"We've been in this current location since 1951," said Sterling Fordham, one of four rangers who oversee operations at the range. "But I think the Club itself operated elsewhere before that." Safety is the number one aspect that all members and rangers of the club look out for. No one is allowed in front of the guns when they are loaded and ready. All shooters have to unload, leave their weapons open, and laid down before any targets are adjusted.

"You don't have to be a member here to shoot," Fordham continued. "Lots of people come by for some practice." The noise from heavy caliber guns is deafening, which explains the earplugs he wears at all times when on duty. At the far end a group of five 'trap' shooters is firing off at their flying orange targets with twelve-gauge shotguns.

"Trap shooting is different from skeet shooting, as the targets fly up into the air and with skeet, sometimes the target goes along the ground," Forham explained. The president of the club, John Mangione sits in an umpire's chair firing off the targets at the call of "Pull," from each shooter. The targets are released by a remote control, and he keeps score of the number of hits and misses.

Dorothy Sirk and her husband have been trap shooting since 1995. "This is a Remington 8700 shot gun," she said. "I fire it most weekends up here. I like the sport very much." It was noticeable that Dorothy was more accurate from the right hand side of the semicircle of shooters than the left. "I don't really know why that is," she said.

Static target shooting is very popular at the club and a number of shooters can be seen crouching over the long tables aiming their weapons at the bull's eyes in the distance. "I like the .22 caliber rifle best," said Dr. Kathlene Dallaire, an environmental specialist, and weekend visitor from Orange County. "They're not so noisy and the kick isn't as great." She fired off a round into the center of the bull, and checked her aim through a small telescope. "I've been shooting for about three years," she added.

All types of guns are fired at the Sportsman's Club, and there are only a few restrictions. "We don't allow certain types of ammunition on certain types of targets," range master Fordham stated. "Mostly though we can accommodate everyone's needs." It is a non-profit organization and members and staff all turn their hands to keeping the place in good condition.

Access to the range is up an unmade road, which is not very friendly to low slung luxury vehicles. It is just opposite Division Road on the north side of the lake, and open from 10 a.m. to 5 p.m. Saturdays and Sundays. "We keep strictly to the times as we have an arrangement with the locals so that the noise doesn't disturb them," Fordham said. It is also open on holidays that coincide with the weekend period.

Where: Big Bear Sportsman's Club
              Highway 38 at Division Road
              Big Bear Lake, CA 92315

Web site: www.bbvsc.org

OAK GLEN

An Oak Glen Resident

LOTS OF PEOPLE in corporate life wonder what it would be like to give it all up and do something completely different. Very few actually do it at the top of their careers but four years ago, Terry Fox visited Oak Tree Village with three of her close relatives and made a career change. Furthermore the three relatives also left the corporate world and became partners in the Oak Tree Village in Oak Glen, where all the apples grow.

"It was just an idea to begin with, but soon we all agreed to take this on and we've been here ever since," Fox said as she strolled around the

14 acres that constitute the resort. She now wears jeans as her corporate uniform rather than the official workplace clothes of yesterday. "I used to run a 400 person call center for one of America's largest and most prestigious organizations, now I look after a staff of 40 and a lot of animals."

The staff of 40 dwindles to about ten when they are not in their busiest period, but it still means a lot has to get done to keep Oak Tree the popular destination it has always been since it was created in 1948. "I was amazed when I first came here," Fox continued. "I never knew the place existed before, although I'd spent many years in Southern California."

The entire Oak Glen region does come as a bit of a shock to lots of people the first time they visit. With the extensive apple orchards, and the rolling hills beneath the mountains, the area looks like it belongs more to New England, or even Switzerland.

Oak Tree Village has a little of everything. It is a zoo, a resort, a shopping place, and an entertainment center. The country music playing quietly throughout gives one the feeling of another time, where country fun took pride of place and simple pleasure were there to be had by all. Pretty Boy and Pretty Girl, two large Macaws are at the entrance booth and their cheerful calls put you in the mood for something a little different. Don't put your fingers in the cage, however, as they can bite.

In the same building, there is a reptile cave and Oak Glen History Exhibition. Here you can wander around looking at live and stuffed exotic animals as well as visit a number of small shops. These are some of the eight retail businesses that operate within the confines of the park; restaurants and hand-made candy stores are there too.

Pride of place goes to the zoo portion of the resort however, and there are some new animals that have just arrived here. "We're very excited about some of the new arrivals," Melissa Caughey, the resident animal expert reported. "Particularly the New Guinea Singing Dog. It actually does sing, as it needs to communicate with its fellows across mountains. The correct term for the sound is 'keening.'" Caughey's company is called Animal Ambassadors Incorporated and since Memorial Day she has been caring for many of the animals at Oak Tree Village, including the three times a day shows that are put on at peak times.

At the petting zoo there are lots of interesting creatures for youngsters to get up close with. "We're very fond of our pigs here," Fox said. "In fact we hand rear them with bottles along with lots of the other animals, who need special care." The treatment seems to agree with them as there are regular pig races around a small track. "It's a very popular event," Fox added. "So too is the Barn where goats are milked, and you can learn to do it too."

Visitors pile through the gates on the weekends and on holidays, when they can get an atmosphere of happy country times. With crafts, fishing contests from the well-stocked pools, the Johnny Appleseed cabin, and gold panning from the rippling stream, it will be hard to tear yourself back to corporate life once again. No doubt Fox and her relatives will smile in sympathy as you drive away. She said she doesn't miss her previous life a bit.

Where: 38480 Oak Glen Road
         PO Box 1285
         Yucaipa, CA 92399

Hours: Open every day
10a.m. to 5 p.m.

For more information call (909) 797-4020
Or visit the Web site www.oaktree-village.com

ORANGE SHOW

THE PROBLEM WITH most exhibition sites is that for most of the time they are quite empty, and have little atmosphere. The organizers spend considerable efforts trying to redress that situation by acquiring as many bookings as they can, but still large areas of their domain remain empty, albeit for short periods.

San Bernardino is fortunate to have the National Orange Show Events Center so close by, as it is a true resource that many diverse groups find of great help in holding their events. From modest weddings to huge rallies, the NOS can host it all and still have plenty of room to go around. "We have about 120 acres here," said Laurel Erickson, who has been marketing director for the last year. "There are six separate buildings, and, of course, the famous speedway."

This quarter-mile racetrack is perhaps the best known facility to those who pass by the gates on South E Street. NOS holds some 35 different motorsport events each year when the normally still atmosphere is filled with the sound of crackling exhausts and squealing tires. At these time fans flock from all over to witness daring feats of speed in a variety of races. Drivers and crews work tirelessly to try and gain an extra second's advantage as cars and trucks tear around the track. "We are holding the Monster Truck Jam here on November 1st and 2nd," Erickson said. "We expect an appearance by the well known vehicle called 'Gravedigger.'"

At the other end of the spectrum, NOS can put on an intimate wedding setting on the grassy areas overlooking attractive water, with just a hint of traffic in the background, as business continues near the center of the busy city. A larger gathering is expected shortly, as Representative Jerry Lewis is booked to use the Orange Pavilion to hold an anniversary of his entrance into Congress.

The name 'Orange Show' comes from a celebration of citrus growing in the area that dates back to the founding of these premises in 1911. But those types of events went on in the previous century. "We still have a large show every Memorial Weekend," Erickson stated. "It's probably what we're most famous for, but we do so much more, and we have something going on 365 days a year."

In fact with a large satellite wagering center there is always activity at one part of the facility. "The custom building was completed in the late eighties," Erickson added, "and we always have lots of people there." On October 25th a full house is expected to watch on satellite the famous Breeders Cup. There is a separate entrance for this building on Arrowhead Avenue and a cover charge of $3 is made with $2 for parking.

The staff specializes in making the huge banqueting and show facilities come alive in a short space of time. The Damus Building is the largest multi-purpose structure on the property and can host sporting events, car shows exhibitions and such gatherings within its 40,000 clear span space. It can cater for 5,000 people and there is a 4,000 person seating capacity for its built-in theater.

Perhaps the most interesting structure at the NOS is the Dome. This is a 120 feet diameter circular facility that can handle small gatherings for receptions and also small concerts. As with most of the buildings there is room for concessions to go along with the activities.

Readily available information from the organizers states that up to 60,000 people can be managed efficiently at the show grounds, but weddings of only 50 are also well within the capabilities of the organization. From concerts to car races, and conventions to satellite wagering, the NOS Events Center has the flexibility to deal with a huge range of activities. Even though it may be quiet for periods, it can spring into very effective life once a date is set.

The NOS Events Center
689 South 'E' Street
San Bernardino, CA 92408
(909) 888-6788
Web site: www.NOSevents.com

MENTONE

IT'S HARD FOR people not to smile at the mention of Mentone. "Ah, Mentone Beach," they will say." But where is Mentone Beach exactly? Even residents are a little hazy about the funny reputation this small community of 7,308 (according to the 2000 census) has.

"We're an independent bunch, I think," said Mary Ellen Panken, who is the production manager of The Book Craftsman located on Mentone Boulevard. A resident of eight years, Panken oversees the daily work of this unusual book binding and printing business. Like the town that surrounds it, it is something of a throwback to earlier times.

"The business was originally started by a man from Switzerland, called Wesley Aplanalp, and then it passed on to Don and Joan Morrill. Since Don's demise Joan has continued to hold the reins," said Panken. All the staff has been apprenticed there by the owners and previous owners, and the work is mostly hand done and of very high quality. As to the location of their famous beach, Panken smiled, and said: "I think it refers to a previous time."

In fact, Mentone used to be quite a resort for taking the waters. It was the forerunner of Palm Springs, and in the 1890's, the Santa Fe Railway had a direct line out of Los Angeles to bring people here. Unfortunately the water company in Redlands drew most of the local water away and left Mentone high and dry. There then began a form of rivalry with the much larger town to the east and south.

Annexation is always on Mentonians minds and they do feel dominated by the large city of Redlands. "I left the bright lights and big city three years ago with no regrets," said Dionne King, the administrative assistant of the local chamber of commerce. "It's a very quiet place here. One day I accidentally left my keys in the trunk all night. I was amazed to find them there in the morning."

There are some fifty plus members in the local chamber and they reflect small town America, with a healthy mix of plumbers, gas station owners and shopkeepers, all of whom want to keep Mentone the integrated community it has always been. As for the famous beach: "I think it was a place on a reservoir where people could swim," King remarked. "But that was a very long time ago."

There are six Mentones in the World. They are in Texas, Indiana, Alabama, California, Australia and the original one on the French Riviera, which is spelled Menton. The founders of the town hoped to reflect the beauty of the first one in France, and many of the street names have an exotic continental sound to them.

Much of the business of Mentone is agriculture, and it raises crops of citrus, avocado, Christmas trees and honey. It also has a lot of rocks. Many of these white even rocks were used in early construction in Los Angeles, San Diego and were used to build the San Pedro breakwater. An often seen bumper sticker proclaims: Make Mentone beautiful – take a rock to Redlands!

But as for the beach, owner of the Greenspot Grocery Store, Gary Jacinto smiled. "I've lived here all my life, and it's always coming up." Supplier of 'World Famous Beef Jerky,' he provides locals and passers by with all that they need to sustain life at the foot of the mountains. "We don't make the jerky in house anymore," he said. "The meat department closed back in the seventies, and so now we outsource it. But the same man has been making it for thirty years. It's very good."

When pressed about the location of the seemingly mysterious local attraction, most of the residents will direct inquirers to the Santa Ana Wash that runs to the north of the main boulevard. With the current drought conditions however, there is little water to be seen and not too much beach either.

The Book Craftsman
1866 Mentone Blvd
Mentone, CA 92359
(800) 794–1856
www.bookcraftsman.com

Mentone Chamber of Commerce
1899 Mentone Blvd
Mentone, CA 92359
(909) 794-0086
www.mentonechamber.com

Greenspot Market
2402 Mill Creek Road (Highway 38)
Mentone, CA 92359
(909) 794-1511

GRAND TERRACE

"I HAVE TO admit that when people hear I'm from Grand Terrace, they often don't know where it is." Said Tom Schwab, City Manager for the last 17 years. But it doesn't seem to bother him. "It's a nice quiet place," he adds. That seems to be the sentiment of many of the 13,000 residents of this small community perched between two mountain ranges and two freeways.

Originally called just The Terrace because of its elevation of 1065 feet, it became Grand Terrace as the population grew in 1898 and residents could enjoy the views across San Bernardino and the Inland Empire. But the expansion in name did not stop the small town feeling. "We're known for our neighborhoods and our residential suburban locality," Schwab continued. "We're just ten minutes from either San Bernardino and Riverside. In fact people here usually have an orientation toward one or other of those cities."

It seems that half the town buy their cars and their major items from one city or the other and don't seem to change that focus. "I started out being more favorable towards San Bernardino," Schwab said. "But over the years I'm starting to go more often south to Riverside. Although I haven't bought a car there yet."

Called the Blue Mountain City on all its letterhead, Grand Terrace enjoys wonderful views at its eastern end as it is built between the Blue Mountains and the La Loma Hills. The 215 freeway hums along at its western end just a couple of miles south from the 10 exchange. It is a very convenient location, but many people don't even know it's there. "Including the criminals!" Added Schwab, with a smile. "I can't remember the last time we had a murder here."

Once they find out about it, people are very keen to move here. "We just don't have enough houses at the moment to support the demand," said Wayne Young, Realtor with Grand Terrace Real Estate. "Houses go in a day," he continued. "And the same goes for rental properties. It's a real shame for the people from the recent fires who have lost their homes. We just can't help them." Grand Terrace is enjoying the same property boom as the rest of Southern California, with entry houses starting at around $200,000 and going up to $500,000.

Not much expansion is expected in the coming years. "Maybe we'll go to 15,000 or 16,000 residents in the next ten years but then we'll be completely built out." City Manager Schwab added.

The town enjoys some small town events in a self-confessed sort of corny, old-fashioned way. "We've just had a country fair," Schwab pointed out. "And on December 11th we'll celebrate our silver anniversary." Grand Terrace was incorporated in 1978, by a majority vote of 82% in favor. There is still a slight feeling of animosity towards its neighbor, Colton, to the west, but it's disappearing fast with the years. The town is only 3.6 square miles and it is easy to feel swamped by the larger entity.

Most of the residents commute to San Bernardino or Riverside area and Los Angeles is still a long way away. However, more and more commercial opportunities are developing in the Inland Empire and no doubt Grand Terrace will be able to be a part of that. In the meantime, like any small Midwest town, it will continue with its chili cook-offs and craft fairs, happy with its atmosphere and its feeling of anonymity. It may have accepted the name 'Grand' but its aspirations are perhaps a little less.

City of Grand Terrace
22795 Barton Road
Grand Terrace, CA 92313-5295
(909) 430-2245
www.grandterrace-ca.org

Grand Terrace Real Estate
22533 Barton Road
Grand Terrace, CA 92313
(909) 825-8888

YUCAIPA

COMMUNITIES IN SOUTHERN California all seem to be expanding these days. But 'burgeoning' is an adjective that can really be applied to the city of Yucaipa. Originally it was a farming and orange growing area, but today it houses more and more people who enjoy the quick commute to the Inland Empire's larger cities, and the relaxed atmosphere under the hills that surround its northeastern side.

"We're really a bedroom community," said Gary Richards, a real estate broker who has lived in the city for 40 years. "There have been a lot of changes recently, but expansion is inevitable."

The journey time to San Bernardino and Redlands is just twenty minutes, and so Yucaipa is ideal for those who work along the 10 freeway. Attractive red roofed houses are rising up from the grassy slopes like the crops of yesteryear. "Entry level homes are in the $185,000 to $200,000 range, but we have an area now where they will go up to the millions," Richards added.

"We have relatively low crime here, the place is quiet and I think we have more parks than anywhere else in Southern California," he said. Richard's office is in the old downtown area, the main street of which is undergoing a renovation.

In keeping with its overall change, there is a new City Hall being erected alongside the current temporary premises. The joke among civic employees is that their present home is the biggest trailer in Yucaipa. A joke only enjoyed by those who remember the reputation the town once had for retirement and mobile homes.

That reputation is ending now with developments like Chapman Heights, a new up market single family home area, where houses are surrounded by grass and golf courses. "There are 2,200 homes planned in the development," CeCe Alvarado–Sallee, the executive Director of the local Chamber of Commerce said. "So far we have about 900 already built." As a resident herself, Alvarado–Sallee, came from Grand Terrace six years ago and has been at the Chamber for four of them.

"We have a cap on the number of residents in Yucaipa. We are at 45,412 now and we are only allowed to go up to 60,000. So we will always have plenty of space," she reported. And there does seem a lot of space along the wide streets. With the backdrop of the San Bernardino Mountains, and the newer boundary of the 10 freeway to the south, Yucaipa seems to have natural borders, but the openness of the city is one of its most attractive features.

Newer shopping areas are growing to the west to cater to the new residents, and suburban traffic is beginning to make its presence felt. New homes however, are being viewed by the authorities with an eye on density. "We anticipate a number of mansion type homes," Alvarado–Sallee said. And up along the Oak Glen area there is likely to be no change in the rural appearance.

There are 350 members that make up the Yucaipa Valley Chamber of Commerce, and they reflect the diversity of business in the area. It reports that it has been working with business since 1915, and so has great experience with the community in helping to position firms and their search for good people to work. "The largest employer here is the School District," Alvarado–Sallee said. "Then we have Sorensen Engineering as the second highest. But there are many small business that serve the town."

Called the 'City of Parks,' Yucaipa has so far enjoyed a modest reputation, but the secret is already out, and it can anticipate several newcomers looking for good schools, and a peaceful life at the foot of the big mountains to the east.

Gary Richards Real Estate
12113 California Street
Yucaipa, CA 92399
(909) 790-5003

Yucaipa Valley Chamber of Commerce
35139 Yucaipa Boulevard
Yucaipa, CA 92399
(909) 790-1841

FOREST HOME

WHEN HENRIETTA MEARS was looking for a Christian retreat back in 1937, she thought the valley in Forest Falls was ideal, but the asking price of $350,000 was way outside her limits. However, a storm, which many believed was brought on by divine intervention, resulted in the price being dropped to $30,000, and Forest Home was born and began its work.

Today, this 500-acre facility provides 'A retreat from the distractions of the world, where people can contemplate...' so says the opening of their mission statement. There is no doubt that the original plan of Henrietta Mears has been fulfilled in total, and the number of visitors to the site bears out its success.

President and CEO, Ridge Burns, oversees what has become a large and impressive institution. "We host some 70,000 guests here every year, and many of them return again and again," he said from his comfortable office in the heart of the Canyon. "We run a variety of programs for many different types of people. We also have another 150-acre site in Ojai." Burns also reported that with a staff of 500 in the summer, the facility keeps a full time equivalent of 200 year round.

"Our summer camp activities are very popular," he continued. "We have an Indian Village for third to fourth graders, Adventure Mountain for fifth and sixth graders, Creekside for junior high school level and Lakeview for the high schoolers." There is also a seven-room bed and breakfast facility, and one with 1800 beds in the conference facility. It is an impressive place, but manages to give off an intimate atmosphere of quietness and reflection, even though there are 176 structures necessary to cater for everyone.

"This is truly a wonderful place for families to come," Burns smiled as he recounted the many success stories he had of the types of groups that gather here. "We have had great success with fathers and sons, mothers and daughters, and most recently we had a large group of single parents. They shared many of the problems they all had with their lives, and were able to pass on a lot of support and help to each other. It was truly a wonderful thing."

Forest Home is very much a Christian center, although it is a non-profit and non-denominational resort. The bucolic atmosphere surrounded by the majestic mountains can only help one adjust to life, as it was envisaged by its founder, Henrietta Mears. During rains, the Santa Ana River rushes by, and further up Valley of the Falls Drive is the waterfall that gives the village its name. Once inside however, there is no need to leave the place until the end of the visit. All food and recreation are provided by a very competent staff, and the agenda is packed for those who need activities along with relaxation.

During the summer months there is a large swimming pool, and also a lake with a beach. This lake was once California's first fish farm but now has other more leisurely uses. Senior Executive Director's Assistant, Buffy Bowman pointed out a special spot. "Billy Graham preached here in April 1965, and we have a plaque on the place where he delivered his sermon." Bowman has worked here at Forest Home for five years, starting out as the manager for recreation. "It's just a marvelous place," was her simple summing up.

Bookings for weekends and other longer stays can be made through the attractive and informative Web site, or through their booking service. Rates and availability vary, and the 2004 season is filling up fast with people needing a different outlook on normally busy lives.

Forest Home Ministries
40,000 Valley of the Falls
Forest Falls, CA 92339
(909) 389-2300
Web Site: www.foresthome.org

BARSTOW

BARSTOW SOMETIMES GETS an unfair review. Most of the 23,100 residents are happy to call the high desert city home, however, and of the 17 million vehicles that pass along Route 15 to and from Los Angeles and the far away places to the east, several stop for a break. It seems to be a natural place to rest and eat, or stay the night.

Jeanette Hayhurst has a simple answer to those who query her place of residence. "It's always been a very positive experience for me and my family," she said. As a twenty-year resident of Barstow, she has a good deal of that experience, and also as the Housing Program Coordinator for the City, she sees a lot of what goes on. "I was born and raised in the Newport Beach area of Orange County, and so I have some comparisons to make."

In the last few years Barstow is actually one of the few Southern California cities to have shrunk in size. "We used to have a lot of people from Fort Irwin living here, but since the base expanded their facilities, many of those people now live on base." Hayhurst explained. In spite of that, Barstow still has a sort of military feel to it, and right in the middle of the old Main Street, which used to be a part of Route 66, stands a military recruiting office.

Although the City of Barstow only covers 40 square miles, the recruiting area goes much further. "We look after the recruitment of military personnel for over 16,000 square miles," reported Sergeant First Class Brian Homme. A veteran of 12 years service in the Army, he has been in the recruitment business for the last three. "We're here because we have the right sort of population, and the right conditions to attract applicants."

Homme shares premises with the other four branches of the military, although the Marines and the Navy only have satellite operations in Barstow. "There are a number of misconceptions about joining up," he said. "One of them is that you can only enlist when you're in your twenties. In fact you can join when you're 17 and right through age 34. You have to still be 34 before you go on the nine weeks basic training. Thirty-five is just beyond the cut off date."

For those hesitant to enlist for fear of being in harm's way, Homme points out: "You have to choose a job before you sign up." And he is there to help in that process. He also pointed out that with the wide range of skills now needed there is no such thing as the 'army type.' His work in Barstow is to assist in the selection of good candidates from every walk of life. These come from 25% walk-ins, and 75% introductions and other potential recruits.

Strangely enough, a similar percentage of walk ins is reported by the new Holiday Inn Express a couple of miles down the road at Lenwood. This is the well-known outlet-shopping branch of Barstow. "We get really busy on the weekends when there is racing out in the desert," Jamie Emerson, from the front desk of the brand new hotel, explained. "We've been open since January this year as our other location was just not big enough for us.

The Holiday Inn Express is easy to spot from the busy freeway and offers an additional 110 rooms to the already 1700 hotel and motel rooms available in Barstow. Once again the military has an influence in the business, as there is a lodging need for visitors to the nearby base. "But we are here for everyone, and our goal is to be the best place in town," Emerson smiled.

In the old center of Barstow there is a large mural on a wall between second and first streets. It shows an interesting scene of its early history, when a group of soldiers in 1857 experimented with the use of camels to haul goods from New Mexico to California. They were found to be very good at the task and could go for three days without water. Unfortunately, the start of the Civil War brought the trial to an end, although it was much to the relief of the traditional mule carriers.

The route these early carriers took was superceded by the railroad, the tracks of which still go over the original area. Then followed Route

66, and finally the roads we all know today. It seems as if Barstow has always been a passing through sort of place, but the residents accept their lot with a smile, as long as many of the travelers continue to stop and stay awhile.

The City of Barstow
220 East Mountain View
Barstow, CA 92311
(760) 256-3511
www.barstowca.org

DESERT DISCOVERY CENTER

THE DESERT IS a big place and very empty, and the Desert Discovery Center in Barstow looks out across much of it. But it's not an empty place to the organizers of this compact museum located at 831 Barstow Road. In fact it's teeming with life and interesting things. And the mission of the center is to encourage more people to share their enthusiasm.

"We're changing a little of our focus these days to attract more children," said Liana Sonne, a student intern for the last month. "I find the desert fascinating, and we have lots of things for people to look at on a visit here." The board outside proclaims this is the home of 'The Old Woman Meteorite,' and sitting on a stand is this large rock from out of the skies.

This mixture of iron and other metals weighs three tons and is not something you would want to hit the roof of the SUV when out for a spin. Fortunately, the meteorite landed billions of years ago and also in the Old Woman Mountains, where few SUV's would go. It was found in 1975 by three prospectors, but because it was on Federal land, it was commandeered by the Smithsonian Museum for analysis. Some 15% of its bulk was removed for research purposes, but the rock now has a home at the Desert Discovery Center. It is an impressive item.

William J. Cook, the director of the museum also pointed out a little known fact: "The Mojave Desert has the most complex ecosystem in the world after the rainforests," he said. "It's our mission to teach people how it all works, and how they can follow up our programs to investigate on their own."

The new accent on attracting children is providing programs on the diversity of life of all the species that make the desert their home. Participants of the third grade will begin the series with a study of the

Desert Tortoise. Then they incrementally pass through to the fifth grade level on 'Leave no Trace Ethics.' Even a large and empty desert needs protecting from neglect and overuse. In order to acquire certification in the DCC Junior Naturalist Program, students must secure a mentor and complete requirements in nine categories.

There is a new effort to upgrade the trails that surround the center, and the neat desert garden is also undergoing expansion of its facilities. A spell within the walls however will teach visitors a little more about the environment in which so many species flourish. A free leaflet tells how the surrounding Barstow area is home to the Creosote Bush, and is the name given to the local ecosystem. After rain, a pungent odor of creosote is given off by this plant, hence its name. It is used for many different products. Its properties allow oils and butters from turning rancid. The Creosote Bush covers 80% of California deserts and is extremely valuable to all wildlife.

Director Cook's drive to open a world of discovery was begun some years ago when he saw a little girl pointing to the night sky. "What are those up there, Daddy?" The father replied that they were stars and planets. Cook realized that lots of children lack even the most basic understanding of the natural world, and he now hopes his museum will start a journey of a lifetime. Such a journey will help everyone understand that although it appears a vast open place, the desert is far from empty.

Where: 831 Barstow Road
          Barstow, CA 92311

Hours: 11 a.m. – 4 p.m. Tuesday to Saturday

Cost entrance and programs are FREE

For more information: (760) 252-6060
Or www.desertdiscoverycenter.com

ROUTE 66 MUSEUM, BARSTOW

THE NAME OF Route 66 still conjures up memories of journeys and feelings by even those who never took a trip along America's Mother Road. There is a nostalgia associated with it, even if it's just the Nat 'King' Cole song, or the tinkling orchestration of Richard Rogers music.

The new museum located at the Harvey House in Barstow encourages visitors to feast in full on those memories when they enter this sanctum. Curator, Debra Hodkin, will do everything she can to help you understand the importance of this vital route in America's history.

Debra Hodkin of the Rte 66 Museum

"We get a lot of foreigners too," she said. "We even had a couple from Switzerland visit us twice in two days. They had traveled down all the way from Utah just to come here." Historians too make their way to the spot along with Harley clubs, antique and classic car enthusiasts, and just people who have lived with the image of Route 66 in their minds for a long time.

The museum is well stocked with memorabilia, and even though there is another one located in Victorville some twenty-five miles to the south, there is no shortage of materials to go around. "We have a very good relationship with Victorville," Hodkin added. "Lots of people visit both locations."

The museum houses some interesting examples of transportation from the era of the great road. A 1917 Model T Ford is shown in pristine condition. "There were only 244,181 made, but there are still plenty out there in good working order," Hodkin said. Also there is a 1947 Harley Davidson Servicar, which draws a lot of interest from the motorcycle crowd. It sits alongside a more modern 1966 Electra Glide, which naturally is in blue.

If you have the time there is a continuous showing within the small movie area, which explains some of the history of the route from the early Indian trails to the mule trains, the short experiment with camels, which preceded the railroad, and then finally the road itself. People have been traveling along this way for a long time.

An interesting display charts the story of the Strickland family, who, like the Joads in the famous Steinbeck novel made the harsh journey out west from their Oklahoma roots. The effects of the dry dust conditions, which stripped all life out of the soil, caused the Stricklands to load up and travel to more prosperous land. In their case it was to Bakersfield. Route 66 did not always have happy results for families who made the trek, and the long straight road often took its toll on people and machines as they struggled against severe odds.

In happier times, during the early sixties the exploits of two young men in their Corvette brought weekly excitement to the television screens of people all around the world. It broadcast much of the American way of life to a generation, which could only hope that one day they might visit this exciting land. "We have many of the videos of those programs here," Hodkin said. "We also have a full range of other materials in our gift shop."

Recently, the Roy Rogers Museum moved out of the area due to a falling off of the people who remembered him and his era. This does not seem to be happening to followers of the history of Route 66. Although by the mid-eighties nearly all the signs had been removed, there seems to be a continuing regard for the times that the road was in its heyday. No matter whether you are an enthusiast, or just have a passing interest, there is a real welcome for you at the Mother Road Museum in Barstow.

Where: Harvey House
              681 North First Avenue
              Barstow, CA 92311

Hours: Friday – Sunday 11 a.m. to 4 p.m. Cost: Free

For more information call (760) 255-1890
Or www.route66museum.org

UNIVERSITY OF REDLANDS

Redlands University

THE CITY OF Redlands is a well-maintained and historic place for people to live and work. The population of close to 70,000 has a lot for all to do and enjoy. The downtown area has been well cared for and features many attractions for visitors and residents alike. However unlike many of the county's other cities, Redlands has within its borders a city within a city.

The University of Redlands is a private four-year university that has a regular population of around 4,300 students with a full faculty to care for their every need. "We have a ratio of 14 to 1," said Deborah Mandabach, Director of Public Relations at the school. "That would make our population about 5,000." However the University is a spacious place and it does not give the impression of ever being overcrowded.

Founded in 1907, the setting has as a feel of antiquity about it, and can hold its head up among some of the country's other seats of high learning. "A recent US News and World Report's survey had us at number seven in the Western Region," Mandabach reported. The magazine's annual survey is highly regarded by all those interested in university standards.

Costs to attend are not modest. A year's fees will set a family back around $30,000, but currently around 85% are receiving some sort of financial aid. "We have some students working on campus to assist with their financial aid package," Mandabach said. The brochure provided by the institution provides lists of alternatives to help with schooling fees, and councilors are only too willing to provide advice.

The syllabus is very comprehensive, but leans somewhat towards education, arts and sciences, and business with separate schools devoted to each.

The School of Education produces a yearly batch of first class teachers who have worked on bachelor's degrees, before taking courses on education. Similarly, work will have been completed on qualifications for communication disorders, which are another specialty of Redlands.

The President has been in his current position since 1987, and overseen many changes in the last decade and a half. "James R. Appleton made his career path through student affairs, fundraising and development," Mandabach reported. "He currently teaches a class on educational leadership."

Within the university is a separate campus called The Johnston Center. Here, students work from a less formal syllabus. A founding member of this alternative education explained it this way: Rather than ordering from the menu, we ask students to come into the kitchen and help make the meal." This innovative approach to learning allows students to explore the full range of their talents with such courses as Death and Postmodernism, and Powder Puff Auto Mechanics. Graduates go into a diverse world ranging from films and TV to academia.

The University of Redlands library is a principal resource for all on campus as well as people from outside. "We have well over 250,000 volumes here, all designed to compliment the curriculum," said Bill Kennedy, the acting library director, who has worked at the university since 1980. "We are also a federal depository housing numerous works from the government on CD's, DVD's, paper and microfiche."

With a full sports program and many teams competing throughout the nation, the University of Redlands is truly a world within a city, which itself has plenty of activity going on. The lucky young people passing through the halls learning the skills for later in life will have much to be grateful for.

University of Redlands
1200 E. Colton Avenue
PO Box 3080
Redlands, CA 92373-0999
www.redlands.edu
(909) 793-2121

GRABER OLIVE HOUSE

ONTARIO'S OLDEST BUSINESS sits quietly within a discreet residential neighborhood. It looks like it belongs there, and this is probably because Ontario has grown up around it, and not the other way around. Clifford Graber purchased the land back in 1892, and intended to farm oranges in this rich citrus growing area. But he soon found olives growing in the region and that they were very popular with his friends and neighbors.

"He also found that if you let the olives ripen on the tree, instead of picking them early, the flavor was wonderful." Said Kathleen Spear, who has worked at the establishment for the last thirty years. "The black canned olives you often find in stores have been picked early and actually dyed to get that color. Graber olives are handled in a different way."

The firm began in earnest in 1894, and olives soon represented a major part of the fruit crop. "But it was the idea of old Mr. Clifford to keep the olives on the tree for longer than normal. Then the fruit is picked by hand, very carefully," Spear added. It was not long before the motto of the company became 'Quality, not quantity,' and this has helped promote the crop as far away as Japan, Europe and attracted buyers from all over the United States.

Olive picking has a comparatively short season – just October through December. "It was a small crop this year and we were done picking early, Spear explained. "Our olives are not grown here any more, but up at our ranch north of Bakersfield, in the San Joaquin Valley. Then they are brought down here for selection and packing." Each olive is passed through a process that grades them by size, and although the largest are most sought after, small ones taste just as good.

Inez Bjorkman has worked here for 35 years. "This is a real family business," she said, "I look after the sales room and I also do a lot of the buying," she said. And there's a lot of buying to do, as the shops sell a wide range of different items. There are two shops at the site; one, which specializes in souvenirs and memorabilia, and food items sold at the other. Graber's produces a wide range of different food baskets with olives only being part of the display. An illustrated catalogue is sent out all over the country to interested buyers, many of whom are buying corporate gifts.

In 2003, the company won a gold medal at the Los Angeles County Fair for its olive oil. Personnel Director, Florence Duncan, who at only six years service considers herself quite a newcomer, said: "The oil is extra virgin, and is the first cold pressing of the fruit." Of course, such oil is readily available to buy at the shop.

Although the curing and packing are done at the location, there is very little hint of much industrial activity for visitors, who are there to just browse in the shops or walk round the small neat and tidy museum. Tours however of the factory are always available, and a visitor can be taken around with no notice necessary. Much of the original equipment is still in use and functioning perfectly.

Olives are one of those readily available items in the local market that most people don't take a lot of notice of. But a trip to Graber's will elevate your interest and help you understand one of mankind's most ancient enjoyments.

Where: 315 E. Fourth Street, Ontario. CA 91762
           (1 1/2 blocks east of Euclid.)

Hours: Weekdays 9 a.m. to 5.30 p.m.
          Sundays 9.30 a.m. to 6 p.m.

For more information call (909) 983-1761
Or visit the Web site: www.graberolives.com

ONTARIO MUSEUM

IF THE ORIGINAL plans of the Chaffey brothers had remained in place, Ontario would have been called Etiwanda. This was how they saw it when they came out to visit their parents, who had retired to Riverside. But all this was back in the late 1880's when the two brothers left their home in Ontario, Canada to seek pastures new.

Ontario Museum

Ontario Museum attendant, Mary Duffy, who has worked there for 13 years is happy to explain the history of the place. "Originally this building was constructed in 1937 as part of the Works Progress Administration under Franklin Roosevelt," she said. "It was the original City Hall, but it's been a museum of the area since 1979." The building is styled Mediterranean-Revival and Duffy reported that its appearance is one of the principal reasons people come by.

Displays on the walls explain the early history of Ontario, since the Chaffey brothers arrived. Back then the region was a haven of citrus farms and some of the displays feature exhibits from that time and industry. An old packing box is on display from the Graber Olive House, which is located just a few blocks away. But the museum is more than just a harbor of artifacts from the old days.

"We change our exhibits about every three months," Duffy reported. "And about half our museum is permanent with the other half changeable." Currently a quilt exhibition is coming to an end. This features rooms of black and white quilts of many different designs. But it will be over on January 25th.

A permanent exhibition is on display showing the effects that road systems have had on our lives. Called 'Road Ways,' it illustrates how the automobile has impacted all of us. Two visitors, Darlene Pitman and her daughter, Emilie, were examining these effects. "We only traveled from Cucamonga," Darlene explained. But it would have been impossible to imagine their short journey without the aid of a car. Back in 1892, the Chaffeys' journeys would have been far more difficult.

As visitors wander around the Road Ways exhibit, they will hear the sound of 'old timers' talking in the background, taking one back to a time when travel was nearly always a challenge. An introduction explains: Here you will explore how the road winds through our history and helps drive our culture. A look at the landscape in the Chaffeys' time shows the massive changes that have occurred.

From February 4 to March 7, a new exhibit will be available featuring the work of a Swiss artist, Karl Bodmer, from the 1800's. He accompanied German scientist Prince Maximillian on a two-year journey across North America and up the Missouri River. At the time the two travelers met with many different settlers, and several of the Native Americans who populated the land.

The works produced from this journey in 1883 and 1884 show in dramatic detail the life that was enjoyed by the early people. The well-known Frederic Remington remarked about Bodmer's work: "It is much better than 'modern' artists, who depicted the West from the heart rather than the head." Entrance to the upcoming exhibit is, like all of the Ontario Museum shows, free.

The Ontario area has changed almost beyond recognition from the days when two Canadian brothers came out of the frozen north to spend time in the California sunshine. Their venture grew and they decided to remember their original homeland by calling the place by the name we all know today. Otherwise, modern visitors to the local airport would be flying into Etiwanda, rather than Ontario.

Where: Ontario Museum of History and Art
         225 South Euclid Avenue
         Ontario, CA 91762

Hours: 12 p.m. to 4 p.m. Wednesdays through Sundays.

Cost: Free

For more information call (909) 983-8978
Or visit the Web site www.ci.ontario.ca.us and look under 'Departments.'

ADELANTO

THE CITY OF Adelanto seems to be in a period of transition. Without doubt it has a lot of potential but such potential is still some distance away from fulfillment. Highway 395 acts as a huge conduit rolling through the community effectively splitting it east and west. But there is another split which is more along social lines and that lies north and south.

"We have a lot of new homes built at the south end," said Stacy Cole of Desert Sand Realty, "but the north end is the old Adelanto and has few new buildings." Cole and his two partners run the realty firm located roughly midway between all points of both split areas. "We all were in the Air Force at one time and we joined up here to run this business," Cole stated.

Airplanes are a part of Adelanto life with the George base so close. Unfortunately the base was scheduled for closure in the nineties and created a vacuum, which is only now being filled. "We're all hoping for cargo flights to use the airfield, but that's a little in the future," Cole added. For the moment, several major airlines use the area to store aircraft that were surplus to requirements after the 9/11 attack caused a slump in the industry. The dry desert air makes storage ideal.

Ex mayor, Ed Dondelinger, one of the partners at Desert Realty, no longer lives in the community as he now shares a home with his son outside the town. "I was the longest serving council member in the history of the town," he said. "And I served as mayor from 1988 to 1992." He came to the desert community in the early seventies and has seen a lot of changes in the area. "There's been tremendous expansion here," he said.

A lot of the expansion is not immediately apparent however, as Adelanto has a lot of ground to hide places. One of which is a large industrial development along Rancho Road to the west. Here, a number of companies have set up, taking advantage of attractive offers by the town authorities.

"Our company moved out here in 1991," said Greg Bourque, sales manager for Cabo Yachts. It might seem an odd place to build luxury sport fishing boats, but Bourque seems very happy with the location. "I've been with the firm since 1993," he says. "We have a large facility here." Cabo Yachts occupies some 200,000 square feet to build its gleaming craft. "Our prices range from about $300,000 up to a million," Bourque said. "Lots of our customers live on the East Coast, and overseas." The company reported a sales turnover in 1998 of over $24 million and received the 'Exporter of the Year' award.

Cabo Yachts is just one firm enjoying the benefits of Adelanto's business climate, but you would not know it was there unless you looked hard. Similarly the town's other claim to fame is the location of three separate prisons. "They're all run by private companies," Realtor Cole said. "Sometimes the prisoners come out to help clean up the roads, but other than that we never see them."

Adelanto was founded in 1915 by the inventor of the Hotpoint Electric Iron. The city's name means "I advance, improve or go ahead." The place looks set for advancement and several plans are already in place. The new City Hall overlooks the crowded 395 corridor and is busying for advancement. We still have land for sale," Realtor Cole said. Perhaps the improvement inherent in Adelanto's name is just around the corner.

Desert Sand Realty
11599 Bartlett Avenue
Adelanto, CA 92310
(760) 246-5012
email: eddesert@mscomm.com

Cabo Yachts
9780 Rancho Road
Adelanto, CA 92301
(760) 246-8917
www.caboyachts.com

City of Adelanto
11600 Air Expressway
Adelanto, CA 92301
(760) 246-2300

ANTELOPE VALLEY INDIAN MUSEUM

EDRA L. MOORE has watched over the Antelope Valley Indian Museum as curator since 1994. "But I've been here since 1989," she said. "Initially as a museum technician." Her responsibilities are to care for both a unique location and also for a collection of artifacts unrivalled in the area. "The museum has gone through three different phases," she said. "Firstly it was the home of Howard Arden Edwards." He was one of the first people to show an active interest in the early peoples of this country, who had established cultures long before the European settlers swept their way across the land. Edwards was an artist and amateur anthropologist, and in 1928 he took advantage of the current law to homestead 160 acres out in this region of the desert.

Unfortunately for his wife and son, this meant full time occupation of the land in order to comply with the regulations. He could only come to his desert home on the weekends, and for the first winter, his dependants had to live in a tent strung up between some boulders. "Perhaps this early experience contributed to Mrs. Edwards not being too fond of the place." Moore said. However, her husband was a determined, though somewhat eccentric man, and he saw the site as a wonderful place for his many interests. And he started with the boulders. Edwards incorporated these huge stones into the structure of the house, and they became an integral part of the living room, which now houses an eclectic assortment of Indian artifacts attractively displayed so that visitors can examine them closely.

"In 1939 the estate, along with most of the artifacts, was sold to a woman called Grace Oliver, who used it as a retreat." Moore said. "And in 1940 it was turned into a full museum, although it had to wait until 1979, before then Governor, Jerry Brown, acquired it on behalf of the California State Parks. It was managed entirely by volunteers until I came along as the first full time employee." Volunteers are still the major resource for manning the museum and its grounds, which overlooks the town of Lake Los Angeles, just off the Pearblossom Highway. "And we're still looking for energetic, enthusiastic people to help us with the work."

The third phase this interesting museum has entered is what Curator Moore calls the Interpretive Stage. "Today we are very interested in the trade routes that occurred here in the Great Basin. It seems that the tribes were very powerful, even what you could call 'wheeler dealers.' A permanent village was established here and it conducted a vigorous trade with other tribes from quite far away." Moore also points out the 'romantic' view of many of the pieces on display. "Edwards shared the rather myopic European ideas of the time," she said. "We have come to understand so much more about the life of former cultures, and have tried hard to ensure that today's descendants of these early people are not offended by wrongful interpretations." Nonetheless, it would be impossible to alter completely all the influences of the original owner's views, and they are of interest in their own right. "Many people come to visit just to see the Chalet like buildings, and the interesting home that was built here." Moore said.

Where: The Antelope Valley Indian Museum is located 17 miles east of the Antelope Valley Freeway (Highway 14), on Avenue M, between 150th and 170the Streets East.

Hours: Weekends Mid September to Mid June from 11 a.m. to 4 p.m.

For more information: (661) 946-3055

Web site: www.avim.parks.ca.gov

FORT IRWIN

SAN BERNARDINO COUNTY has many varied and diverse communities within it, but perhaps none so as one located in the far north of the County. Here surrounded by desert sand and scrub, some 5,000 souls work and toil at their dedicated task of keeping the country safe from foreign harm. And yet it is one of those rare places where visitors are not exactly welcome and a serious pass is needed for entry.

Fort Irwin houses the United States Army National Training Center, and it's 5,000 permanent population swells to twice that size for ten months of the year. "We have ten rotations every year," Captain Belcher of the Public Affairs Office said. "That's one every month, except for December and July." Capt. Belcher is days away from being promoted to the rank of Major, and has 13 years of service to the country.

Fort Irwin has some 1200 square miles of land, and they need all of it. Tanks and assorted Humvees, with serious looking soldiers at the controls, are everywhere. Incoming troops are rotated with maximum efficiently in order to learn more of their craft of warfare and protection. Nothing goes to chance, even port-a-potties are in smart regular lines for disbursement to the field of operations. It is a rarified world to a civilian. And yet there are many civilians on the base - many of them spouses of serving personnel.

There are over 2,000 family homes constructed on base. "We have a waiting list of 450 families to move in here though," said Garrison Commander Lieutenant Colonel Richard L. Sobrato. "At the moment we have to house them off base in Barstow and surrounding communities, but they really need to be here." And here is what is referred to as the 'cantonment' area of the base. This is one of many specialized words used by the army and refers to the actual area of five square miles, which contains the living quarters of the troops and their families, and also the administration.

"I'm not sure if I would be the mayor or the city manager of the location," Sobrato said. "There's a budget of some $100 million for the fort and that's just the actual infrastructure, not the combat side." With the shops, schools – there are two of them – restaurants, roads, sewers, water lines and the like, Fort Irwin in many ways does perform like a city.

"It's a lot different from when I was here," said 'Sarge' Miskell, a visiting retired Sergeant with 21 years of service. "I did a tour of duty here in the seventies and it was a lot different back then." Miskell, as a veteran is allowed on base, and likes to visit the clothing store for essentials to keep his uniform up to date. Years of service make it difficult to shake off the discipline and confidence that comes with the job.

There is no mistaking the different atmosphere that cloaks Fort Irwin. Whether in uniform or not, people have a smartness about them and an obvious pride in what they are doing. Although to the uninitiated, the camouflaged dress is much the same, the smallest insignia is immediately apparent to the troops. Salutes are snapped off smartly to higher ranks, and badges denoting skills and service are recognized immediately by even the newest recruit.

Currently a rotation belonging to the 3rd Infantry is completing exercises after a turn of duty in Iraq. They will return to Fort Banning in Georgia, and more soldiers will take their place. Each rotation is a brigade, which totals some 4,500 to 6,000 troops, all of whom receive the most modern instruction in the art of war available on the planet.

LTC Sobrato is delighted with his position, which he has held since last June. He returned here after five years serving with the European Command. His duties took him to Bosnia and Germany. "I've been here before though," he said. "I was here in 1993, and I would often wonder why something wasn't done about a certain aspect of life here. Now I have the chance to do something about it. It's a great opportunity."

It's easy to forget the object of Fort Irwin's existence, as life here is much the same as in other communities. If it were not for the occasional rumbling of a military vehicle rolling past, one could imagine one was in any other city – one that had a rather strict dress code however. With its veterinary clinic, furniture store, fast food, car washes and the like, it performs much like other towns.

However Fort Irwin is dedicated to one aspect of life that the rest of us can mostly forget, because of its existence. Namely to train the dedicated men and women, who devote their lives to the service of this country to be even better than they can be, with the best training of the best army in the world.

National Training Center and Fort Irwin
PO Box 105067
Fort Irwin, CA 92310
(760) 380-1111
www.irwin.army.mil

GOLDSTONE

THERE'S A CERTAIN glinty-eyed enthusiasm noticeable with the folks at the Goldstone Deep Space Communications Center, off in the desert north of Barstow. "We track 30 different space craft here," said Marie Massey, one of two out-reach coordinators at the site. But it's not all of the 30 vehicles that are causing the current excitement. No, it's really just two of them, the Mars robots, Spirit and Opportunity, that are causing the hearts of the crew at Goldstone to beat a little faster these days. "We have a lot of interest in the other craft, of course," Massey continued, "but the recent successful Mars landings are really wonderful."

Located thirty miles out into the desert and far from traffic and other distractions, Goldstone has been a part of N.A.S.A. for forty years, acting as the eyes and ears of the earthly mortals, who look beyond our skies in search of deep exploration.

"We try to inspire a new generation of scientists to this field of expertise," added Karla Warner, who is the other coordinator for tours to the center. "Right now we're in a sort of lock down situation as so much of our focus is on the Mars landings, but on March 1st we'll start our regular tours once again."

Goldstone is one of three stations around the world tracking spacecraft. "We have one in Madrid, Spain, and another in Canberra, Australia," Massey explained. "With all three we can mount a 24 hour watch on the skies, and our operation here runs 24/7." Since joining the station in 1978, Massey has been an enthusiast of all things to do with space, and speaks knowledgeably about the various programs that are under the watchful eyes of the powerful telescopes.

"We are looking forward very much to another mission; the return of the Genesis satellite," she explained. "On September 8th, it will return from passing through some solar dust fields, where it collected very valuable samples. The arrival will be quite unique for us." After the craft enters the Earth's atmosphere, and the parachutes are opened, it will be collected by a helicopter in mid-air. "The dust is potentially so fragile that we can't risk a normal landing." Massey explained.

Both Massey and Warner recall the sounds of Neil Armstrong's words from the moon in 1969 of one small step for man and one giant leap for mankind. They were obviously the touch papers for a lifelong passion for the worlds beyond us. Their excitement for the various Goldstone tracking projects is transmitted into their teachings at the center. "On our tours, we can take from one visitor to 60," Warner explained. "Everyone receives a good grounding in what we do."

The museum on site contains scale models of the many projects launched into space, and charts explain the progress of the various probes. There is much to see and witness at the center. A tire from a recent space shuttle is against one wall. "It was designed to be used over and over, but once was enough," Warner showed.

Science and space travel are complicated issues and no doubt many visitors to Goldstone wish they had paid more attention at school, or perhaps kept up with their reading more on leaving. However, the two coordinators make it all sound easy to understand while being able to answer fellow enthusiasts' questions. The hard work that was put into the recent landings with the resulting great success explains the upbeat outlook of these dedicated space technicians.

Where: 35 miles north of Barstow on the Fort Irwin Military Base

Restrictions: You must have a valid driver's license, car registration and insurance to enter the base. All adults need a current ID with them.

Cost: Free

For more information call (760) 255-8687 or visit the Web site www.deepspace.jpl.nasa.gov

EL PRADO

"IT'S THE FIRST time in four weeks I've smiled!" Said Jorge Aguilera, after his lesson in the capable hands of golf professional Karl Schubert. Both were enjoying the unmatched views and casual atmosphere of El Prado Public Golf Course, at the bottom left hand corner of San Bernardino County.

El Prado in Spanish means meadow or field and although a meadow is a field with water in it, the location of the golf courses at this small country club is one of outstanding beauty. It was opened in 1976, and has two full sized regulation par 72 golf courses, and attracts a steady stream of enthusiasts to this quiet area in Chino.

"We do lots of banquets and wedding receptions here too," said Bruce Janke, the PGA General Manager. "We also hold reunion dances and other formal occasions." But it is the golf that is the constant draw for people looking for relaxation and the satisfaction of hitting that annoying little white ball as far and as straight as possible.

That is where Schubert the director of tournament operations comes in for lessons and tips on achieving that sometimes elusive goal. "We're very keen here on promoting the sport to youngsters," he said. "We visit the local high schools and we offer a free junior clinic to encourage them."

The club is a limited partnership and is run by six general partners. Dr. Walter Heuler is the managing general partner. "We are open six days a week from sun up to sun down," he said. "We have seven T-times per hour." Both walkers and those in golf carts are welcome at either of the two courses that lay side by side. "We have the Butterfield Stage Course and also the Chino Creek Course." Schubert added. The Butterfield Course is named after the well-known Butterfield stage coach that used to run through the area with important stops in the fields and citrus growing area of the Inland Empire.

Dr. Heuler explained that there are a number of public golf courses in the area and that things had been affected economically for a time, but numbers are picking up, and now there seemed to be no shortage of people swinging their clubs at the small white targets at their feet. "We have two putting greens here and also areas for practice. There is also a chipping area with a sand trap," Schubert said. "We are fairly quiet Monday through Friday mornings, but then things get busier."

It seems that golfers who have finished for the day find lunchtime on Friday to be a good start to their games, and the prices reflect the demand. There also seemed to be a ready crowd using the grass driving range.

Weekdays the cost for walkers is ten dollars cheaper as an incentive to come by for a round. But if you prefer to watch the game rather than play it, there are several opportunities at El Prado to watch those with perfect swings and deadly accuracy do their thing. Tournaments are regularly held here.

"We host the Chino City Amateur Championship every year," Schubert reported. "And we also have the Pro Tournament each fall called the Chino Fall Classic. We get about 60 to 80 good players for that every year." The facility works hard at promoting activities, and offers discounted green fees for seniors and juniors alike.

Plans are afoot for lighting the driving range, as winter daylight does restrict outdoor sport.

But the beauty of El Prado is simply that, the beauty. With the rolling hills to the south and the snow-capped mountains framing the golfing activity to the north, it is a perfect location to enjoy the best that Southern California has to offer. Of course, in order to fully enjoy the views and scenery, it might be necessary to leave those pesky clubs behind.

Where: El Prado Golf Courses
         6555 Pine Avenue
         Chino, CA 91710

Web site: elpradogolfcourses.com
Hours: Sun up to Sun down
For more information: (909) 597-1751

ONTARIO AIRPORT

IT'S UNLIKELY THAT the first flyers to enter Ontario Airport in 1923 would recognize it today. Both Archie Delwood Daniels and Waldo Waterman along with their few friends started flying into a dirt patch near San Antonio Avenue and the Union Pacific tracks in those first few days of aeronautical bravery. "The plane they used was the Curtiss JN 4," director of community relations Dennis Watson said. "It was known to all as the Jenny, and it was the WWI equivalent of the Willy Jeep, only for the air."

The original strip was named Latimer Field after the orange packing company of the time located right alongside it. But within six years the airfield moved three miles away to the southwest corner of the present location and changed its name to Ontario Municipal Airport. "Of course, this was way before LAX was even thought about," Watson continued.

With the start of the war, Ontario began to expand, and was used to assemble aircraft from many sites around the south of the state. "It was really the military that helped the airport expand," Watson said. "The early jets in the fifties needed longer and longer runways, and there was plenty of space out here."

Ontario has the longest runways in Southern California and planes land on a pair of parallel two-mile strips, giving them plenty of room. They no longer use the original method of gauging wind direction by looking for the smokestacks on nearby railroad engines. Ontario is the ultimate in modern airports.

To look at, Ontario Airport is a very modern affair, built in the eighties, with lots of room. The two terminal buildings have plenty of space between them. "It was designed that way," Watson said. "Once we reach 10 million passengers a year for two years we will begin talking about the extra third terminal to be built between the present two." Currently the facility has some six million passing through its doors annually.

With 2200 acres, the airport is the size of some of San Bernardino County's smaller cities. "We only use 1700 acres at the moment, but we have another 500 which we call our land bank." Watson said. It is a big place but it has plenty of space, and few crowds, which makes it a favorite with its customers.

"I've been flying in here regularly for about two years," reported Juan Ortega, who lives in West Covina. "I always used to drive to LAX, but once I started using Ontario it made a big difference to my life." Many have also found the lack of crush, the easy access roads and the space for all very attractive.

Ontario Airport is also a master of the modern trend of outsourcing. "We have many contractors among the 6,500 people who work here," Watson continued. "Of course, we lease out space to the various airlines and then there are the many vehicles used by contracting companies to ferry passengers around, as well as the concessions." But the number one moneymaker for the facility is the parking. "It's the same for every airport," Watson said. There are 11,500 places for parked cars and each one is a potential earner.

Ontario is also a favorite landing place for freight aircraft. UPS and Federal Express all use the airport and UPS represents 75% of the airport's annual freight revenues. On the passenger side, Southwest Airlines make up 50% of passenger flights in and out of the field.

"We're hoping to increase our passenger numbers, but the Inland Empire is still developing," Watson said. "Most of the local population are still getting their feet on the first rung of life. Not many are yet the frequent flyers that make up the airline's favorite passengers."

Such facts make Ontario a pleasant alternative to other crowded and crushed terminals in the Southland. A flight out of here is a far more pleasant experience and it feels more the way we were intended to fly. The staff seem unhurried, and even the ubiquitous security checks seem to pass with less agitation on the part of both passengers and guards.

Back in the early days, on approach, aviators always looked for the diagonal of Mission Boulevard, and many pilots these days still do although their instruments are more accurate. Long gone are the signs warning flyers to KEEP CLEAR OF THE CHICKEN HOUSES, but the principle reason for Ontario being there in the first place still stands. There is more space out here.

Ontario International Airport
1900 East Airport Drive
Ontario, CA 91761
(909) 937-2700
Web site: airport-ontario.com

SLASH X

WHEN LEE BERRY started his ranch deep out into the desert, south of Barstow in 1954, he could not have imagined the activity that is due to occur here on Saturday, March 13. He was a cowboy plain and simple, and he ran cattle across the range that he bought from the railway for $2.75 an acre. His ranch measured a cool two square miles.

The event he would no doubt be astonished to witness is the start of the DARPA race that is scheduled to begin at 6 a.m. From the quiet sounds that Berry would have known and loved will erupt the roar of engines belonging to a crowd of serious competitors racing for a prize of one million dollars. And as they say: That's not chicken feed!

Slash X Café and Ranch

DARPA stands for Defense Advanced Research Products Agency, a branch of the military. And the prize money is awarded by the government in what is a very serious venture. As their Web site explains, this is to "leverage American ingenuity to accelerate the development of autonomous vehicle technologies that can be applied to military requirements." For autonomous vehicle technologies read robots, and they are big ones; not the types that are followed by the driver with a radio and a joy stick. These are machines that have been modified to navigate via satellite over rough terrain, until they reach their goal, which in this case is Primm, Nevada.

The starting point for this expensive race is Lee Berry's Slash X cafe, the name of which is the / X brand he put on his cattle. Located some twelve miles out of Barstow towards Lucerne Valley on route 247, the Slash X is a stopping point for many travelers. This was one of Berry's plans when he built the café and saloon.

"The other reason he built the place was so that his cowboys would have somewhere to go rather than into Barstow," said Dave Krumbine, the owner for the last 21 years. "Lee had to go and fetch them when they got too drunk to come home, so he decided to put a stop to that."

The Slash X was the second building that Berry erected out in the wilds. It immediately followed the building of his house. "His wife wouldn't let him have a beer in the home, so he build a saloon next door," Krumbine laughed.

The facility has become a haven for off-roaders of all types. On any given weekend, rows of dirt bikes can be seen lined up for excursions into the Stoddard Valley whose entrance is located next to the café. Four-wheel drives and quads share the 54,000 acres of land now administered by the Bureau of Land Management, where Berry's cattle used to graze.

One recent two-day event gave all its proceeds to the Barstow charities. It was a poker run where participant selected a card from various points along the route and the ones with the highest poker hand win the prizes. As with many of these types of activities the prize is really not the main attraction, as the fun and camaraderie make up for any possible disappointment in a bad hand.

A recent event held a dinner on the Saturday night and there were plenty of facilities for camping. Strict outdoor rules will be enforced, as safety is at the top of the list to ensure a good time for spectators and participants alike.

No doubt Lee Berry would smile at the changeover from horses and cattle to dirt bikes and quads out on his range. But what he would make of the high tech machines competing for the million-dollar prize we can only speculate about. One thing is certain, once the dust has settled and the crowds gone home, the desert's quietness and the beauty of the night skies would be instantly recognizable to the old cowboy.

Slash X
12 miles south of Barstow on Highway 247
PO Box 1948
Barstow, CA 92312-1948
(909) 252-1197

BUREAU OF LAND MANAGEMENT

THE BUREAU OF Land Management admits that they're not the most popular agency around. "We have to walk a very thin line," John Yates, the public contact representative said. "Many times we have to place ourselves between two very opposite factions."

The local BLM has to administer over 25 million acres of public land in some of the most diverse conditions on earth. And often they have to stand fast against many different groups. "You have the environmentalists, and then you have the off-roaders," Yates continued. "Both have an interest in the land for their specific interests. And we have to insure that the land doesn't suffer."

Just twelve miles down the road from the local Barstow office is the Stoddard Valley area, and here, ATV's, Quads, and dirt bikes all want to use the wide open spaces to explore the scenery and enjoy their particular sports. A few miles further away is the Johnson Valley which is one of the largest off road areas in California. "It's about 185,000 acres of the best land for this activity," Yates added.

Overseeing this enormous area takes a lot of work and manpower to make sure the owners' interests are looked after, and we are all the owners as it is public land.

BLM's start goes back to 1785 and the Northwest Ordinance. These laws provided for the exploration and settlement of the lands that the original 13 colonies ceded to the Federal government after the War of Independence. In the 20th century, grazing rights, mineral rights and mining all merged to produce the modern BLM in 1946.

Today, the BLM has to oversee some of the fastest growing areas in the country and cope with an unplanned population explosion. When people start to endanger what is good for nature and the land, then someone has to step in. It's a big job, and nationally the total amount of area the Bureau administers is 262 million acres, which is about one eighth of the entire United States.

Locally, the Barstow office is pleased to help the public with any inquiries they might have before setting out to explore the region. The maps on the walls show a wide area, with a bewildering range of ownership. "The blue areas are owned by the county," Yates pointed out. Other areas belong to cities and others are privately owned. The diversity is testament to the development of the region and the random settlement back in the old days of the West.

Currently the BLM is watching the anticipated plans of Fort Irwin, who wish to expand their area of operation. To the uninitiated it seems from the maps, that this could do no harm. However, out in the desert roams the desert tortoise, and its existence is very protected. It is no match for an Abrams tank and it's not too quick on its feet either. Studies continue before the military can make its move.

The Bureau has information on where to camp and where to hike. It can tell you where to take your all terrain vehicle, and also your binoculars. They have maps to sell, and can give directions. One of the favorite spots is out on the dunes area off Highway 127, 25 miles north of Baker. "It's 5000 to 7000 feet high and can be quite a dangerous place," Yates continued. Only recently a man was killed when his vehicle tipped over on him.

The Bureau clean up the areas where man has left an unwelcome mess, and they oversee areas where it is safe to discharge firearms. They also watch over much of the filming that goes on for outdoor shots. "A lot of the land north of Adelanto in El Mirage is used for car adverts," Yates added.

It may have to tread a fine line between various competing interests, but with its long history and its dedicated staff. Barstow office employs fifty, and it never forgets who it ultimately works for - us!

Bureau of Land Management
2160 Barstow Road
Barstow, CA 92312
(760) 252-6000
Open Monday - Friday 7:45 a.m. to 4: 30 p.m.
Web site www.ca.blm.gov/barstow

BAKER

THERE IS ONLY one visitor comment on the Virtual Tourist Web site for Baker, California. It's from a person named Polaris 1. It says: "You may suffer from extreme boredom!" This seems a little harsh for a place that is possibly the biggest pit stop in the state. Because Baker does not try to disguise that it is just that.

The small township nestles alongside Interstate 15 some fifty miles from the line with Nevada, and the traffic is mostly tearing off to the two cities of Las Vegas or Los Angeles. Inevitably some have to stop; for gas, for food or for rest, but many motorists and their passengers have Baker in their minds as a natural halfway place along the desert highway.

When asked about the reason for settling here the current Mad Greek, Larry Dabour smiled: "Oh, we had to mend a flat tire." But he is joking. The son of immigrants from Greece, he explained that in fact an opportunity to buy the restaurant that bears the family logo came up. "It was 17 years ago, and we moved out here from Riverside to take it over."

"The name The Mad Greek is on several restaurants across the Southland and it was the idea of Larry's father, Michael, to franchise the operation in the eighties. But today both the father and the franchise business are retired. This is not to say that the family is content to rest on its laurels - even Greek Olympic laurels! "We own a motel here, and also the gas station and the store," Dabour explained. As for the original Greek restaurant, he mentioned that Mediterranean cooking was becoming a lot more popular than it was even a few years ago. This is good news for lovers of Mousaka, Dolmades and Taramasalata.

The family also owns and runs the Bun Boy restaurant across the street, and as such is responsible for what many people know as Baker's premier feature, 'The World's Tallest Thermometer.' Visible from many miles away, the 134 feet obelisk reaches high into the sky, with its electric lights competing with the desert glare to proclaim high numbers, particularly in the summer.

"It has gone as high as 136 degrees," said Mary Dabé, who recently opened a shop on the main boulevard. "That may not have been the top temperature in Death Valley, but we get pretty close." Dabé's shop began in early May this year and holds an interesting collection of gifts and artifacts for the passer by looking to memorialize the stop.

"I've lived here since 1987," Dabé said. "I used to run the shop in Calico, and when this property became available I jumped at the chance." She is one of the 500 residents that call Baker their home and are not passing through. "But that number includes the inmates at the local prison," she added. The prison is not immediately noticeable on a short stay in the town as it is discretely placed over the hill.

Pat Ginter, who had stopped at the new store, agreed that Baker was a pretty small place. "I don't live here any more," she said. "But somehow I keep coming back." Perhaps once you get used to the isolation, the heat and the constant change of people rushing to be on their way, Baker weaves its own special magic on those who stick it out.

For the most part however, unless automobile engineers double the size of gas tanks, and biologists somehow increase the range of humans, who have consumed too many sodas, Baker will continue to offer a pit stop par excellence to those in need. The alternative is to continue the drive for another fifty miles to the next major stop along the way at Barstow, or Primm, NV.

The Mad Greek
Baker Highway & Hwy 127
Baker, CA 92309
(760) 733-4354

Gamma Ray's
72252 Baker Highway
Baker, CA 92309
(760) 733-4080

Bun Boy
Baker Highway & Hwy 127
Baker, CA 92309
(760) 733 4660

ZZYZX

THE CURIOUS NAME of Zzyzx is written large close to the town of Baker, halfway between Primm, NE, and Barstow, CA. It is an invented name given to the place by one Curtis Howe Springer, who decided it would be the ideal spot to start his business. In his own words, the land to the east was "… a mosquito swamp." But he felt it would be a place he could begin a health resort, and so began the Zzyzx Mineral Springs and Health Resort in 1944.

Springer became a celebrity, lauded by some and hated by others. He was both a radio evangelist and a businessman; a healer and a quack. But he managed to carve out a place for his services and his Zzyzx products. The name he conjured up was designed to be the last word in any dictionary. There is some argument as to whether it refers to his product motto or the fact that he was inclined to have the final word in any argument.

Today, Soda Springs as it was formally known is a haven for those interested in the study of desert matters rather than the almighty dollar. "We have a very rich history here, well before the Springer days," said Robert Fuller, the manager of the facility. "There has always been an abundance of surface water here, and so it attracts a wide variety of wildlife."

In fact, studies have shown that Soda Springs has been an important part of desert life going back to pre-historical times. "The first recorded European to visit was Fransisco Garces, who broke away from the main party coming through, and he was escorted through by local Mojave Indians," Fuller continued.

Today, the Desert Studies Center is under the control of the California State University with a cooperative agreement with the Department of the Interior. Seven Cal State campuses share responsibility for the facility.

"We are at the termination of the Mojave River," Fuller explained. It travels 150 miles inland from the San Bernardino Mountains and ends up here." The large salt bed was flooded until 9000 years ago, and water is still very close to the surface. In fact the Center is really an oasis, with green areas and ponds to attract a variety of creatures. "We get coyotes, gray foxes, big horn sheep and spotted skunks," Fuller said. "We also have 220 species of birds that use the place for a lay over. Predators know that they come and so we have a lot of them, too."

Speckled rattlesnakes are also in the area, as well as sidewinders. But the most dangerous snake to be seen is the Mojave green rattlesnake. "They're nine times the potency of a regular rattlesnake, so it's best to give them a very wide berth," Fuller added.

Currently the Center for Desert Studies offers a wide variety of courses. With room for up to 80 students and lecture facilities it can provide a unique learning experience for all those interested in studying its special environment and atmosphere. "We sometimes have schoolchildren here for an entire week. Those that come from a purely urban area, are very surprised by what they see and learn," continued Fuller. "We even have visitors from overseas to learn what they can from this place."

Within the well-kept display rooms are exhibits showing how the area has changed and developed in the thousands of years of its existence. Brochures, maps, books and charts all detail the history, and within one case is a prized display of some of Springer's products, billed naturally as "The Last Word in Health."

Where: Desert Studies Center
        Zzyzx Road,
        Baker, CA 92309
        (714) 836-0461

For more information of courses, and hours visit the Web site: http://biology.fullerton.edu/ or call (909) 880-5981

REDLANDS ART

THE CITY OF Redlands has always been a thriving place for art. "We were started in 1938," Sandy Davies, the Publicity Director of the Redlands Art Association said. "Then we had a sort of lull and really became active in 1964, that's when the association was incorporated." Today the Art Association is a center for artists to show off their work and also help younger people with their developing skills.

"We have about 250 members in the Association, and they all have the chance to show off their work here at the Gallery," Davies continued. The Gallery is located in the heart of the historical district of Redlands on the tree-lined State Street. "The sale of works allows the Association to provide classes for children and those interested in art."

Some 80% of the classes are for young children and there are often many of them in the classroom learning about colors, textures and shapes from a number of enthusiastic teachers.

"We are run on a completely volunteer basis," Davies added. And not everybody is an artist. Some just like the involvement and also to help promote art." Joan Wiley, the current co-treasurer, however, is an artist of considerable talent. "I work mostly in water colors and also drawing," she said. "Two of my paintings are on show here at the moment." Wiley pointed to a muted picture of Big Sur in the classroom, no doubt acting as an inspiration for the young students near by.

Redlands is a unique city with a special mix of the traditional and also the new. "We have a good combination of preservation and new development," Davies said. A look at the variety of work within the Gallery shows a similar mix of the new and the old.

The Margaret Clark Fund is one of a number of opportunities for people to receive grants from the Association. "Margaret Clark was a teacher and the fund allows us to assist with education," Davies explained. "Recently we helped five teachers attend courses on children's literacy. The fund took care of the cost of replacement teachers."

Much of the activity for the Association takes place in the cooler months.

There is a semi-annual outdoor show scheduled for November at the old Santa Fe depot, and there is to be a 40th anniversary art auction. However, the Gallery's works are always changing and visitors come from all over to look at the many different pieces on show.

Not only paintings line the walls, but there are cases of jewelry, and some functional art on display. Prices of the art are usually below $250 although at the moment there are some paintings by local artist Janet Edwards, which are a lot more.

If one is looking for more expensive art, then the EOS Gallery a block away on Citrus maybe the place to visit. Currently, there is an exhibition there by mother and daughter Lucille and Joy von Wolffersdorff. Their work embraces a long period of time - 1942 to the present, with a wide variety of styles and media.

"The paintings on show here are called In Plein Air," Joy Wolffersdorff explained. "They are all from nature and represent a certain stillness." For the next few weeks, the gallery will display the works of both artists, and then the owner, Shirley Harry, will change the art on show.

The Gallery's hours are normally on the weekends from 10 a.m. to 5 p.m., but for the In Plein Air exhibit the gallery is open during the week.

The City of Redlands has always been considered attractive. With the mountains as a backdrop, and the old style buildings that make up the historic part of the city, it is no wonder that artists are drawn to the scenery. For those looking for a chance to enjoy the work of such artists, the two galleries in the center are worth spending some time in.

Redlands Art Association
215 E. State Street
Redlands, CA 92373
(909) 792-8435
www.redlands-art.org

EOS Gallery
304 E. Citrus, Suite A
Redlands, CA 92373
(909) 798-3200

BEAR VALLEY STAGE LINES

BEAR VALLEY STAGE LINES- GUIDE TO STAGECOACH ETIQUETTE

Adherence to the Following Rules Will Insure a Pleasant Trip for All

1. Abstinence from liquor is requested, but if you must drink, share the bottle. To do otherwise makes you appear selfish and unneighborly. And, don't overlook the driver.

2. If ladies are present, gentlemen are urged to forego smoking cigars and pipes as the odor of same is repugnant to the Gentle Sex. Chewing tobacco is permitted but spit WITH the wind, not against it.

3. Gentlemen must refrain from the use of rough language in the presence of ladies and children. This rule does not apply to the driver, whose team may not be able to understand genteel language.

4. Buffalo robes are provided for your comfort during cold weather. Hogging robes will not be tolerated and the offender will be made to ride with the driver.

5. Don't snore loudly while sleeping or use your fellow passenger's shoulder for a pillow; he or she may not understand and friction may result.

6. Firearms may be kept on your person for use in emergencies. Do not fire them for pleasure or shoot at wild animals along the roadside. The noise riles the horses.

7. In the event of runaway horses, remain calm. Leaping from the coach in panic will leave you injured, at the mercy of the elements, hostile Indians and hungry coyotes.
8. Forbidden topics of discussion are stagecoach robberies and Indian uprisings.
9. Gents guilty of unchivalrous behavior toward lady passengers will be put off the stage. It's a long walk back. A word to the wise is sufficient.

Two of the largest residents of Big Bear are often to be seen standing quietly in the middle of the village munching from their lunch bags. Both Diane and Thumbelina stand six feet tall at the shoulders, or as those in the know say: "At the withers." For the two females are English Shore horses and belong to Michael Homan, who has cared for them for the last decade of their lives.

Diane and Thumbelina are half sisters and they are a little different in size. Diane is the larger of the two and is measured at a full seventeen hands, whereas Thumbelina is only sixteen and a half. Homan has two other large horses, a couple of Belgian Draught horses, which he uses as well.

"I've worked with horses all my life," Homan said. "So when I went into this business it was fairly easy for me." Homan is a native of Missouri, but has lived in the Big Bear Valley for the last fifteen years. "I saw an ad in the paper for carriage drivers, and applied." He now owns Bear Valley Stage Lines, and regularly drives his various carriages and coaches for those interested in capturing a little of how it used to be a hundred years or more ago.

Bear Valley Stage Coach

The stage coach, which is the usual vehicle which the two large black horses pull, is one that Homan bought from a beer distributor in St. Louis, MO. "It was once owned by Joe Montana, who had a Coors Beer business, he was in partnership with some other people but eventually decided to sell the coach. I went down there and bought it." Homan then changed the decoration of the coach and he was ready to go.

"I've had a couple of modifications done to the steering," he said. "In order for the horses to be able to back up in a small space, I've made a shorter turning circle." Seeing the pair carry out this maneuver in weekend traffic is truly spectacular, as they seem to understand the difficulties and behave with great deliberation.

Bear Valley Stage Lines have other rigs for a variety of customers' needs. Bridal pairs are often seen settled into the plush seats of a white carriage, pulled by Thumbelina, who is the horse for such occasions.

Homan himself as the driver is decked out, and the carriage is also beribboned and flowered. It's quite a transportation for that special day and is guarantee to make a couple feel really grand.

Horses are simple when it comes to feeding. "I give them bales of alfalfa normally," Homan explained. "But if it's really cold or they've been working hard I also give them grain." Each horse eats 35 pounds of hay a day or a third of a bale each.

Diane and Thumbelina's mother was a vaulting horse, carrying acrobats around a ring, and their sister is a trail horse, all desirable positions for these giants of the horse world. "They don't like to be touched much," Homan said. "When they're just standing and waiting, people do come up and try to pet them, but I tell them to keep away." He is assisted in this by his two daughters, Keli, 13, and Kailyn, 11. It's not that the horses are unfriendly, it's just that they can get startled and those big feet could do some damage. Also occasionally one of the horses nods her head up and down quite noticeably. "That means 'get out of my space.'" Homan smiled.

"Thumbelina has a funny way with her too," he continued. "When she walks, sometimes her top lip goes left and right, while her bottom lip goes up and down. It's quite unique."

Bear Valley Lines hopes to continue carrying out functions for the foreseeable future. With weddings and functions on and off the hill, Homan and his various charges will draw people back to an older time.

For more information call (909) 584-2277

REDLANDS AIRPORT

YOU WOULD BE forgiven for thinking that Redlands Airport was not actually in Redlands. It's quite a long way out of town, and off to the east and north. "It used to belong to Mentone," said Charlotte Kranenburg, the airport manager for the last year. "But it's belonged to Redlands now, since 1967. It is run by the Municipal Utilities Department."

Its comparative remoteness has perhaps caused the airport to lack some of the crowd pulling amenities that other airports have. It has no restaurant or bar, and the facilities there are strictly for aircraft enthusiasts only. "It's hard to have a decent restaurant, when you only have around thirty potential customers a day," Kranenburg continued. However, we do expect the facility to increase its appeal in the next few years."

Redlands Airport lays along the east west lowlands of the San Bernardino Mountains, and attracts pilots who need a break or who share the facilities there. There are fuel pumps available and a large well set-up lounge overlooking the runway. "We are categorized as a small General aviation (GA) airport," Kranenburg explained. "That category is dominated by the length of the runway, which is 4,750 feet. Later on in the year we have some pavement reconstruction and that will increase the length to 5005 feet."

It is also an uncontrolled airport, which means that pilots are not assisted from the ground, and talk to other pilots in the immediate area via a Unicom system. This is an antenna which operates on a frequency controlled by the FCC.

The airport has a large number of flight operations for its small size. "We have over 40,000 take offs and landings a year," Kranenburg said. "But that is mostly due to the two flight schools we have." One of these teaches acrobatic flying, and the other trains pilots on helicopters and also fixed wing aircraft.

The airport management's mission is to make people more aware of the airport and increase its function. It has an advisory board to help in this and they now host three events annually, with one of the most popular being for The Young Eagles arranged by the Experimental Aircraft Association. It is run quarterly and encourages young people to ride in these aircraft to increase the interest in the activity.

There are approximately 200 planes at the airport and twelve businesses operate there. Perhaps the most interesting of these is the Mission Aviation Fellowship. "We have a world wide safety office here in Redlands," reported Dennis Hoekstra. The Director of Aviation for the mission. "We were founded in 1945 in Los Angeles and moved to Redlands in 1980. We train missionaries to operate in remote and difficult places all over the world." They have 54 aircraft operating in 20 different countries, and the base in Redlands is there to teach their personnel how to maintain and fly aircraft in very difficult circumstances.

"Many of our people are ex-military, who have a calling," Hoekstra reported. "We have to teach them how to maintain their aircraft and fly them where normal maintenance is a problem." He also said that their standards are a little higher and their tolerances are little closer than here in the US. Their red and white Cessna 209 planes have to operate far from home.

A look round the Redlands airport shows that flying has not altered a great deal in the last couple of decades. Aircraft design at the smaller end seems to have altered very little, although electronics have improved enormously. "We expect a huge change soon though," Kranenburg said. "This will be with the introduction of Very Light Jets." This new category is an exciting development and it is hoped it will introduce a new breed of flyers to the scene. "We expect it will be within a year," she added. It seems this new form or propulsion will be quieter and also more within the financial range of people wanting to get into the air.

Redlands Airport may have enjoyed a remoteness that was once enjoyed only by the few who controlled light aircraft, but the single family homes creeping slowly out of the communities of Highland and

Redlands will introduce more and more to the delights of leaving the ground. And with a new form of jet arriving soon it may be the push the authorities are looking for to encourage more visitors.

Redlands Airport
1745 Sessums Drive
Redlands, CA 92374
(909) 798-7668
Web site: http://www.cityofredlands.org/qol/airport

KIMBERLY CREST

Kimberly Crest

EUROPEANS OFTEN FEEL a little smug when visiting California. Particularly when they are looking at some of the historical places and replica buildings. Let's face it, California is not that old when compared to the ancient cultures of Europe, and some of the replicas are only built as ideas of what other places look and feel like.

However, when visitors walk the hundred yards from the parking lot to the house known as Kimberly Crest in Redlands, there is no doubt at all that the building that so elegantly comes into view is a seventeenth century chateau. Granted, it is smaller than its counterparts along the Loire Valley in France, but it is nonetheless built exactly along the lines of the old French architects, except it was done in the last years of the nineteenth century by Mrs. Cornelia A. Hill. She was a widow who had a particular fondness for the French region.

Her tenure at the magnificent house she built was short lived however, as it became the property of the successful paper magnate Alfred Kimberly of Kimberly-Clark fame, in 1905.

"The house was given to the people of Redlands in 1968," said Paula Dill, a docent at the house. "It was continuously lived in for 75 years and the youngest daughter of the Kimberly's, Mrs. Mary Shirk, was the last owner."

Several improvements were made by the Kimberly's both to the house and the magnificent gardens that are now under the direction of Terry Hernestrom. It looks out across well tended grounds to the valley below, giving an ideal setting to the many events scheduled there, particularly weddings.

Inside the house, all the furnishings are of the time of the original occupants. "We take great care to match the fabrics when we have to do repairs," continued Dill. "In the Pink Parlor, which Mrs. Shirk always loved, we needed to change some of the drapes. We had to have special fabric made to blend in with the décor."

The house is full of perfect examples of Victorian life and the elegance associated with the graceful living of the time. In the dining room the current place settings are for just six people, but the table could extend to serve 18. One can only guess at the conversations that must have gone on in such surroundings. A discreet bell push is located on the floor at the head of the table, so that the host could inform the servants of any guest's needs.

The large main parlor faces out across the gardens and was the scene of elegant afternoons. "Mrs. Shirk liked to serve tea here," Dill added. "She particularly liked ginger biscuits, which her cook kept a good supply of."

Kimberly Crest hosts guided tours Thursdays through Sundays from 1 p.m. to 4 p.m. Each tour lasts approximately 30 minutes. There are some 90 voluntary docents to take care of every request by visitors.

The latest docent classes have just finished for this year but will begin again next January.

Europeans may smile when visiting some of California's historical landmarks, but in the case of Kimberly Crest, they will no doubt notice that it has one major advantage over the original chateaux in France. It is full of furniture. Nearly all the French furniture used by the aristocracy, who built their castles along the river Loire, was burned or stolen during the revolution, and unlike this Redlands monument, they are mostly empty of life and atmosphere.

Where: Kimberly Crest House and Gardens
         1325 Prospect Drive, Redlands, CA 92373
         For more information call (909) 792-2111 or kimberleycrest.org

NIXON LIBRARY

Nixon Library

"I WAS BORN in a house my father built," were words often spoken by Richard M. Nixon. And from San Bernardino it's a short forty miles or so of freeway driving to reach the City of Yorba Linda, where Nixon's Library and Birthplace are located.

We are very lucky to have two presidential libraries in the Southland, although the Reagan Library is a little more of a drive to reach. It's also a lot more imposing.

Nixon's Library seems more intimate, and perhaps it's the proximity of the small home built house that was the scene of his birth in 1913 that makes it feel that way.

It is a nice house, modest and tidy as it must have been through the nine years that the young Richard lived in it. His father Frank had built the house from a kit, and the family lived modestly there before having to move to Whittier. Nixon never lost his affection for the area however.

The museum's exhibits are arranged in an interesting way, and the deep voice so well known for so many years is often heard from the many TV screens located throughout the building. Via the latest in touch screen technology, there are opportunities to ask the ex-President questions directly – at least provided they fall within the 300 programmed into the system.

"I've been here for about two years," said Susan Muir, a docent at the Library. "We get a lot of very interesting people that come to see everything here." Muir was at the time close to the presidential limousine that is often a draw to the car enthusiasts from all over the world.

The limousine that served four Presidents – Johnson, Nixon, Ford and Carter – sits empty of its prestigious passengers now, but it still remains an impressive machine. Often called The Rolling Fortress, the car was shipped to China for Nixon's ground-breaking trip there. It was capable of traveling 50 miles on flat tires at its top speed and could stop a 30-calibre rifle bullet. At the time it was the most expensive car in the world and cost an estimated $500,000.

Nixon was into his second term when the cloud of Watergate swept over his Administration. Rather than gloss over this unfortunate event that wracked the nation so greatly, the Library has a display that allows the visitor to understand the build up to the famous "break-in," and subsequent "cover-up." There is a commentary and also well documented photographs of that important period until Nixon waved farewell from the aircraft steps for the final time on August 9th, 1974, before returning to California.

Nixon's Original Home

That Nixon was a complicated man is of no doubt, but his importance in the world was never in question. A room of life sized statues gives testament to his place among such world leaders as Churchill, De Gaulle, Adenauer, and Chairman Mao, with whom he made such an historic visit.

In the words of Executive Director, John H. Taylor: "It was the President's specific wish that the Library complex not be a sleepy, stodgy museum, but rather a vibrant, ever changing landscape against which visitors, particularly young people, could learn more about the Presidency, our country and the world."

There is a view across the English style garden, where both Richard M. Nixon and his beloved wife Pat are now buried side by side next to the little house his father built. It is a very small distance, but between the dates in 1913 when he was born, to 1994 when he died, this Californian from such modest beginnings made giant steps across a world that he affected greatly.

The Richard Nixon Library & Birthplace
18001 Yorba Linda Boulevard
Yorba Linda, CA 92886
(714) 993-5075
For more information visit the Web site: www.nixonlibrary.org

THE HUNTINGTON LIBRARY

THE ACQUISITION OF great wealth is something that most people have probably contemplated in their lives; but acquiring enormous wealth comes with its own set of challenges, and responsibilities.

Henry Edwards Huntington came to California in the nineteenth century with the express goal of becoming rich. He succeeded beyond his most creative dreams. In fact, although no one today refers to the term, he was one of those robber barons who helped to shape the nation.

When Huntington moved from the San Francisco area to Los Angeles, he began his next ambition. He was passionately interested in three things: books, gardens and art.

Having stayed once on a ranch in the San Gabriel valley, he became impressed with the opportunities of the area and when this same ranch became available he bought it and in 1903 moved in.

Today, The Huntington Library has become a world famous institution renowned for the three original interests of its founder; horticulture, art and rare books.

Having driven through the very well appointed area of San Marino, just South East of Pasadena, a visitor enters the estate once owned by this great benefactor, and also his life of splendor.

Just wandering around the extensive 120-acre cultivated gardens in the 207 acres of the grounds can only make one marvel at the original plans of this super industrialist, whose main wealth came from the world of energy and transportation. At one time, Huntington controlled 23 companies in the Los Angeles area including the Pacific Light and Power Company and the Alhambra Water Company.

Among the works of art are Gainsborough's Blue Boy, Lawrence's Pinkie, Reynolds' Mrs. Siddons as the Tragic Muse, and Constable's

View on the Stour. All of these are accepted as being of the best of the particular genre, and are part of the finest collection of British art outside of London

Within the art collection also are truly wonderful examples of European art, furniture, silver and other delights, too numerous to examine in detail during one visit. The Huntington calls for many visits and it would be impossible to overdo the time spent there.

As a center of research, the institution attracts some 1,700 scholars from all over the world to study the rare books in the library. It houses an edition of an original Gutenberg Bible from 1450, and also a manuscript of Chaucer's Tales printed in 1410. There are letters from Benjamin Franklin, George Washington, and Abraham Lincoln, as well as many first editions.

Henry Edwards Huntington was not born into poverty, and his early life in New York was not one of privilege. Once he began making his fortune, he, like many of his generation, decided to lift his efforts to self-improvement and use his wealth for the greater good.

If one won the lottery or otherwise came into a great fortune, would one have the dedication or ambition to use that money to create a truly unique experience for over half-a-million people to enjoy annually many years after one has passed away?

The Huntington Library, Art Collection, and Botanical Gardens
1151 Oxford Road,
San Marino, CA 91108
(626) 405-2100
Web site: www.huntington.org

The Huntington Library

INLAND EMPIRE
MILITARY MUSEUM

MANY MUSEUMS ARE so large that they can be overwhelming, with huge galleries and halls full of so much that it is almost impossible to focus on individual exhibits. As it has only been open for fourteen months, the Inland Empire Military Museum is still in its building stage, and it is possible to spend quality time there looking in detail at its many pieces.

"We get lots of veterans here, and they often donate items to us," said Mario Montecino, the curator and founder of the museum. Montecino is himself a vet from the sixties having served with the First Cavalry Division in Korea before spending time in Vietnam.

"We are also sponsored by Albert Okura of the Juan Pollo Corporation," Montecino added. "He had this space next door to his premises and he helped us to come up with the idea of something with a military theme." The Juan Pollo Corporation owns the original McDonalds premises and runs the museum there.

"Once the word got out in late 2004, the vets and other people just started coming in, and the military museum really took off," Montecino explained. "We're also helped by James R. Valdez, who is a veteran of the Navy, and also served in Vietnam."

The museum is divided into sections dealing with each branch of the services. Being ex-army himself Montecino expresses a particular fondness for a cabinet displaying some artifacts from the WWII era. "The items in this display cabinet were given to us by Jim Murphy and his wife, Audrey," said Montecino. "Murphy was one of the crew who had to make sure all the defenders were out of the caves in Okinawa.

He brought home a Japanese flag and also some of the other things that had been left behind."

Also in the cabinet is a selection of medals from Audrey Murphy's brother, Charles Tannehill, who was listed missing in action in Korea in 1950.

The prize of the collection is without doubt one of the most successful war machines that everyone is familiar with – a Willis Jeep. "This one is a completely restored 1953 version," said Montecino. He is obviously very proud of the machine and also careful as he climbed in for a photo op.

The military museum is active in events in San Bernardino, and promotes a number of happenings. "We help sponsor the 'Cruzing E Street' Veterans' Day Parade, which is very popular," said Montecino. "The street is closed and we have all kinds of things going on. We have car shows, and booths with lots of music too. It's like a mini Route 66 Parade." This event is held on the Saturday before Veterans' Day which is held every year in early November.

The museum also hosts regular meetings for the Inland Empire Military Vehicle Restoration Association on the 2nd Saturday of every month. The Vietnam Vets of America Chapter 47 also holds its meeting there.

Currently the museum is only open on the weekends, but Montecino is please to open it up for anyone who would like to come along at another time. "Just call me up and we can set a date and time," he said. Several groups do come along on such occasions, and if more volunteers are prepared to assist with the running of the place opening hours could expand as well.

Inland Empire Military Museum
1394 North 'E' Street,
San Bernardino, CA
(909) 885-6324
Hours: 11:00 a.m. to 5:00 p.m. Saturday and Sunday. Admission – Free.

EDWARD-DEAN MUSEUM

THERE'S AN OLD joke about a parson stopping by a man's garden gate on his way back from church. "We don't see you much in church these days, Bill," he says. "Too much work to do in the garden," Bill replies. The parson smiles: "Ah yes, God's work is marvelous." "I dunno," said Bill. "He didn't do much with this place before I got hold of it!"

A short drive through the Oak Glen area will pay tribute to both views of bucolic bliss, as with the season approaching, the apple orchards are in the full swing of producing their annual crops, and visitors are roaming around the well kept gardens and attractions. The scene is perhaps more reminiscent of Europe or the East Coast than California.

But the road twists on, and at the far end in the small town of Cherry Valley we come to another monument, but this time one to man's quest for culture and taste, and in particular, design.

J. Edward Eberle and Dean Stout were two of Hollywood's foremost designers and they came to the area to set up a weekend retreat and family vacation home.

Perhaps people with this simple idea in mind could rest with the location and a few small items around them; but these were two of the finest cultured minds of the era and they were not content with just any old stuff, they were driven to form a house of outstanding beauty, both inside and out.

"They built it in 1957 during Hollywood's hey day," said RaLana Gurney, the Exhibition and Event Coordinator. "It was often used by the stars on their way down to Palm Springs; it was something of a party place."

The Edward-Dean Museum contains between 2,500 and 3,000 pieces of art from the sixteenth to the nineteenth century, and most of it is European. The collection has also been added to by other people's prized possessions over the years.

"It's a wonderful place to work," said Gurney. "I've worked here since 1994, and I never get tired of the place."

This is not surprising as every piece on show is a gem of the craftsman's art, be it paintings, sculpture or furniture.

Eventually the two partners moved into it full time after selling their businesses. The Blue Room is a replica of their home in Pasadena, and shows a very elegant form of living. Stout died in 1967 and Eberle in 1980, when the property was gifted to the county.

Within the main building are seven rooms, beautifully laid out to display a lifetime of dedicated collecting. The salon is called the Pine Room, as its walls are covered in a paneling of pine. This paneling was purchased by William Randolph Hurst to be used in his friend Marion Davis' house. When that house was to be demolished Dean and Stout managed to acquire the paneling which they had admired for many years, and had the room built to accommodate it.

From a personal point of view I was interested to see the Pine Room as the panels had originally come from an area in England called Cassiobury Park, which is in a town just north of London where I grew up. The park had first been mentioned in the Doomsday Book and then had passed to King Henry VIII. Eventually it was sold to the town of Watford in 1927, and converted to a 900-acre park for the use of the citizens. I passed many happy hours in the park and was pleased to have had some further contact, albeit from a very tenuous point of view.

In an alcove of the basement is a fine bust of Napoleon. This was given to Admiral Lord Nelson by a grateful French citizen after the country had been rid of the self-crowned Emperor. As it was one of many such gifts to the famous English seaman, one wonders where he put them all.

This fine museum is a wonderful testament to man's development of culture and the arts. It is almost impossible to spend as much time with each item as it demands, but the two men who gave their lives in pursuit of the excellence of art had that time and have left us a monument to such grace.

Wandering around the rooms and the downstairs library, gives one a strong feeling of a distant world where elegance was often at the expense of many hours of creativity. It is impossible not to be attracted to such a collection. From the passive and gentle country life outside the doors, it is a shock to enter a world of formal discipline and man's attempt to tame the forces around him.

Edward-Dean Museum and Gardens
9401 Oak Glen Road
Cherry Valley, CA 92223
Hours: Friday, Sat & Sun 10 a.m. to 5 p.m.
For More Information call (900) 845-2626
Or visit the Web site: edward-deanmuseum.org

SCANDIA

SCANDINAVIA IS RECOGNIZED by the world as a very clean and tidy place – even by those who haven't been there. While walking me through the grounds of the Scandia Amusement Park in Ontario, one of the executives made a small detour to pick up a small piece of scrap paper that had escaped from one of the many bins located around. Such is the dedication of the staff to keeping this place exemplary in its presentation.

"I've worked here for over 14 years," said Connie Rojas, the Marketing Director. "I came here to work as a student and kind of stayed on afterwards." It is a place devoted to fun, and the many customers who return time after time seem to find the place ideal for a number of their family events.

"We do a big line in birthday parties and other celebrations," Rojas continued. "For about $10 you can come here and enjoy most of the rides and the atmosphere." They provide vouchers for rides and attractions depending on the value of the package, and a hostess is dedicated to your group from the moment of booking to the last celebrant leaving the park.

Scandia even hosts company events too, with team building activities taking place on the lush grassy areas dedicated to such activities. "It's nice for people to take a break and go on a few rides after corporate work," Rojas added. Yes, perhaps a few minutes on The Screamer would help to readjust a team to its new role in corporate affairs.

For those who would like to develop their sporting skills, there are several batting cages where one can face top speed hard balls or the more sedate slow pitches for softball. These can be rented by the hour or with tokens.

There are two 18-hole miniature golf courses that wind their way through interesting and challenging scenery, and everywhere the quaint Scandinavian theme is present. Copenhagen's little mermaid overlooks one of the holes and the small street scenes only lack the sing-song accents of the countries far to the north of us.

The Larsen family owns Scandia, and their family obviously has links to the Sweden/Norway/Denmark/Finland area joined to the European landmass. They also own a similar Scandia park in Sacramento and Victorville, both no doubt with the same accent on fun, safety and cleanliness.

If you want to duck out of the rides and celebrations going on all around there is an indoor amusement area with air conditioning, and every game that is known to boost one's adrenaline. Air hockey, pinball machines and other arcade delights are on hand aplenty – there's as much noise as in Las Vegas.

Whether you plan a grad night, a company picnic or just a few rides with your family, Scandia is easy to reach being just off the 15 Freeway between the 10 and the 60. Prices are very reasonable and they pride themselves on their flexibility as well as their safety and of course, cleanliness.

11665 Wanamaker Avenue
Ontario, CA 91761
Hours: Summer Hours Weekdays 10 a.m. to midnight
Weekends and holidays 10 a.m. to 1 a.m.
For more information (909) 390-3092
Web site: www.scandiafun.com

SAN BERNARDINO MUSEUM

THE SAN BERNARDINO Museum is doing well. A lot of visitors find the site of great interest, and as a result some reorganizing must be done in the near future. "In fact, we're having to upgrade a lot of the galleries soon," said Jennifer Reynolds, marketing specialist with the institution. "But that's after we've shown our new exhibit downstairs."

This exhibit, which runs through June 18, 2006, is everything to do with the Salton Sea, that strange desert phenomenon just eighty miles to the south east.

"We have all the facts available for visitors," said Reynolds. "It's a very interesting place. The displays represent the past, present and future of the Sea."

The Salton Sea is the largest lake in California – twice the size of Tahoe. It's also below sea level and 25% more salty than the ocean. "They used to race boats on it," added Reynolds. "The salt content made the boats ride up higher in the water."

Today, the Salton Sea is one of the wonders of California, but has never fulfilled the promise that a number of developers made in the fifties and sixties. Due to the agriculture run off in the area, the level seems to hold and not evaporate, but with a twelve foot depth there is a limit to the size of craft that can use it.

If you prefer not to have to make the journey however, then the San Bernardino Museum will take the driving away from you, and you can find out everything you need with as many details as you could wish for.

Beyond the Salton Sea exhibit, the permanent collection is housed within three well-spaced floors, and offers a unique look at some of the more interesting aspects of natural life. The upper level is mostly devoted to birds, and the museum is constantly used as a reference for scholars, who need information for their work.

Within the airy rooms, the sounds of nature blend in as a background, while visitors check out what a cuckoo really looks like, and how big a bald eagle is compared to a tiny humming bird. It doesn't seem possible that the two could belong to the same family. Within this area is the fifth largest collection of birds' eggs in the entire world; there are 40,000. "And it keeps on growing," said Reynolds. "They keep on laying," she quipped.

If you are interested in something closer to terra firma, then the museum's extensive exhibition of minerals will be more to your liking. Along with petrified wood, the exhibit of gemstones and rocks from all over the region and beyond are displayed with well laid-out descriptions. There is even a set of dinosaur tracks close to the mammal section.

Outside the main museum is a large outdoor exhibit with a steam locomotive and Santa Fe caboose, the F105 Thunderchief, and also a lumber wagon from the local mountains. The cactus garden displays many plants from the immediate region and is an area where you should keep your eyes open for the wildlife that visits here. You are likely to spot lizards scampering around, and see the swooping of flycatchers, orioles and phoebes. If you aren't sure which is which, just return to the upper level of the museum and check out the samples inside.

Even though the Museum is very popular, there is plenty of room to linger over the well-stocked cabinets and come away from your visit knowing a lot more than when you entered.

San Bernardino County Museum
2024 Orange Tree Lane (California Street off ramp from I-10.)
Redlands, CA 92374
(909) 307-2669
Website: sbcounty.gov/museum

MARCH AIR MUSEUM 1

THE NEW EXECUTIVE Director at the March Field Air Museum comes from a different background to that of an ex-flyer. "I used to be with the Redlands Symphony," said Patricia Korzec. "But I've always been very interested in aviation." Korzec in fact has qualifications in the museum business and that is exactly the sort of skill that this busy museum devoted to the aircraft of yesterday needs.

"We have over 70 planes here," Korzec explained. "What we need is to present them to the public in an organized way." There is no shortage of volunteers at the museum; in fact there are more than a hundred of them. Most of them have an aviation past and it is Korzec's mission to harness the huge talent available to the facility, and direct it to make this interesting place a continuing success.

"We have applied to the American Association of Museums for accreditation," Korzec continued. "This will help us with funding and we're very excited about the possibilities."

Visitors to the site will currently find a selection of planes from all the ages of aviation, and the differences are quite marked. One can stand underneath the wings of a giant USAF B 52, or look down on the tiny Folland Gnat, which is there courtesy of the UK's Royal Air Force. "It's a great favorite with the children," said Korzec. "The bright red color attracts them and they often want to know if it can actually fly; it most certainly can."

In fact, one of the changes that has occurred since the appointment of the new executive director is a stress on making the museum more attractive to the entire family. The last Saturday in every month is designated as family day, where different subjects of aviation are promoted. "The most recent was: 'If Peter Pan can fly, why can't I?'"

said Korzec. "It was a great favorite with the children and taught them a lot about the species on earth that have the ability to fly, and how humans have managed to do it."

Outside the main building is a special area devoted to military dogs and their handlers. For the last five years on the Sunday before President's Day, a crowd has gathered to offer tributes and memories to those pairs who joined together to protect America.

"They've saved at least 10,000 lives," said Mike McKelroy, retired master sergeant and dog handler, United States Marine Corps. "Together with their handlers, we honor their work in all branches of the military."

Usually the protection took the form of patrolling installations, but that is not the only job of war dogs and their handlers. "The Air Force is the biggest user of dogs," McKelroy explained. "They guard ammo dumps, and search for mines, they are excellent at what they do. Their noses are forty times stronger than ours, their ears 20 times more powerful, and their eyes are ten times as sharp."

The relationship between a dog and its handler goes very deep. Often eating, working and sleeping together in hostile territory, the two become very close. Soon after the memorial was dedicated six years ago two bronze stars were left behind by unknown dog handlers, who felt compelled to honor their canine charges.

But it is aircraft that dominate this large museum, and inside the main hangar is an exhibition of flying machines and the people who made such science possible. Currently the facility is engaged on a project to finish renovating a Sikorsky Helicopter V83A. This well known machine is possibly the most photographed helicopter of all time; it carried the departing President Nixon from the White House lawn on his exit from power in 1974. Once finished it will take its place alongside the other memorabilia at the Nixon Library and Birthplace in Yorba Linda.

Where: I-215 at Van Buren Blvd Exit
Hours: 9:00 a.m. to 4:00 p.m. every day.
For more information call (951) 697-6604
Website: marchfield.org

MARCH AIR MUSEUM 2

IT IS A sad fact that over the last few months we have witnessed TV shots of the vapor trails left in foreign skies of B52 bombers doing their work to fight terrorism. Modern warfare is often done at long distance and it is not often that the public has the chance to see its armaments "up close and personal." Fortunately for those of us in the Southland there is a group of dedicated volunteers who want you to see some very interesting exhibits up close, and a B52 bomber is one of them.

Just a few miles down the 215 Freeway brings you to the March Air Field Museum, where more than 60 military airplanes are on display. The site covers a total of 60 acres, and here it is easy to stand beneath the wings of a giant USAF B52 or look down on a tiny Folland Gnat jet, courtesy of the UK's Royal Air Force.

March Field was first used as an airfield in 1918 at the end of the First World War. Then it was a cross-country stop for aviators from the San Diego area. On March 1st of that year the first official aircraft landed piloted by a Cadet Compere. Twenty days later the field was given its current name in remembrance of the death of an early hero of the air called Lt. Peyton March. In fact there are many memorials in this historic sight devoted to those who have gone before.

Outside the entrance to the museum is a Memorial Courtyard dedicated by the P-38 National Association and the 15th Air Force to those who died in service. The Freedom Shrine's wall also features engravings of America's most important documents. Alongside this garden is a tall dignified statue commemorating the West Coast National War Dogs, which is dedicated to all the dogs and handlers who have played their part in keeping us safe, and our installations secure.

But it is planes of all types that draw the many visitors to this open and interesting museum throughout the year. And what a varied collection it is. The 135 volunteers labor to upkeep and restore the antiques to keep them as perpetual reminders of a science that has been with us for barely 100 years. And yet the improvements that the science has brought are many and obvious. From the early models of string, wire, canvas and wood to the black matte sleekness of the SR-71 Blackbird.

The Blackbird is perhaps the most popular exhibit as it is a plane whose performance defies imagination. With a published top speed of 2,310 miles per hour, it streaked across the skies of all continents during the hay days of the cold war, speeding its passengers in great secrecy to their destinations. People who lived near the Air Force base in Cambridge, England regularly reported sightings of these black rockets leaving at breakfast and returning at lunchtime. It was well known they had flown to Washington DC and back in the time. No wonder they still hold a mystique even though they were retired many years ago.

To see some of the aircraft on "the other side," March Field is very proud of an area they call MIG Alley. Here a number of Russian MIG's are on display with some of their escorts. An Antonov from 1947 squats menacingly. Its bulk makes it look as if it would never lift off the ground, but it's still being made in certain parts of the former USSR.

The facts of every plane are clearly displayed so that visitors can catch up on the details, and if one wants to get even closer, there are four days held every year called Open Cockpit Days where you can get into a number of the planes and really look around. The website gives details of these days and also all the planes on exhibit. Currently, there is a display in the main museum hall called Women in Aviation. Here you can see the role women have played in keeping our skies safe and those of our enemies under pressure. It was Albert Speer, Hitler's armaments minister, who said it was the women in the Allies war effort who made the real difference.

On May 25th the annual Trains to Planes Day takes place. Here March Field links up with the Orange Empire Railway Museum to ferry visitors from Perris to the airfield for a day of travel delights. March Field Air Museum is located at the Van Buren exit of Interstate 215 in Riverside. Telephone (909) 697-6600. Website is Marchfield. org. Hours of opening are 10.00am to 4.00pm, 5.00pm in the summer.

YUCAIPA ADOBE

THERE SEEMS TO be some controversy about the original builder and owner of the Yucaipa Adobe. The information sheet maintains that the neat farm building located just off the 10 freeway on Dunlap Street was built by James Waters in 1858. However, the curator of the museum, Tony Webb is certain that it was the original home of Don Diego Sepulveda and his wife Maria.

Webb has lived at the site for twelve years and is something of an expert in what is after all his own home. "If you look at the construction of the walls and the windows downstairs you can see how crooked they are," he said. "Upstairs, things are completely different."

He also points out the construction of the walls, which are true adobe, and the floors, which are mostly original. In fact the nice thing about this old house is that it has not been rebuilt or renovated. It gives it a feeling of authenticity, which is sometimes missing from other old sites.

"One of the interesting things about the interior is its cool temperature," Webb continued. "It's never gone over 81 degrees inside, and we've often had temperatures outside of over one hundred. It's the old fashioned construction that does it."

The three rooms are laid out in the fashion of the day and the effect is of a real home. The bedroom however is not its original designation as there is a serving hatch in the back wall, which led directly to the kitchen; this therefore must have been the dining room.

Don Sepulveda's portrait looks down from the mantle, and his wife stares at us over the head of the bed itself. Sepulveda went on to build a business with services from Long Beach to Los Angeles – and the longest street in the city is named after him.

Whether the house was built by the famous don or not, the land around it was granted to the Sepulveda and Lugo families in 1842 by the Mexican government. But in 1850 the Mormons bought it all. It was from this sale that the land and the house then transferred to James Waters. His picture hangs in the living room.

"Waters was from New York, but became a mountain man," Webb explained. "He raised pigs and sheep, but eventually became the San Bernardino County supervisor."

The living room contains a small wind organ which is used for weddings in the house, and also there is a family bible from the last owners of the house, the Dunlaps. "They also had a history book of the Scottish Royal family," Webb said. "If you look at the condition of both you can see that the bible is well used, whereas the history book is in a much better state; they read the bible all the time."

The Dunlap family stayed in the house until the mid-fifties, when it was vacated. The Yucaipa Woman's Club raised money to save the deteriorated building and eventually they gave it to the County of San Bernardino to be cared for as part of the Museum system. It holds the number 528 as one of California's State Historical landmarks.

Whether the Waters or Sepulveda families first built the house may still be speculation, but what is agreed upon is that long before their time it was the Serrano Indians who gave the name Yucaipa to the area. It means Wetlands.

The Yucaipa Adobe
32183 Kentucky Street and Dunlap Street
Yucaipa, CA 92399
(909) 795-3485

Open Tuesday through Saturday 10 a.m. to 3 p.m.
Admission is free.

JOSHUA TREE

SAN BERNARDINO HAS plenty of desert areas, but in the South East corner, is possibly the finest example such an eco system as exists anywhere on the planet; it is the Joshua Tree National Monument, whose geographical boundary we share with our neighbors, Riverside County.

The name of Joshua Tree came from the early Mormons, who thought the strange plants looked like Joshua praying to Heaven with his arms outstretched. The park was also helped along by a desert enthusiast called Minerva Hamilton Hoyt, who had lost her husband and son, and in her grief turned to the desert for consolation. She believed that others should have the same access to enjoy this expansive place, and in 1936 the conservation-minded President Roosevelt signed the proclamation establishing the park

Before wondering off in this hot, wonderful place it is best to remember one very important thing – people get lost here.

The desert can be a dangerous place and Cindy Von Halle, who supervises the visitor center, explained that most of the people who become lost are in fact experienced, or at least aware of the dangers.

It is easy to understand how it happens. A couple of people leave their cars and set off across the desert park with its boulders and dunes. Perhaps they are in deep conversation or are thinking hard about something; after half an hour or so they decide to turn around. Not having noticed any particular land marks they are now in a totally different looking place from where they began – the shadows are all different and the terrain looks hostile. They see nothing they recognize. They panic. It gets worse. It is very hot.

Nearly everybody can relate to the panic attack that is bound to hit under these circumstances, but that is the first dangerous thing you have to control. The next is the heat and the worst of all, dehydration.

"We all need water, and in a hot environment lots of it." Von Halle explained the body's need for water and exactly how much. "You need to start out hydrated, and then drink plenty on your hike," she explained. "Don't allow yourself to get thirsty, as by then you're already beginning to become dehydrated."

In fact, it could be said that in order to survive in the desert you need two principle things – water and common sense. But then if common sense is so common, why isn't it used more often?

There are courses that are run at the Monument to help visitors understand the dangers that exist and also how to best enjoy the experience of this place.

The visitor center is located in Twenty-nine Palms and is full of interesting information to help those coming to the monument to get the best out of their stay. "The Monument, as it is referred to, is run by two entities," said Nancy Downer, Executive Director. "There is the Joshua Tree National Park and also the Joshua Tree National Park Association. The former is run by the Department of the Interior, and their mission is to protect and preserve the national parks for everyone to enjoy."

Today 1.3 million visitors come to enjoy the 800,000 acres of pristine desert and there is so much to enjoy in terms of wildlife, scenery, and an atmosphere that will fill the needs of the most ardent nature lover.

"We run several tours to some of the more interesting sites," said Downer. "For instance, there is one to the Desert Queen Ranch, which is about 40 minutes from the center. It has an old school house, a dam and an orchard. It is where one of the early residents, Bill Keys, made his home, and it is full of quite rare artifacts."

Most of the tours are free, but the Desert Queen tour has a $5 extra charge as it requires travel. Like everything else, this fee is dedicated to keeping the Monument in first class condition. "Recently, we've had an increase in our collections, and also a 10% increase in membership has helped with our funding," Downer continued. "We have also received corporate donations from Toyota and Walmart, all of which allows us to give added support to the park."

Joshua Tree National Monument
74485 National Park Drive
Twentynine Palms, CA 92277
For more information call: (760) 367-5525
Web site: joshuatree.org

WRIGHTWOOD

YOU HAVE TO admit that when looking around at the history of the region, the Serano Indians certainly covered a lot of ground, and in some of the best places too. Had they know about the upward tick in real estate values they may have stayed a little longer.

Take for instance the mountain community of Wrightwood, which is advertised as the easiest resort to reach being just 15 miles off Interstate 15. Naturally the Serano Indians spend a lot of quality time in this beautiful place before modern man found it.

The Mormons came along in the mid-nineteenth century, and it was a couple of brothers called Swarthout who settled here for a few years before they returned to Salt Lake City in 1857. The Valley still holds their name although a Mr. Wright eventually started up a ranch and it was his name that the small community eventually took.

Wrightwood, located in the San Gabriel Mountains is a fine place with much of the same attributes as Big Bear Lake across in the San Bernardino Mountains. It has a smaller population but it enjoys the same bright blue sky and clear air that covers the area. There is no lake of course, well, not like its rival. It does have a Country Club and that has a lake, but quite a small one.

"It used to be two lakes at one time," said Pam Mortimer, a local realtor. "In fact the club used to be called Twin Lakes, but the upper lake was filled in and is now a baseball field."

The Country Club is a great place for kids with its water, tennis courts and well kept grassy areas. It's for members only of course, but enquiries are always welcome.

There is also a lake not far down the road, called Jackson Lake. It's another quiet place for children to play in safety and helps make up for the lack of a central water spot in Wrightwood.

In other respects, there is a lot to do in this town. Attractive shops share compact space with realtors and outside dining restaurants. "We have about four thousand residents," Mortimer continued. "But we're really full on the weekends." And this is with the Angeles Crest Highway closed as it is at the moment due to snowmelt sweeping away the surface. The road is normally a favorite route for motorcyclists, and now they have to take the long way around.

In the winter, Wrightwood cater to skiers that frequent Mountain High Ski Resort just along the highway. Lodges are full and vacation homes ripple with the sound of winter sportsmen and women looking for thrills on the slopes. It's a busy time for all.

As with all communities in Southern California, residents look with some concern at new housing developments taking place, but so far there seems no need to worry as there is a lot of space up at 6,000 feet.

Wrightwood bills itself as a town with no traffic light and that places it in a different category from its rival Big Bear, which has just installed yet another to cope with traffic flow. It now has over half a dozen.

Visitors to Wrightwood have a lot of choice in hiking trails, and wonderful scenic views of the Angeles National Forest which surrounds them. If shopping is not on the agenda, the town is manageable enough to stroll around completely, or maybe stop for a spell and watch the world go past.

Perhaps if the Seranos had the chance they would have stayed in Wrightwood a little longer and continued to enjoy what must also have been to them a marvelous experience in the mountains.

FLYING MODELS

THE OTHER DAY on a walk I noticed a plane doing some amazing acrobatic maneuvers. It was a while before I realized that the plane was a lot closer than I thought, and also that the terrain over which it was flying was hardly suitable for such goings on.

We were at Baldwin Lake, which is a dry lake at the East End of Big Bear Valley and although there has been water in it for some time since the rains and storms of the last two years, it is now returning to its normal arid self. Eventually, I saw that the plane was a model one and that there was another in the sky as well.

Now, when I was a boy model airplanes were a part of growing up, and like many of my peers, I spent many happy hours hunched over a model board, cutting and sanding and painting in pursuit of man's dream of leaving terra firma: even while one's feet stayed permanently on the ground, of course. But the pilots of the planes that day were full grown men, and there was nothing childlike in their aircraft.

"I've been doing this now for about 20 years," said Jim Newkirk, who when he's not looping the loop and soaring up higher and higher into the blue sky above, runs a jeweler's shop in Big Bear Lake. He is a keen aficionado of this sport and even calls the name of his shop Wings.

"I have about twenty models at home," he said. "I keep the crashed and broken ones on one side, and the ready-to-fly ones on the other. My wife thinks I have far too many."

As a boy, he looked up to his father who used to fly real P-51's around the world with his work in the US military. "I guess it got into my blood that way," he said. His own son, James, who works alongside him in the business, is also an ardent flyer of remote planes too.

"I've just finished a new model," James said. "It's a U-Can-Do 3D plane with a five feet wingspan. It's pretty big."

This plane is one of several that are taking advantage of a giant technological breakthrough that occurred two years ago. "The size of electric motors suddenly became smaller and lighter," Jim said. They went from being 500 grams to 100 grams and this made them highly suitable for model plane use.

They also became more powerful and easy to charge. By connecting the battery to a car's electrical output, the power pack can be charged rapidly and will give around twelve minutes flying time. They are also virtually silent, which removes the insect buzzing of the normal gasoline powered engines of old.

Of course, the old engines still exist and perhaps remain the favorites of the true enthusiast, but can they hold back progress? No doubt the electrics will become even more powerful and lighter still.

Bill Gray is also one of the flyers who gather at the site. His favorite plane is one that his father started building twenty years ago. It's a bi-plane and uses a gas engine. "My father is really pleased that I've finished it," he said.

Unlike real planes, there are no regulations required and any place with a piece of flat ground will do for take offs and landings. Of course, it helps if there are not too many buildings around, nor mountains. Landings are still fraught with tension as the frail craft come in low and maybe with no power if the battery has run out. Knowing the length of flight is still a matter of judgment.

To become airborne for the first time one needs a relatively small investment. The Newkirk's reckon $250 to $300 will do it, but naturally there is almost no end in sight to build a kit or a "scratchbuilt" as one is called if it is made off a plan from scrap materials.

As for accidents, James says they sometime come from a technical fault or using the wrong frequency on the sets. "Mostly though they come from pilot error," he said. So even in a small world the human element can get in the way.

FULLERTON ART MUSEUM (RAFFMA)

UNIVERSITIES CAN BE confusing places to visit. California State University San Bernardino is no exception as it's as big as a small city. But the Robert V. Fullerton Art Museum is fairly easy to find although it is deep within the campus. And any extra gas you use to get there is made up for the very reasonable entrance fee – which doesn't exist, as it's free.

Under the direction of Eva Kirsch this fine exhibition consists of three separate aspects of art; artifacts from the ancient world, ceramics, and contemporary art. This latter category is always an interesting one as a large space is devoted to displaying some of the very best in modern art. And although some of this is challenging to look at, it is shown in the best of lights to help the process.

Eva Kirsch herself is a devotee of all that is on show here, but her particular favorites come from the ancient world of Egypt and also some of the ceramics. Kirsch has been in charge of things at the Fullerton since 1998, and is currently working hard to provide all the necessary documentation to have the museum accredited by the American Association of Museums. Of 15,000 museums around the country only 800 have reached this standard, and once it is achieved it provides easier access to funding and also for borrowing art from other museums. It also helps to cement the institution more firmly within the university.

"This year has been a year of celebrations," said Kirsch. "CSUSB itself is in the midst of its 40-year birthday, and 2006 marks the tenth anniversary of the museum." One celebration that took place a year ago was the arrival of a very important permanent visitor. It was a sarcophagus from Egypt which once contained the remains of a man called Neter Haneb, who lived at the time of the great pharaohs. Haneb was no longer within his small home but the exterior of his shelter confirmed that he had been a very important person.

"He made several offerings to the temple of geese and oxen." Kirsch explained. "This generosity resulted in his wonderful coffin." The somewhat hermaphroditic features nonetheless show that Haneb was a Mr. and not a Ms. "His face is portrayed as being quite dark," Kirsch continued. "Females were painted much lighter in shade."

Currently they have a show of photographic art called Photography Unbound, which exhibits the work of contemporary photographers. It promises to be a challenging exhibition as these are four artists who have pushed the boundaries of their art. Located within the large hall visitors will find the work stimulating and rewarding.

At the other end of the time-line are 350 pieces of jewelry on loan from the University of Indiana. Entitled "A Golden Legacy," these exquisite gems in gold come from as long ago as 3000 B.C. up until the 10th and 11th century. The wearers of the time were from the very highest levels of their societies.

These two exhibits run concurrently until early December at which time two more artists will have their work on show. From China and Poland the two lived outside their own countries and were in fact stateless, although their work finds a comfortable home here.

Museums can be intimidating places and the subjects might not always be at the top of the list of things people want to see, but at the Fullerton, the atmosphere and the setting of the artifacts is so attractive that any visitor will come away with some permanent memories of their time spent there.

Where: Robert V. Fullerton Museum
CSUSB 5500 University Parkway
San Bernardino, CA 92407-2397
Closed on Sundays and Mondays
Cost: Free but parking is $1.50 per car.

For more information call (909) 880-5007
Or visit the Web site: museum.csusb.edu

MCDONALDS MUSEUM

IF YOU HAPPEN to be driving north along E Street in San Bernardino and you're feeling a little peckish, don't be seduced by the sign at 14th Street advertising burgers for 15 cents; you'll be somewhat disappointed. But if you go inside the premises, you'll be confronted by some very interesting memorabilia from the past; for this is the original home of McDonald's.

Today, it is the head office of Mr. Albert Okura's Juan Pollo, and although it could be said he is in competition with McDonalds he still promotes this birthplace of American fast food.

It was way back in 1937 that the McDonald brothers opened their first food place. It was called the Airdrome and it was located in Monrovia. They initially operated a movie theater when they came to California in 1920 but they noticed that the lines of people waiting to get in were going to a nearby hot dog place, and they decided to start one themselves; it soon became their primary focus.

In 1940 the McDonald's had their Airdrome hauled to the current location in San Bernardino. It had to be cut in half to pass under a low bridge, but eventually it was reassembled and open for business as McDonald's Famous Bar-B-Que. But they also sold hot dogs and some burgers.

They became the number one teen hang-out within a year and by their tenth anniversary, they were tired of the pressure of operating a big place with all the staff problems and extensive menus. In December 1948, they opened the original McDonald's offering a "speedee service system," with hamburgers for 15 cents and fries for 10 cents. It began to take off.

By mid–May 1953 they opened a branch in Phoenix and then later on that year one in North Hollywood, California, and one more in Downey.

It was in 1954 that Ray Kroc came by to sell the brothers some drink mixing equipment and he was so impressed with what he saw that he persuaded the two brothers to let him start a McDonald's franchise restaurant back in Des Plaines, Illinois.

In 1961, Kroc bought out the brothers for $2.7 million and the rest, as they say, is history. The franchised business has grown from strength to strength and is now all over the world as one of America's most recognized symbols. By 1998, there were 23,000 restaurants worldwide. Once Kroc owned the chain he set a marketing department the task of increasing sales with cartoon characters. Speedee had been the one the original owners has used to promote their new service back in 1948, but now Kroc introduced the Hamburglar, and he can still be seen on top of the sign at the museum. More characters were to follow and children's cartoons still help boost kid's meals at the restaurants.

Within the original restaurant the walls loaded with items from the rich history of McDonald's and also a number of items from the days of the Mother Road, Route 66. "This street was designated as the business loop, by the City of San Bernardino," said Jack Marcus, the curator of the museum. "The actual route went another way, but the business loop was along E Street. So we have quite a lot of things from those memorable days."

Marcus, apart from being highly knowledgeable on all things McDonalds, knows a lot about the times that made them famous. "Mr. Albert, as he's referred to, also owns much of Amboy – right out in the desert," he added. "It's a place that's often used for films and other photographic pieces."

The original building in San Bernardino has been replaced a few times in its 70 year history, the one there now was completed in 1974, and the man who took McDonald's to the top of the business world, Ray Kroc, died in 1984 at age 81.

The museum is an interesting place to come to and will certainly not disappoint visitors, even if they are in search of the fifteen cent meal, which sadly no longer exists.

Where: 1398 N.E. St., San Bernardino. CA 92405
Hours: 10 a.m. to 5 p.m. daily
Cost: Free.
For more information call (909) 885-6324

PARAFLYING

SINCE BEFORE ICARUS tried to fly with wings stuck to his back with wax, man has always had an eye on the skies to see if there is any way he can shake the ties of gravity and get up there. Today it's no different, except that we know how to do it now, and it's just a question of allocating the time and money.

Unfortunately, an aircraft is expensive and also obtaining a pilot's license is not something that comes cheap or easy. However there is another way to get aloft, and enjoy the freedom of the birds. It's called paraflying.

In simple terms, paraflying is a combination of parachuting and flying, with a small aircraft built from tubular metal and a large oblong chute; all powered by an engine. It sounds a little odd, but it really works and it's a great way to fly.

"I first heard about it from my brother back in 1992," said Phil Dietro, paraflyer extraordinaire and licensed instructor for the sport. "It requires a permit to fly but that's not nearly as rigorous to get as, say, a full pilot's license."

In fact you can be aloft in as soon as 12 hours; ten of which are in the company of an instructor. After that you can be up on your own. It's really that easy.

"You spread the chute out behind you," Dietro explained. "Then you start to move the plane forward, which causes to chute to fill with air. Once the wing is built, you go faster and then you will lift up and you're on your way." Nothing to it, right?

In fact it is quite a simple process as the chute is a larger version of the type that skydivers use and is able to support the plane completely. It does the job so well that should there be a mechanical malfunction the entire rig can just float down to earth.

Deitro's machine is called a Powrachute Pegasus which has been in manufacture since 2002. It is a skeletal rig in bright orange, with an "N" number proudly painted on its rear end. "It's registered just like any other aircraft," added Dietro. But there the similarity ends.

The plane has a top speed somewhere between 25 and 30 miles per hour. It's not a fast method of travel, but at least it's well above the traffic.

The Powrachute needs about 300 feet to take off and can do this from pretty well any level surface; landings can be a lot shorter and only need 50 feet. It has a range of 80 to 100 miles and can go as high as 10,000 feet. Dietro said that the minimum height for travel over populated areas is 1000 feet. But as we know, in San Bernardino County there is a lot of open space for such a fun device.

Phil Dietro's company provides instruction out of Apple Valley Airport, and his Web site explains a lot of the details and pricing. An introductory lesson costs $85 for half an hour. He is a fully licensed sport pilot instructor and actually teaches other instructors how to instruct. He's been an enthusiastic leader in the sport for over ten years.

If you were to decide to buy your own plane, you can have a single seat, or a double seat machine. The engine is either two-stroke or four stroke; 65 or 100 horsepower, using ordinary automobile gasoline – so you can fill up anywhere. The purchase price begins at about $10,000, and can go up to $30,000. Also you can easily trailer the plane to just about any suitable location.

No license is necessary, just a permit and the simple instruction to get off the ground and steer the device. To take off you increase the speed; to land you just slow down. It's a little more complicated than poor Icarus's wings, but you won't have to worry about the wax melting. If only he had known about that parachute idea.

Inland Paraflite
Apple Valley Airport
Corwin Road
Apple Valley, CA 92307
(760) 242-3359
Web site: www.paraplane.com

THE RIVER

I MUST CONFESS that after 25 years in Southern California, there is one major trip that I have failed to achieve until very recently. I have always been amazed at the number of people here who are constantly going off to "The River." For some time I wasn't quite sure of which river they meant as it was always called "The River."

Of course, I soon found out that the target of their final destination was the Colorado River, and more exactly the bit of the Colorado River between the dam just north of Laughlin and as far down as, say, Blythe. All of these sites were at least three hours drive away too.

Naturally I was aware of the great waterway's course as it meanders and rushes its way down from its source in Colorado; sometimes running free and sometimes stopped by man at dams, diversions, lakes and other well intentioned projects. Also I've seen the activity at Laughlin during busy times with jet skis, speed boats, rafts and it seems every form of water craft that has been invented and can float. But it's taken me a long time before I've actually been to "The River."

However an occasion arrived recently to visit some friends who have a house on "The River" at Bullhead City and a fine place it is too. Also in keeping with the needs of people in that location they have lots of water toys with which to indulge your fancy, waterwise.

After a period of watching other craft drifting, tearing and downright speeding up and down the fast moving current, it became time for me to get out on the surface of the clear water as well.

For my initiation a pair of kayaks were chosen for me and my host to slowly take our way downstream to a fine little establishment known for excellent food and adult beverages called Lazy Harry's. It seemed a simple enough task, and I was eager to get out there and enjoy the trip.

Now my previous experience in such a small personal craft was many years ago in Hawaii, where I was warned of the difficulty of the river and the slipperiness of the rocks over which we would be moving. The resulting disaster was sufficient for Mrs. Summons to have such hysterics it created an atmosphere between us which lasted almost as long as it took me to stop bleeding.

This at least was deeper water, with very little need to paddle as it was to be all down stream – a simple task indeed. Also my wife was to be dispatched to our destination with a video camera to catch the arriving explorers and help ferry the kayaks back to base afterwards on an awaiting truck.

I was doing rather well once we pushed off. In fact, I even strutted my stuff, and did a bit of up stream paddling just to see if I could do it. I was feeling extremely relaxed and confident in my new found skills and looking forward to my eventual arrival and liquid reward at journey's end.

It was about then that The River God decided that after two and a half decades of neglect, a forfeit and a price had to paid. For some inexplicable reason I started to roll on the starboard side – for those not familiar with the correct nautical term that's the right-hand side. Unlike riding a motorcycle where you can steer your way out of such a situation no such method seemed to be available. As I slipped off, I was struck with two thoughts: I was extremely glad that I had cast off the macho ness of youth and accepted a life preserver, and also I wished I had paid more attention to those programs showing how with a deft flick of the paddle you could somehow twist yourself up the other side of the capsizing kayak.

These thoughts only lasted a micro second as the coldness of the water soon took over everything else. But up I popped, and with some help from my friend managed to get to a nearby dock, right the craft and get back in. My arrival at our destination caused that look on my wife that said: Oh no, not again! But all was well apart from very wet clothes, which soon dried out.

I can now hold my head up proudly when people say they have been, or are going to "The River." Not only do I know where it is, and what goes on there, but I can also say I am intimately familiar with it.

20 MULE TEAM MUSEUM

"COUNT YOUR BLESSINGS," is one of those annoying little maxims usually trotted out by interfering people at a time when it's the very last thing you want to do. However it is maybe a good thing to remember occasionally as we can often forget how lucky we all are; particularly when we compare our lives to those who came before us.

The next time you are stuck in traffic with the A/C pumping, but you can't find the right radio station, or the in-car iPod is not playing the tune you want spare a thought for one Ed Stiles.

Now poor old Ed was a muleskinner and his life was no doubt seriously lacking in blessings as he helped to drive a team of twenty mules 165 miles across the Mojave Desert from Death Valley to the small town of Mojave itself. His job was to sit astride one of the last two animals in the train, often in temperatures of 130° F in summer; the twenty extremely stubborn creatures under his control must have created quite a challenge for anyone.

Apparently maneuvering this wagon train around was one of the sights that spectators would turn out for – Ed and his two fellow handlers would use short tugs on the reins to go right and steady pulls to go left. Quite how responsive the mules were is not mentioned but you can be sure they didn't always perform according to the owner's manual.

Along with him was a driver, who sat aloft the huge wagons and at the back was the "Swamper," who was responsible for manning the breaks and also the cooking and dishwashing.

The exploits of this piece of California history are well documented, photographed and otherwise exhibited at a small museum in Boron just to the west of Kramer's Four Corners on Route 395. It traces the development of the train from its inception in 1881 to the end of its time in 1898.

The loads they were carrying were borax, which today is used in over 1000 products. At the time most of the borax in the world came from Tibet and Italy, so for California it was an important find out in Death Valley. It just needed to be mined and then shipped.

Working with the limitations of man, mules, horses, and wagons a William T. Coleman calculated that 20 mules could haul a load of 36 tons with ease, and a design by John Perry at the Harmony Borax works created each team's cargo of two wagons. Of course, crossing the desert with such a load, both mules and men needed water, so 500 gallons of that was hauled along too; making the load even heavier.

The round trip took 20 days and one can only imagine the discomfort of such a life out there in some of the most difficult terrain in the country. Sleeping was done rough on the ground, and meals consisted of bacon and beans. The pay wasn't up to much either and came in at between $100 and $150 a month, but then bacon and beans in those days were no doubt fairly cheap.

The muleskinner and his two helpers were generally described as "quiet, bad tempered men," and fights often broke out among them. Is this surprising?

"The shame of it is that there were huge borax deposits right here in Boron," said Dorothy J. Pratt, the director of the museum. "But they didn't find it until much later." Such a discovery would have cut the entire journey by about two thirds.

"My family came here in 1932," Pratt continued. "I was twelve at the time." She has seen quite a few changes in that time and now oversees this small neat museum with a caring hand, and a lot of information on this chapter in our past.

Here there are scenes depicted of the life of a muleskinner and the teams that helped California's economy. There are paintings of the mules that were at the end of the long lines of leather reins – most of them with a benign expression that no doubt Ed Stiles and his colleagues rarely saw when they dismounted from a sore and hot day on their various positions.

We don't know what went on in the minds of these men who drove these 20-mule teams across the desert in such stultifying boredom, but we do know that it must have been an exceptionally grim life. One thing is certain; the view from out in the windswept, scorching Mojave must have contained few blessings for Ed Stiles to count.

20 Mule Team Museum
20 Mule Team Road,
Boron, CA 93516
(760) 762-5810

AMBOY

The Famous Roy's Sign at Amboy

IT'S NOT VERY often on a trip that I am disappointed by what I'm looking for. And in this case, my primary target was not disappointing at all, but the little side trip I had planned turned out not to be much use.

On my way to Amboy on the old Route 66, I had intended to stop at the small dot on the map called Baghdad; in fact I had already worked out a few slightly amusing phrases to describe what I was sure would be a very different scene to the place we so sadly see every day on our TV sets. As things turned out Baghdad, California was one of those places that people say: "If you blink, you'll miss it!"

I must have blinked because even though I kept a sharp look out for it, nothing materialized on my way to the much larger town of Amboy a few miles further on. Now "larger" is a very relative term as there is not very much of Amboy to be seen at all these days – but at least it does exist.

According to the metal plate on the door of Roy's Café, Amboy was settled as far back as 1858 as a water stop for the Southern Pacific Railroad as it laid its tracks through the Cadiz Valley. It survived and with the opening of the Mother Road, Route 66 in 1926, it began to do quite nicely.

The plate continued that there was from then on "a steady stream of flivvers, dust bowl emigrants, soldiers and vacationers." A flivver was the term for an old cheap car, and you can be sure that such drivers were glad of the sight of some population after a long hot drive through the dusty desert from Needles nearly 75 miles away.

More recently Amboy has had a somewhat interesting history. Following the completion of Interstate 40 and the bypassing of Route 66 in 1973, Buster Burris, the son-in-law of the original founder and owner Roy Growl, is said to have bulldozed much of the town in temper at its certain demise. Finally, in 2005 it was put on e-bay for $1.1 million and failed to attract any bids of that size.

Mr. Albert Okura, owner of the fast food chain Juan Pollo, had his bid for $425,000 accepted and he became the new owner of the town, and the renovation of this famous stop began.

"Apart from the motel and filling station and café there are about half a dozen houses here," said Larry Stevens, the manager of the project. "Also there's a school."

But there was no water, and no proper electricity, all of which had to brought in, plus a serious upgrade to the facilities in order to bring the buildings up to modern day code.

The new owner has expressed his concern at all this extra work, but as the new savior of the town he must be pleased that it's only a few more weeks before gasoline will flow out of the shiny new pumps outside Roy's famous café. The old motel too should not have to wait too long before it can open its doors to clientele for the 24 rooms and six cabins.

"We fully expect half of the rooms to go to local businesses in the area," said Stevens. He also said that he expected most of the clients for the café and gas station to be locals as well, and that traveling Route 66 aficionados would be just the icing on the cake. Hopefully they will be able to enjoy a bowl of the delicious chili that was always a staple of the old menus.

As for my side trip, I asked Stevens what had happened to Baghdad. He said: "Well, it's just a couple of trees and a railroad crossing these days; but you might find an old cemetery if you look hard enough for it." A shame, but I don't often get disappointed.

Roy's Motel and Café
Route 66, Amboy,
CA 92304
(909) 653-5842
E-mail: amboyroute66.com

GOFFS SCHOOLHOUSE

"SCHOOLDAYS ARE THE happiest days of your life." Well, that's what they say, but maybe it's another case of: "Distance lends enchantment to the view," although Jo Ann Casebier who now oversees the Goffs Schoolhouse said: "They had a good time here, I think."

Out in the middle of the Mojave Desert, Goffs is one of those dusty, almost forgotten places where people gathered in years gone by to try their luck with the harsh terrain.

It was the railroad coming through that gave some of their workers the idea of a school, and in 1914 the present structure was built on an acre of land to cater to the children of the employees of the Santa Fe Railroad.

Jo Ann and her husband Dennis bought the schoolhouse and surrounding area back in 1990, and have spent the last 17 years turning it into an interesting look back at the past.

The schoolhouse itself is a sanctuary to life back almost a century ago, when a dozen or so children would be sitting at their desks under the control of a single teacher. The first of these was Clara Rippeto, and the last when the school closed in 1937 were Anna and Daniel Stern. By then two teachers were employed to teach the first through eighth grades in the single room.

Over the following years the building was at one time used as a cafeteria by WWII troops in the area, but then it gradually fell into disrepair. It was in 1982 that Dennis Casebier passed through the area. He was saddened by what he saw and said that being convinced that it would eventually completely disappear; he took several photos of the dilapidated scene.

A couple called Jim and Bertha Wold bought the place soon after this and began to restore it before they put it on the market in 1990. It seemed prophetic that the Casebiers should then become the owners of the site, and their important work began.

Today the schoolhouse contains many of the artifacts that were so familiar to the original occupants, and there is an atmosphere of caring and vibrancy that must have been totally absent when Casebier took his pictures.

The name of Goffs is cause for some speculation. It was one of the alphabet towns preceded by Fenner and followed by Homer. These towns were planned to stretch east of Amboy by Southern Pacific Railroad who were in deadly competition with Santa Fe. Almost certainly it was named after a particular man, and in the records, there is one called Isaac Goff, who was a railroad locator for A & P, a subsidiary of Santa Fe Railroad, who eventually pushed the line through to the Pacific Ocean.

The present scene is laid out as it was intended but there were other uses for the building. It was occasionally used for dances, and back in 1928, during one such event, a shot was fired from a Colt .45 and a man was killed. The victim, Leo Sweeney died at the scene and a suspected perpetrator, Doug Craig was charged with murder. The charge was eventually dismissed and Craig went free.

This was not the only piece of violence in the remote desert area; there is one grizzly artifact on the back wall of the schoolhouse. In 1908, one Joseph "Hootch" Simpson was hung in Death Valley County by an angry citizenry, tired of his ways. The Press tore out to witness the scene but Hootch had already been cut down. Nonetheless, in pursuit of a hot story the press persuaded those in attendance to re-hang Hootch so they could get photos. One of these is in the case with the actual noose that sent Hootch to the hereafter.

For the regular youngsters – 412 in all – who passed their days at the schoolhouse, no doubt there were some happy times away from the heat and dust of the desert, and a lot of evidence to that fact has been gathered by the enthusiastic owners of the site.

Goffs Schoolhouse is opened by appointment and you can find more information at (760) 733-4848 or on the Web site: www.mdhca.org.

CONCRETE

MOST OF US are surrounded by it, few of us like it, but we couldn't live without it. "It" of course, is concrete, and the basis of that is cement.

Nestled into the base of a corner of the San Bernardino Mountains, just few miles from Lucerne Valley is the Mitsubishi Cement Works. Over the years the management has done wonders to hide its appearance from the hundreds of motorists driving up and down to the higher elevations on Route 18, but the fact remains that it's not a very pretty place.

"Mitsubishi bought the plant in 1988 from the then owners and founders, Kaiser Cement," said Douglas Shumway, Mining Manager, who has worked here since 1985. "Originally it was built in 1957 to provide limestone for the Kaiser Steel Works in Fontana."

Limestone was used as a flux for steel mills in those days, and the discovery of large quantities of the material in the hills started the work there.

"The Kaiser Steel Works themselves were located at Fontana for a specific reason," Shumway continued. "The military leaders at the time of WWII wanted it there as it was out of the range of the enemy's battleship guns."

However, today the limestone that is taken out of the ground on a 24/7 basis is used for concrete. Together with iron, silica, and bauxite which is imported from Australia, it is mixed together to make the concrete which we all need to lead our 21st century lives.

Down at the mine level the quality of the limestone is different depending on how deep one goes. Lower down it is white and pure, higher up the strata shows gray, which is used for such work as highway construction. The levels are called benches and they are just that, with each bench being about 45 to 50 feet high and 30 to 40 feet wide.

Once the material is dug out then the rocks are poured into a crusher prior to mixing, which is a highly controlled process. "It's a bit like making a Betty Crocker cake," Shumway explained. "Our chemist takes samples every ten minutes to make sure the mix is right."

Incidentally, each year there is enough cement transported around on the roads of the U.S.A. to build 100 Hoover dams - and that's a lot of concrete.

Fortunately there is sufficient material at the Mitsubishi Plant to last another fifty years, so they won't run out any time soon.

Of course, digging out rocks and then moving them around is hard work, and particularly for the trucks that are used on site. They are huge, and they're expensive. "Nearly everything to do with mining is expensive," Shumway said. And these Caterpillar monsters cost $1 million each. "Even the tires are expensive at around $6,500 each," he added.

Tires too are part of the furnace mix that is in use here. Shumway explained: "Every year in California a tire is discarded for every man woman and child. We use many of these old tires in our blending. It burns cleaner than coal and helps the environment too." In fact there is the equivalent of two gallons of fuel in each tire.

Mitsubishi is happy to arrange tours of their facility and you can either contact them directly or through the Discovery Center in Big Bear Lake.

The next time you drive up on Route 18 and the wind is blowing a little dust out over you; try to remember that they are hard at work inside mixing up a huge Betty Crocker cake – one that is made of cement.

Mitsubishi Cement Corporation
5808 State Highway 18,
Lucerne Valley, CA 92356
(760) 248–5136

CYCLING

PERHAPS THE ONLY real casualty of my move to California was a serious slowing down of my usual early morning run. This had been a practice for many years which I believed would keep me fit, and once completed would allow me to pass the remainder of the day in comparative idleness. Sadly the previous amount of use and also the hardness of California pavements gave me a level of pain in the knees that sent me to an orthopedic surgeon who confirmed my own diagnosis. My running days were over.

Once the understanding seeped in, I regretted the loss of my quiet time each day, and this set me to finding a replacement activity. It didn't take long for me go back to my old love when I was a pre-teenager — cycling. Here one only needed a bike, decent; preferably traffic-free routes, and the discipline to get on and ride. Many years later this is still my preferred way of exercising and even when the weather is poor I feel better doing it than lazing around finding excuses.

I expect that if most people inspect their garages, inside they will find somewhere a bicycle. They are remarkably little changed since their invention in 1815. Naturally there are improvements galore, and wonderful new light materials, but to a distant observer, they look much the same as when someone first put pedals and a drive chain on the original design where one simply sat on and scooted along with one's feet. Their evolvements included the quaint and rather ungainly high-wheels, or as the British call them penny-farthings.

Every July, my long suffering wife knows that she will be subjected to daily TV broadcasts of the Tour de France; cycling's finest sporting achievement and also an opportunity to look at the continent that I once called my home.

I'm not sure if it's the outstanding scenery of France, or the actual racing coupled with the English commentators' voices that keep me watching year after year, but I try never to miss a moment of this event.

Held since 1903, the Tour is perhaps the ultimate athletic test, with the route taking close to 200 participants through individual time trials, across some of the flat zones of the country; followed by lung-bursting climbs in the Alps and the Pyrenees, and ending with a sprint through the streets of central Paris. All of this intense activity takes place over three weeks and some 2,200 miles of cycling – exhausting!

Perhaps with the retirement of Lance Armstrong and the doubtful win of last year's contender for the yellow jersey, America may have to hand the top prize back over to the Europeans. They have rather resented Armstrong's seven successive wins in this race as they like to think it their own. Currently, two Americans, Levi Leipheimer, and George Hincapie are doing their best to come through, but with one week to go it doesn't look too good.

Nonetheless, once the final has taken place within the shadow of the Arc de Triumph, and the winners' rostrums have said farewell to the kissing girls and the cheering crowds, the estimated worldwide audience of 120 million will no doubt be a little lost with no Tour to latch on to each day.

Maybe San Bernardino doesn't have a ride like the 15 miles up the Alpe d'Huez or even some of the old architecture of Montpelier or Arle to enjoy, but the local mountains can attract a lot of enthusiasts, like local racer, Steve Kinney; smart in his look-alike Tour de France outfit.

If you Google "bicycle trails in San Bernardino County" there are 286,000 sites where you can find places to ride that bike you've been trying to ignore every time you try to stuff another item in your garage.

All it needs is a little oil on the chain and a dusting off to be able to take you out and about in a way that allows you to enjoy the scenery and the many sights that otherwise you would miss in the car. And I can tell you that provided you adjust the machine correctly, you won't suffer any knee damage, which is indeed a real bonus.

LANE HOUSE & MUSEUM

IT'S RATHER SURPRISING that the Lane House has survived all this time. It was built as one of four adobe buildings in the 1880's in the middle of Calico. What with fires and earthquakes, by rights it should have fallen down decades ago. But those old engineers obviously knew a thing or two about construction; and long before code inspectors came on the scene.

Calico is a hot place at the moment and that makes it perhaps the best time to visit. Not too many crowds and a chance to live the experience as it should be; with a little inconvenience and sweat. After all, life back in the old days was a tough experience and not viewed through the windows of an air-conditioned bus.

The Lane House and Museum is a developing exhibition where visitors can enjoy the true atmosphere of the old Calico during the boom days of silver and borax mining.

In 1884 a miner called George King made a start in Bismark, which overlooked the town of Calico, the center of mining operations at the time. His ten-year old daughter, Lucy used to walk and slide down the steep slope to school every day, and during a conversation with a journalist in 1961, she remembered that the walk back home at night was very tiring.

After a number of relocations for health reasons, Lucy returned to Calico and became engaged to John Robert Lane, who at the time was the waterworks engineer

After their wedding, the Lane's opened a general store to help provision the mining population. Most of this stock was tinned goods, although potatoes were sold in bulk. Cloth, nails and other important items were on hand but the bulkier things such as stoves and furniture were ordered from catalogues and delivered to the customers.

"She lived here for the last forty years of her life," said Serena Stiner, curator of the museum. "From the twenties until the sixties." The current Lane House is divided into four separate rooms and reflects much of the life the Lanes shared in their 64 years together

Visitors making the small diversion to the Museum will find an interesting collection of mining maps and area photos to help orient them to the area which has undergone so many changes since the boom days. The Lane Family Room gives an understanding of how life was lived in the times when running water, gas and electricity were considered more of a luxury then a necessity. Check out the 1930's original electrical wiring. There's no chance that would pass an inspection today.

In order to keep food from going bad, the Spark Iceless Cooler helped Lucy Lane in her escape from the desert heat. A burlap flap caught water dripping down and the evaporation kept eggs from hatching, and butter from turning rancid. A far cry from today's all purpose refrigerators with so many features.

The small Southwest Room holds a number of Native American exhibits from the early times before Calico's deposits were discovered; whereas the Main Room is largely dedicated to those deposits, and the effect they had on life. Miners, opportunists, and entrepreneurs all congregated into this compacted area, hoping to make their fortunes. Many struck it rich but of course, most either did not or lost all their earnings in other ventures, or the demon drink or gambling.

The Lane's managed to hang on and make their lives successful, even though they had to survive the days when the silver ran out. Lucy herself saw out her days until she was 97. She was often seen in the town and would talk to visitors about the old days that she had enjoyed. She died in the late sixties and no doubt would thoroughly approve of the collection of memorabilia now on display.

Where: Lane House and Museum
Main Street, Calico.
For more information call 1 (800) TO CALICO
Or visit the Website http://cms.sbcounty.gov/parks/Parks/
CalicoGhostTown.aspx

SAN DIEGO

SAN DIEGO AS a destination for those of us in the Inland Empire is often overlooked in favor of our nearer big city, Los Angeles. But it is a wonderful place. To consider it as the destination for a day trip is almost too much as it has grown so much in the last couple of decades, when it was home to the U.S. Navy Pacific Fleet. That title has now been changed to Naval Base San Diego, but the flavor of the sea has not gone away with the new name. It is still very much a naval town.

To get acquainted with some naval history a wander along North Harbor Drive will bring you to the Maritime Museum where you can spend a lot of time looking at the ships of the past in a perfect setting.

Sharing space with modern cruise ships of up to 110,000 tons are seven floating vessels aboard which our ancestors chanced their arms in the days before GPS navigation systems and radio. There is a Russian Submarine from 1974 and on the sidewalk too are some new exhibits to interest you.

H.M.S. Surprise at the Maritime Museum

H.M.S. Surprise lies alongside the entrance to the museum and is a replica of an 18th century British Royal Navy warship — the type that built an empire "upon which the sun never set." It was used for the recent film: Master and Commander: The Far Side of the World. Originally called H.M.S. Rose when she was launched in 1970, she was used as a training ship before being commissioned for the movie. The work during the film caused her to become unseaworthy and it is planned to restore her to full operations in the near future. In the meantime it is a testament to the toughness of Nelson's sailors who lived and fought aboard such a craft.

For an original vessel in all her glory, there is no beating the Star of India, just a few steps along the road from the Surprise. It is the world's oldest active ship and goes out once a year to strut her stuff in the bay. The ship is 212 feet in length, displaces 1318 tons and was built in 1863.

Originally called The Euterpe after the Greek muse of music, she started out being a rather unlucky ship having been involved in a collision, a mutiny and a cyclone. Her first captain also died on board prematurely. After 21 voyages carrying emigrants out to New Zealand she finally left her native English shores in 1898, and began ferrying men and supplies up from California to the Bering Sea, returning each fall laden down with tinned salmon.

In 1923, with her commercial operating days over, she was bought by an enthusiast for $9,000 and eventually towed to San Diego where she languished until a fund for renovations began in 1957. Twenty years later she made her debut as a fully rigged sailing vessel, to the cheers of half a million of her fans.

The museum shop is housed in the Berkeley, which is an 1898 steam ferry that used to ply for 60 years on San Francisco Bay. You can see how the engine worked down below decks, but the steam is gone, and the work is now performed realistically by hydraulics and compressed air. Berkeley played an important role in 1906 when she ferried survivors to safety away from the earthquake.

A particular favorite of the museum is the Medea, a small steam yacht. Born in an age of elegance in 1904, she was built in just 51 days which was a record. Her life was that of cruising around Western Scotland for the pleasure of William Macalister Hall, a wealthy Scottish land owner and British Army officer, but she served in both World Wars and ended up here in 1973. She still cruises, going out about twice a month.

With the Wildlife Animal Park, Sea World, a rebuilt downtown, and some of the finest beaches in California it's hard to focus on just one aspect on which to spend the day in this lovely city, but a visit to what has made her the place she is – ships - might be a good start.

Maritime Museum of San Diego
1492 North Harbor Drive
San Diego, CA 92101
(619) 234-9153 Web site: sdmaritime.org

MOJAVE RIVER MUSEUM

THE TRAFFIC ROARS along the 15 Freeway just south of the split before the 40 in Barstow. Concentrating on their drives no doubt the thousands of drivers are largely unaware of the historical significance of the routes they are traveling.

In 1776 Father Francisco Garcés plodded his weary way as the first European to venture into the untamed west. He was followed in 1826 by Jedediah Smith and from then on a regular stream of visitors made their way over the Cajon Pass and down to the flat lands of the high desert.

Eventually the route became the Old Spanish Trail, which existed until 1846 when wagon trains took over the task that had so far been left to single travelers, pack mules, horse thieves and traders looking to benefit from business between New Mexico and developing western cities like Los Angeles.

The Trail was described as "the longest, crookedest, most arduous pack mule trail in the history of America," and it replicated the path taken by many indigenous peoples who also used it as a trading route for thousands of years earlier.

It would be easy to let this piece of genuine Americana disappear completely, if it were not for some enthusiastic workers at museums and associations around the area.

One of the most comprehensive of these is the Mojave River Museum located just above the hum of the Freeway's traffic. It is a compact place with its own history going back to 1964. Today it is crammed with memorabilia of ancient times and the old western settlements in the area.

The museum boasts an extensive collection of old photographs of places long since gone into the dust of the desert through lack of use. They emote a time of struggle and enormous hard work by dedicated people trying to wrench a living out of an unforgiving land.

Jesse Bryrd is a docent at the museum. "I've been here since 2003," he said. "I'm particularly interested in the archeological opportunities of the area." In fact he was introduced to the museum through many of the field trips that occur in and around Barstow.

"We have a regular lecturer here every third Wednesday in the month," he continued. "Mostly they are professors from local colleges and we also get authors."

Throughout the museum are the results of diggings from sites where mankind had been walking for 50,000 years, including Calico early man and Paleo Indians. But more modern exhibits are not neglected with several examples of Victorian living.

Outside the building is a fine example of a caboose, which served as a drovers' wagon during the cattle driving days. The bunks inside don't look very comfortable, but after a long hard day in the saddle, any flat surface no doubt was welcome.

There is a gift shop and an archive of old newspapers, describing life way back when. You will find plenty to interest you on a visit, and the docents have a full understanding of the subjects.

Next time you are on your way to Las Vegas or further east, as you go through the concrete expressways of modern transportation, spare a thought to how life was lived by those early travelers. If you want to find out more about them a trip to the Mojave River Museum will provide all the details.

Mojave River Museum
270 E Virginia Way
PO Box 1282
Barstow, CA 92312-1282
(760) 256-5452
Mojaverivermuseum.org

Open every day except Christmas Day from 11a.m. to 4 p.m.

BANNING

WHEN A HUGE freeway comes by your town it is often a case of good news bad news. When the 10 Freeway was completed it was no doubt both a benefit and also a bane for the town of Banning. Today spreading westwards out of the center and parallel to the freeway is a long line of one of the biggest collections of fast food restaurants and national chain cheap hotels in the State. Not one seems to be missing.

And yet, Banning's tiny center of town has gone through its best and also its worst days and is now going through a rebirth. In order to do this it has needed a vehicle to begin its renaissance and it has successfully chosen art.

"We've got about six galleries open in the center," said Diane Kelly, a docent with the Banning Fine Art Gallery. "In this one we have a regular selection of local artists who submit their work to a committee who then decide which ones to display."

The light, airy gallery over which she was presiding had a full collection of very varied work from pseudo-cubist works to sculpture made from scrap pieces. The featured artist was Edwin Tuazon, who originated from the Philippines and has a gallery himself in the town.

Kelly herself paints and has lived in Banning for more than five years. She explained that the gallery is in fact a co-op of artists and they are all very keen to show off their talents.

Across the street is the Corda Gallery which is run by Joseph Corda, who also paints. "It was really a hobby when I was in construction in the Victorville area," he said. "But we moved here and opened this place right in the center. It's rather a European atmosphere, and we live over the shop."

Often when small towns lose their focus and the population moves out of the center, it can attract a bad element with run-down businesses and a lack of revenue, but Corda says that is not the case with Banning. "We've lived here for about seven years and it's really safe and quiet in the evenings."

Furthermore the town is situated close to a lot of very useful places like Palm Springs, the mountains, and Los Angeles which is less than 90 miles away.

There has been a beautification process going on for the last two years. The city has backed the rebuilding of many of the facades of the town which were suffering with age. They will assist with the cost of replacing these old fronts. Also there are a number of brightly painted murals around the town with historical significance for what is known as Stagecoach Town USA. There is a festival every year in early October to celebrate.

Plans are afoot for a new gallery and building to be called The Haven, which will be at the very center of town at the crossroads of Ramsey and San Gorgonio. Apart from a gallery it will house a working studio, a bookstore and a coffee house selling Banning Blend coffee.

Although the area of Banning is very spread out and seems to almost merge into the adjoining community of Beaumont, you will not need hiking boots and gallons of water in order to spend some time there. Currently the entire refurbished center is only about a block in area. But what is there is beginning to make it a desirable place for a trip, and will give you an interest in future developments.

No doubt as the 10 Freeway began to drain away business from Banning's center it was seen as a serious problem for the residents; but now the same artery is going to bring a new visiting public to a revitalized small attractive town.

Banning Fine Art Gallery
130, N. San Gorgonio Ave
Banning, CA 92220
(951) 849-3393

Corda Art Gallery
137, N. San Gorgonio Ave
Banning, CA 92220
(951) 922-2880

GLEN HELEN REGIONAL PARK

FREEWAYS ARE WONDERFUL things. They whisk you to where you want to go in an orderly and efficient way. Providing there are no jams or hold-ups, of course. However, they do have one disadvantage; they take you very quickly past places that might be worth a stop and a general look around.

For years, I have intended to visit the Glen Helen Regional Park lodged between the I 215, and the I 15, just where the two join south of the Cajon Pass.

Usually I have been on the way to somewhere else, and very often I have said to myself: I really must go and have a look at that place some time. Being on a freeway, I've been keeping up with the traffic and not able to look at what this park may be like, and it does keep its secrets well away from the casual observer packed in with all the other drivers.

So I was quite looking forward to making a special trip to this new place on my list of travels.

I chose a day where the winds were really coming down over the passes, and I met up with rangers, Steve Smith and Neil Gericke at the entrance gate for an interview. Smith was quite familiar to me as it seems I had met him once before when he was at the Mojave Regional Park in Apple Valley. "I've been here now for a few years," he said. "It's a wonderful place to work. It's always changing."

The park sits like a big green emerald between the two freeways. A testament to what constant sunshine and water will do for grass seed. Currently, camping is reduced to groups only as the camping areas are being given a facelift. But for a day out in a wide open area this place has a lot to offer.

There are two lakes for the people hoping to persuade fish to join them, and there is an overall feeling of care that's gone into the park. During the summer months, there is a water park with plenty of challenges on the two water slides.

But during the winter time, people can relax by the lakes or at the well-appointed picnic areas. Lots of rest facilities are on hand and bar-b-que pits available too.

Glen Helen Park is also home to the country's largest outdoor amphitheater, the Hyundai Pavilion. It sits above the park and holds a number of top flight concerts during the summer. There is plenty of parking to cope with the big crowds that come along.

There is the Glen Helen Raceway Park in the immediate area, which provides race condition for motorcycles and motocross.

Newcomer, Neil Gericke, who has been at the park for just six months agrees with his colleague, Smith. "It's a great place to work,: he said. There are always improvements going on here and it's nice to be outside all the time."

Recently the park has hosted the San Bernardino Sheriff's Rodeo which brought a lot of interest to the park, and a lot of well trained horses too.

So next time you are traveling on those busy freeways and you see a sign to the Glen Helen Regional Park, take the time to go along and enjoy the 1600 acres of this restful oasis in its vibrant green surroundings.

Where: Glen Helen Regional Park
2555 Glen Helen Pkwy,
San Bernardino, CA 92407
(909) 887-7540

BASS PRO SHOPS

MOST MEN I know are not keen on shopping. Perhaps we lack a certain gene present in the distaff side of our homes. Many women don't quite understand this deficiency, and regularly drag their unwilling partners along for shopping expeditions, only to be met with an instant look of fear at the suggestion. Of course, there are degrees of desperation in the male, but I think there is no more pitiful sight than some poor fellow sitting outside a store in a mall surrounded by parcels and endlessly waiting.

There is of course the ultimate in misery; that of having to perch on one of those spindly chairs outside the changing rooms of a dress shop, clutching a purse. And woe betide any unfortunate if he doesn't show the right degree of enthusiasm when the object of his affections pirouettes in a new outfit; a horrible scenario indeed.

And yet, there are shopping places where men do feel at home; electronic stores and pretty much anything to do with food. Certain automotive establishments also hold the same allure, as do Harley Davidson dealerships.

During the beginning of the year, anyone passing south down I-15 would have noticed the erection of a very large store on the west side a few miles before the I-10. What could it be?

Eventually, the signs went up – Bass Pro Shops OUTDOOR WORLD. But what exactly was it apart from being one of the biggest buildings in the area?

Soon the rumors began that it was a haven for the outdoor person, and also the hunter and fisherman. I don't hunt, and I am a very bad fisherman, but still there was something about the place that was intriguing. I was determined to go.

The first thing to note about the place is that it is indeed extremely large. It's like a giant hunting lodge on steroids. But it is also very welcoming with its muted, even darkish woods and displays. Yes, they have clothes, but they seem appropriate and not of the variety to cause a panic attack should your female companion get that look forecasting a hefty raid on the credit card.

Let's face it; any store that sells boats on one side and excellent food on the other is on to a winner in the mind of the reluctant male. And they've got guns too – lots of them! But discretely displayed upstairs in a mezzanine area.

"The place began in Springfield, Missouri, in 1972," said Bob Derr, the General Manager since it opened in late July this year. "It was a section of a small liquor store." It's certainly grown since then.

"We try to have as many of our customers as possible share in the outdoors," Derr continued. "And we very much encourage conservation."

Throughout there are tableaux of the wild life the firm promotes – coyotes, deer, raccoons and other critters all pay testament to the taxidermist's art. A huge fish tank sits in the center of the place, and a small stream runs through under an attractive bridge.

A very sizeable part of the store is given over to the capture of similar fish to the ones in the tank. There is even a separate shop dealing with the art of the fly. One has to wonder why so many lures are required for a creature that is not known for its intelligence.

When I first thought about this site as a piece for my column, I decided to check with my editor. She readily agreed, which somewhat surprised me. Perhaps there is some sort of conspiracy out there. Perhaps all women are in on it, and encourage even the most intransigent male to visit a shop - any shop. Perhaps this visit might encourage more regular shopping trips in the future.

As for the Bass Pro Shop in Rancho Cucamonga, I have to say it's worked, as I look forward to my next visit there very much.

Bass Pro Shops – Outdoor World
7777 Victoria Gardens
Cucamonga, CA
(909) 922-5500
Basspro.com

ALPINE SLIDE

I HAVE TO admit that I'm not much of a skier. I have tried it a few times, and taken some lessons as well, but I just haven't taken to it. Perhaps it's because I tried it too late in life and then again perhaps it was due to the last lesson given to me by my eldest son.

The result of this was to prove to me that he was as bad a teacher as I was a skier, and the experience left me with two broken ribs. I completely failed to follow his curse instructions on the intricacies of the turn. The result was not only painful but humiliating as I had to remove my skis and boots and walk down the slope before the watching crowds. That was the last time.

I think the aging process robs one of the visceral thrill of careening downhill at various speeds. But in my youth I well remember doing it on a home made sled wearing freezing rubber boots and soggy socks that had crept down uncomfortably under my instep. But the thrill was such as to not dampen my enthusiasm to clamber up the hill again for another ride.

But such discomfort is not for the youth of today, and if they want a little less equipment and danger than skiing or snow boarding there is another way. At Magic Mountain at the west end of Big Bear Lake there is the ultimate sledding experience.

At the start of every season locals notice a thin carpet of snow appearing long before Mother Nature is able to provide the real stuff. Magic Mountain has begun its snow making and they start it well before Thanksgiving. Usually by the beginning of the holiday season they are ready to provide crowds of young and old alike with the next best thing to a ski run; and with no danger of broken ribs.

The Snow Play section of the site features the ultimate in magic carpet rides before reaching the top of the run. Riders stand on this rubberized walkway, similar to the people movers at airports, and climb steadily upwards. Once at the top seated comfortably on huge inner tubes, they can fly down the hill across freshly groomed snow towards the big ramp at the bottom. Kids love it!

"We've had a very good season," said Julie Eubanks, the assistant general manager. "Incoming storms slow things down a bit, but all in all it's been very busy."

Eubanks, who has been at the facility for eight years in her present position, lends a hand at all the favorite spots. At the time of the interview she was running the snack bar. "We serve a variety of different foods here," she said. The menu offers all the usual hot dogs, chili, soup and pretzels, everything, in fact, to keep hungry people going in between rides.

There is also the ever popular Alpine Slide to enjoy. After a ride on a chairlift, two ¼ mile concrete tracks provide thrills to riders aboard low-slung sleds. "You have to be careful as the turns are quite fast," Eubanks commented. This feature is open year round weather permitting.

The facility also provides miniature golf and a go cart track – in fact there's plenty to do for the entire family whether it's summer or winter.

In the summer the water slide is open for all ages to swish down the twists and turns. It's a little too cold up here for that at the moment, but you can get your thrills in a very safe way on the other amusements at Magic Mountain.

Where: 800 Wildrose Lane and Big Bear Boulevard
Big Bear Lake, CA 92315.
Opens at 10 a.m.
For more information call (909) 866-4626
Or visit the Web site at alpineslidebigbear.com

HEMET MUSEUM

NORMALLY YOU EXPECT the moving parts of railways to be the rolling stock and not the station. But in Hemet, it's the other way around. "This is the old freight office," said Bob Frazier a docent with the Hemet Depot Museum. "It used to be on the other side of the street, but it was moved over here."

The trains stopped rolling too quite a few years ago. "The last train came from San Bernardino to pick up a load of potatoes," Frazier continued. "And the last passenger train came through in 1972." Unfortunately it became unattractive financially and the mournful wail of the whistles stopped for ever.

Today the old freight office is joined onto the original depot which is now a coffee shop, making a long interesting building in the heart of Hemet.

The area has seen more than its fair share of changes apart from its railroad days. It was once home to roaming herds of prehistoric creatures and many thousands of years later Native Americans made it their home. Intricately woven baskets are on display to show some aspects of their life here. "One of the smaller baskets was made by Ramona Lubo," said Frazier. "She was married to Juan Diego and they were quite a well known family in the area."

The small packed museum is spick and span and has a lot on show. The building itself is considered to be one of Hemet's oldest wooden structures and is cared for by a team of docents like Frazier. He has lived in the area since 1958, and admits to being particularly fond of the railway aspects of the place.

Agriculture too was a serious part of Hemet's past being part of the citrus producing industry. Sadly most of the farms have been covered over by houses to cope with Southern California's burgeoning population.

Roses too were an important crop for Hemet. "There was a famous rose grower here," Frazier continued. "They produced a rose called Granada and outside the town hall in Granada, Spain they have a huge garden of them." A poster shows the vibrant red and pink colors of the flower.

But whether it's trains, people, fruit or flowers, the one common thread that runs through this community is water. And in 1895, the Great Hemet Dam was completed making progress in the area possible. It was during its construction that builders started uncovering the remains of the huge creatures that had been here so many thousands of years before.

As you wander around the showcases you will pass by an old telephone switchboard. "There used to be banks of these when I came out from the mid west in the mid fifties," Frazier said. "If you wanted to make a call, it would go through here and one of the phone operators." You can't help but think of the convenience of the cell phone on your belt and its ease of use compared to this big lump of solid technology. But somehow the callers of the day seemed to manage OK.

The wall of artisan's implements and tools is also a long way from the convenience of one of the big box stores that cater to today's homebuilding and gardening needs. And not one of the drills, saws or sanders has a cord hanging from it or even space for a battery.

A little time spent here will take you back in time and allow you to understand how life was lived in this interesting region before and after the trains came through.

Where: Florida Avenue and State Street, Hemet.
Hours: Tuesday – Sunday 11 – 3
Free Admission, but donations gratefully received.
For more information call (951) 929-4409
Web site hemetmuseum.com

WESTERN CENTER MUSEUM

IT SEEMS TO me that dinosaurs have gone slightly out of style. A few years ago you couldn't move for them – there was even a big purple one always jumping around on children's television. But their day seems to have passed.

It's not the first time it has happened of course. They went permanently out of style at the end of the Jurassic period which was about 140 million years ago, give or take five or ten million. That's a lot of zeros for those of us numerically challenged.

But dinosaurs are the generic name used for lots of big frightening stuff that roamed around the earth before we humans got seriously started. And you don't have to go back quite so far before you run into things better left well alone.

"We have to tell kids when they come here, that dinosaurs were before the time of the recent discoveries," said Dr. Richard Giese, the Executive Director of the Western Center Museum for Archaeology and Paleontology in Hemet. "During the Jurassic period, which was the dinosaur time, this area was all under water."

To demonstrate this fact Giese showed a display illuminating the way the sea covered the area and how it receded eventually to allow animals to live here. The remains of such creatures had been left mostly undisturbed until work was started digging the Diamond Valley Lake in the 1990's.

Today the museum houses close to a million artifacts although many of them still need to be catalogued and labeled. The displays however are cleverly constructed to show you the sort of animal living on the great plains outside the very modern building housing them.

"We tried a different approach here," Giese explained. "The bones you see on the models are actually replicas. The real bones are under the display." The mastodon for instance has several ribs and its tusks fitted into a life-size clear plastic shape. The actual remains are in glass cases at its feet, and beneath the glass floor itself are more replicas of the position in which the bones were found.

The hall where the remains are displayed is full of information as to how the animals lived and where they were discovered. The giant land sloth, which stands about twelve feet high, is certainly not the sort of fellow you'd like to meet unexpectedly while out on a country stroll with your tribe.

The first humans in the area are also represented by some of the things they held dear. Baskets and other useful items are on display to remind us that there were people here long before the Europeans arrived. Once again in the back storage area, thousands of Native American pieces await curators and other scholars before they can be put out. "We literally have years and years and years of work ahead of us," said Giese.

The Center welcomes groups and students as well as families who have an interest in what went on before. It's a manageable place benefiting from its newness, with all the latest ways to make a visit memorable and interesting. There is a 270° cinema showing animations and documentaries about the period covered. Its shows are continuous.

Even though it's hard to get one's thoughts around periods so long ago, this museum will leave you with a much better understanding of all things "dinosauristic" even though they were a little earlier.

Where: Western Center for Archaeology and Paleontology
2345 Searl Parkway, Hemet, CA 92543
Hours: 10 a.m. to 5 p.m. Tuesday – Sunday.
For more information call (951) 791-0033
Web site: westerncentermuseum.org

PATTON MUSEUM

"IT ALL BEGAN really when the Bureau of Land Management came out here to put up a monument," said Margit Chiriaco Rusche. "It was in 1985, and that's when it started." The "It" she was referring to is the General Patton Memorial Museum located at Chiriaco Summit some 30 miles east of Indio. It was here in 1942 that General Patton came out to oversee the beginning of the Desert Training Center.

"There was such a response to this that we started the museum," continued Chiriaco Rusche. Today the traffic stops on its journey out of the desert to fill up, rest and also take in some of the exhibits at the museum.

The summit itself has quite a history as it was originally called Shaver Summit when Chiriaco Rusche's father bought it in 1933. He had stayed over after watching a football game at the Rose Bowl and never returned to his native Alabama.

He had originally taken a job with the Metropolitan Water Company that was bringing an aqueduct out to Los Angeles from the Colorado River. It passed quite close to where the stop is. Also there was a new roadway passing through and it was finished the day Chiriaco opened.

In 1942 when Patton was inspecting the area, he came into the café. There was quite a commotion on his arrival. Chiriaco was drinking a cup of coffee at the counter. "My father was quite a feisty man, but when he turned round and saw all the scrambled eggs on the uniform and also the medals, he behaved accordingly," said Chiriaco Rusche.

The Desert Training Area covered 18,000 square miles and in its time together with its 11 sub camps trained over one million men.

Patton knew that the fight against the Axis forces would soon be in North Africa and he needed a place with the same terrain and climate – hot in the day and cold at night.

The museum that bears his name is full of WWII artifacts. Looking at these antiques makes you wonder how the Allies managed to beat Rommel, the Desert Fox, with such equipment. But then his was not much better. There's nothing it seem that dates so much as technology.

Considering that the ages of the veterans of WWII are increasing so much, I wondered if perhaps the numbers attending the museum were falling off. "Not at all," Chiriaco said. "We have a growing number of people here to look at the museum. In fact we are expanding the building soon."

The stop is well placed for travelers and also the museum is not just about Patton, although his presence is everywhere. The accent is also on America's participation in most of the involvements since the Civil War. In fact alongside a replica of Patton's famous ivory handled Colt 45, is a display devoted to that tragic conflict.

Inside the entrance you cannot miss The Big Map. This wooden three-dimensional map of the area was used by engineers to cut the canal for the aqueduct. The map was broken down like a giant jigsaw and taken to Washington D.C. for hearings before permission was given for the project.

A dozen tanks are placed outside the museum building. They fit in well with the scenery. One interesting exhibit is the mock tank that was used to fool the Nazis. It was covered by cloth and driven around on top of a Jeep.

Driving along the busy 10 Freeway through the desert it's easy to ignore the terrain as just being the same old same-o. But within living memory this entire area was once awash with tanks and other machines intent on freeing the world from the tyranny of fascism. Their maneuvers were under the watchful eye of one of the country's most colorful and successful generals, and in the museum named after him there is much to enjoy.

Where: The Patton Museum
Chiriaco Summit, CA 92201
For more information: (760) 227–3483
Web site: generalpattonmuseum.com
Hours: 9:30 a.m. to 4: 30 p.m. Monday through Sunday
Closed Christmas and Thanksgiving.

IDYLLWILD

PERHAPS LIVING IN the San Bernardino Mountains has poisoned me for the other wonderful mountain ranges in our area. Perhaps it's a misplaced sense of regionalism. But the truth is I don't often travel to the San Gabriels, the Tehachapis or the San Jacinto Mountains.

So it was with a sense of exploration and a slightly furtive feeling that I took the 25 miles of mountain road down to the 10 Freeway, the 25 miles of that natural division's course, and then the 25 miles up the other side of the San Jacintos to reach the goal of Idyllwild. As I put my back to the San Bernardino Mountain range I was reminded of crossing the Rubicon, or even coming ashore at Cap Griz Nez in France having crossed the English Channel. It was such a natural barrier.

The early slopes of the San Jacintos are different to their sisters on the north side of the 10. They are peppered with boulders no doubt thrown up by some enormous tectonic burp eons ago. Once you reach 4,000 feet, however, green takes over and the tree population is very rich and thick as you journey on.

About ten miles away from the target town of Idyllwild, you pass Fulmor Lake, and I made a note to stop there on the way back down.

Idyllwild is a small town clustered around a triangle of shops and galleries. A local brochure claims that there are more art galleries there than comparable towns in the area. Some eight were highlighted in the same brochure.

Two natural features dominate the town. It seems that years ago before the Europeans arrived there was an Indian Chief called Tahquitch. A tall handsome man he ruled his tribe well, but it seems the power went to his head and he became difficult. Furthermore he became, shall we say, a little too aggressive and enamored of the ladies. Bodies began to turn up, and the tribe rebelled against him.

He was executed by fire and the story is told that he disappeared in the flames with a big spark leaving the embers and flying up into the mountains where it settled as a huge outcrop. Today it is called Tahquitz Peak and it is a frequent place for rock climbers to hone their skills. I have to say that were I a female climber I might pause a little before starting if I knew the legend of the man who went before so many years ago.

The other natural feature of Idyllwild is the river than runs through it. This is Strawberry Creek and it is marked as the only place in town to fish. During the summer months the water is very low and I doubt many fish are to be had there, but the water sparkles in the mountain air and offers many restful places to stop if you're on a hike.

The town is billed as having a population of 3,500 people and this no doubt rises dramatically on the weekends and during vacation periods. It is also a little lower than it's sister Big Bear across the divide – it is 5,303 feet above sea level.

As I promised myself, I stopped at Fulmor Lake on the way back down. This is a three-acre lake which is no longer regularly stocked with fish. The limit therefore is just five per season. It is a marvelous mountain lake; green, tree-lined, and tranquil. You have to park across the road to get to Fulmor, and remember to put your adventure pass on display.

The return journey was without incident, but I did wonder if years ago I might have needed some papers or perhaps a bribe to cross from one mountain kingdom to another. Today it's just traffic and road repairs.

WIGWAM MOTEL

Wigwam Motel

WE'VE JUST COMPLETED the annual Route 66 festivities in San Bernardino. The main streets have been full of the most wonderful shiny examples of automotive art, and the sounds of souped up engines have been filling the hot evening air with their roars and rumblings

But Route 66 was not just a strip of black asphalt that attracted car loads of families with dreams of a better life out west. It also brought innovative businesses to cope with travelers who needed rest, relaxation and refreshment along the empty highway.

One such innovator was Frank Redford, who having seen a teepee style building in Long Beach on his travels in the '30's became quite obsessed with the design and tried it out on a number of ventures.

Stories are told where he experimented with the shape for an ice cream stall, then a food stand, then a gas station. To this last one he added a food facility and then began building rooms – all in the shape of teepees.

Eventually his ambition led him to build and operate seven motel villages stretching from Kentucky to San Bernardino; with number seven located here and built in 1949.

Now known as the Wigwam Motel, it has been owned and operated by Jagdish Patel since 2003. "I came out from India in 1979," Patel said. "Route 66 became a sort of hobby for me and this is right on the road."

The motel complex is very neat and tidy with 19 wigwams in two semi-circles around a kidney-shaped swimming pool with clear blue water in which tired travelers can relax.

As he proudly showed me his operation it struck me that there was a certain irony in all this.

Some 500 years ago, my European ancestors set out on long arduous voyages to try and meet up with Mr. Patel's ancestors in order to trade in spices, which back then were the items of choice for any discerning consumer. The overland route had proved less than desirable and fraught with danger.

This was risky business, and the small ships were far from comfortable as they pushed out from their rocky coves and storm tossed inlets.

Most of the crew believed that the world was round by then; although a few no doubt had sea-going nightmares that it was flat and they would fall off the edge any day.

As we all know, eventually they ran up against a huge landmass a few weeks out. Without the benefit of any medieval GPS or even a decent Thomas' guide, they naturally thought they had hit the target and this was India.

Of course, they also assumed that the people they spotted running up and down excitedly were Indians, and the name stuck.

But here today we have a real Indian on historic Route 66, owning a business build by a European American in the style of the Native

Americans of so long ago; a true example of the giant melting pot in action.

Unlike the original tents upon which the design is based, these motel rooms are complete with air-conditioning. "And every one has its own water heater making it fully independent," Patel added. The outer semi-circle rooms are a little larger than the inner, but once you're inside and close the door you are in your own cute little wigwam.

"We are always fully booked for the Route 66 event," Patel said. No doubt during their temporary stay, the occupants rarely if ever wonder at the strange circumstances that brought all the different historical elements together to create their abode for the night.

Wigwam Motel
2728 W. Foothill Boulevard
Rialto, CA 92376
(909) 875-3005
Web site: wigwammotel.com

ETIWANDA

IT WAS WAY back in 1877 that George Chaffey Sr. arrived in California. It didn't take him long to realize that the area had a lot of potential and he set about making a fortune for himself and his family.

Apart from this drive to succeed, Chaffey also brought two important names with him. The first was Ontario, which was from his old home up in Canada. The second name is familiar to all those who regularly travel the ten freeway – Etiwanda. This second name that Chaffey brought came from a distant uncle who was an Indian Chief, so it is no surprise that such an arcane name should elicit questions from today's travelers as they rush past.

Etiwanda is now almost swallowed up by the developing tracts of concrete and smart suburban housing. The little city is bounded by the 15 freeway to the east, the new 210 to the north and the 10 to the south. However, it clings to its quiet time of yesteryear and is in fact experiencing a renewal of life assisted by the enthusiastic members of the Etiwanda Historical Society.

"We're hoping for a proclamation soon. It will allow the buildings to be permanently preserved," said Donna Kendrena, who is a member of the board of the Society. "We're actually hoping to get it for our grand annual opening." This is in mid-November and allows visitors to look at five historical buildings from the Chaffey era.

Currently, the two most active of these sites is the Community Church which still functions as its originators designed; and also the Chaffey-Garcia House, which dates back to the time Chaffey Sr. arrived in the area, and was bought for his son from a Captain Garcia.

This small house is a delight for anyone interested in seeing how people of class lived 150 years ago. "The Chaffey's slightly flaunted their wealth," said Marsha Banks, the curator of the museum. "There was a tax on doors at the time, and the Chaffey's went ahead and had lots of them installed."

They also had the latest fashion and convenience added – electric light. "But it wasn't very reliable," Banks continued. "So they had dual systems working."

The society has just installed some original light fittings which have a detail that one could miss on passing through. The two glass housings are facing both up and down. The upward facing one contained a gas element, so that when the electric failed, they could immediately switch to gas.

The members of the society are full of little details like that which help the visitor to bond with the experience of understanding the quirks of an older age. They are all very excited at a recent purchase of brown china door knobs. They will add to the authenticity of this look back to a different time.

A small organ stands in one of the two living rooms; it was originally from the Mennonite Church in Upland, and was no doubt the focal point for a lot of lusty singing when people gathered round. Perhaps the equivalent of today's Tivo!

The other buildings in the less than a block radius that are to be protected by the new proclamation, will be the Pacific Electric Train Depot, across the street, and a couple of other small houses that would have been highly desirable to the families of the day.

If George Chaffey were to look down on the area he founded all those years ago, no doubt he would have a problem figuring out exactly where his son's house would be: there is so much development in the immediate area. But he would undoubtedly approve of the building expansion as it was his dream to make the cities that he named successful and full of profitable activity.

Where: 7150 Etiwanda Avenue
            Etiwanda, CA 91739

Hours: 10a.m. to 3 p.m. Second Saturday each Month.

For more information call (909) 899-8432

WHITEWATER CANYON PRESERVE

MY NATURAL CYNICISM always warns me off people and groups who appear to be working entirely for the common good of the rest of us. Sadly, a look at the financials mostly proves the hollowness of their stated objectives.

Whitewater Preserve

This jaundiced view however is most definitely reversed on meeting The Wildlands Conservancy, which I have bumped into a few times before. These are people truly dedicated to us all by preserving large swathes of our lands, and they do it all on their nickel, and without any government help.

"We were formed in 1995," said Frazier Haney. "We buy, and clean up areas of natural beauty, preserve them, and then encourage the public to visit and enjoy them." And they make no charge for all this.

Within their control is Pipes Canyon Natural Preserve; Windwolf Preserve; which is off Route 166 and Interstate 5; Bluff Lake near Big Bear, and Los Rios Ranchos in Oak Glen. In all the Conservancy cares for 97,000 acres and is the biggest owner of such land outside the government.

Just to the north west of Palm Springs along the ten Freeway is a turning marked Whitewater; thousands pass it every day. The term seems to be something of an oxymoron, as this is right out in the desert and not normally the site of gushing water, unless it's out of a broken sprinkler.

A gentle ride of 4.5 miles north however will take you to the Whitewater Preserve, which is another of Wildlands' sites. "It's a former trout farm," Frazier Haney, the manager, said. "The immediate area is about 300 acres, but it sits in the middle of 2,900 acres of total preserve." In this case they are preserving the watershed which is the flow of rain water that comes down from the mountains all around. This leads to white water at times of flood, and also passes on via the reconstructed trout ponds to help with Palm Springs' water needs.

The original farm is now a lodge which is the center for teaching people all about the scenery around them. And the scenery is magnificent.

It also attracts a large selection of wildlife, and as such in the '80's it was designated by the Bureau of Land Management as an area of "critical environmental concern." The private organization of Wildlands is showing that concern with a dedicated staff under Haney's supervision.

There is a large local population of Big Horn sheep, black bears, reptiles and amphibians. Snakes too abound in the area, and Haney states that several species of rattlesnakes share the rocks with the infamous King Snake, which is striped in equal black and white collars, and is the only one to eat other snakes. Flying overhead you can see a record number of 200 plus species of birds throughout the year.

The renovated ponds are home to hundreds of rainbow trout, and they leap to the surface when fish food is thrown in. Fishing instruction is given to youngsters at various weekend courses, and Haney reports that the fish soon learn not to show the same enthusiasm for lures at the end of a line attached to an excited child.

This interesting group seems to have only one aim in their existence, and that is for people to have the same relish for the outdoors as they do. "We have great camping facilities here," Haney said. "It's a wonderful place for families to come and experience the fun of living in the outdoors." The camping area is well trimmed green grass, and with very handy "facilities" near-by.

There is no doubt that as our lives become ever more urban, there is a need for people to get back to nature more; and especially the kids. The Whitewater Canyon Preserve is a wonderful place to do that, and it's cared for without charge by true philanthropists.

Whitewater Preserve
9160 Whitewater Canyon Road
Whitewater, CA 92282 (760) 325-7222 www.wildlandsconservancy.org

REDLANDS GLASS MUSEUM

THE HOUSE AT 1157 North Orange Street, Redlands is a perfect example of a small late Victorian dwelling. Technically having been built in 1903 it falls outside that illustrious monarch's reign, which ended in 1901. Also due to some unfortunate civil disturbances 125 years earlier, Redlands along with all the other cities in the USA failed to be included among Her Majesty's dominions. Although everybody remained good friends, of course.

The house was built by Jerome Seymour, who owned a local wood mill. Inside are many examples of the wood miller's art as well as lavish paneling throughout the small neat areas.

After Jerome and his wife, Martha, left the house to their daughter, Emma Cryer, she continued to live in it until her death in 1977. The local historical society bought it and after years of work and fund raising it opened its doors as a glass museum in 1985.

Entering the museum from the back door you are plunged into a different world. Before Thomas Edison invented the first commercially practical light bulb in 1878, houses were at best lit by gas, but more normally by candles and open fires. It was usually quite dark.

In order to catch every bit of light available from these relatively dim sources, glass was shaped and cut to give off a sparkling addition to whatever was available. It lead to an era of innovation and beautiful works of art, which are almost gone today.

In the museum, cases display the intricate works that adorned homes and became treasured possessions. One complete wall is devoted to rows of delicate cruets. These small handled jugs were used to hold vinegars or oils on most respectable middle class tables. Alongside them, no decent home would lack knife holders carved into the shapes of pineapples, and other fruits. A display of these is also there.

Frank Herendeen is the president of the Historical Glass Society, and when asked to point out his favorite exhibit, he had no hesitation in showing off a set of thin wine glasses from about 1928. They had small portraits of a lady etched into them. One would feel inhibited to use them for their original purpose as they are so delicate. Definitely not dishwasher safe!

The Victorians were the first people to have the money, opportunity and the desire to bring about social change with a boost to manners; and particularly manners to do with the dining table.

To show the growth of this social change the glass museum has a collection of small cup plates. These were used to put cups of tea upon when the tea had been poured into the saucer to cool it. The cup plate was used to avoid leaving a ring of tea on the table, marking it. The display of 20 little cup plates again shows the ingenuity of the artists involved. I had never heard of such items before.

In a similar vein of charming obsolescence, there is a collection of auto bud vases. Around the turn of the century, early cars were equipped with small vases to hold flowers. These were for decoration and also to freshen the atmosphere of the interior. I am sure even the most rigorous search would be unable to unearth such trinkets in today's auto parts store.

Glass design and manufacture is not totally forgotten in today's world of course, and there are several exhibits of modern times. One such piece is a statue in deep red glass; it's called Prairie Post and at about 24 inches tall it is the biggest piece in the museum.

Opening hours for this interesting small museum are from 12 to 4 on Saturdays and Sundays. There is a reception and fund raiser in September and the entire place will be closed for renovations throughout the month of August. There is no entrance fee, but donations are gratefully welcomed.

The Historical Glass Museum
1157 North Orange Street, Redlands, CA 92373
(909) 798-0868
Web site: glass_museum@yahoo.com

THE INTEGRATRON

The Integratron

IT'S A LONG dusty road from Lucerne Valley out to Landers, and when you get there the scenery doesn't change that much. The desert isn't for everybody, but there are two things that you can guarantee about it, it's quiet and it's hot. It reached 101 degrees on the day I went to visit the Integratron, although sitting in the shade outside it with that canny little water mist thing going, it was very comfortable and enjoyable.

I've been to the Integratron before, but never inside this strange structure. Its history is comparatively recent, but nonetheless, it is

213

quite unique. The construction of the dome is made of wood, in fact to quote one of the three sisters who own it: "…it's constructed along geomagnetic lines. It is a 16-sided dome supported by glue and laminated spines held together by a one-ton block of concrete at its apex. It was made with no metal fasteners in its construction."

George van Tassel was a test pilot for Lockheed, and in 1947 he moved with his wife, Eve, to Big Rock airfield a few miles away from the present site of the Integratron. He opened a café called the Come on Inn and his wife's burgers were famous in the area.

He always had an interest in outer space and UFO's, and his enthusiasm was rewarded by a visit from an extra terrestrial called Solanga, who flew here in his space ship from Venus. Having taken Van Tassel into his ship he gave him the formula for building a rejuvenating machine to help refresh body and soul. It was the start of what is there today and it took him 18 years of dedicated work to build.

As a natural cynic, I found all this extraterrestrial stuff a little hard to take, but the Van Tassels never varied from their story and in fact made a good living lecturing and writing about the entire experience. He described his creation this way: "The Integratron is a machine, a high-voltage electrostatic generator that would supply a broad range of frequencies to recharge the cell structure."

Joanne Karl who met me on site for the second time is not the sort of person who you would expect to be involved with "ufology." In fact she admits she came from corporate life. She and her two sisters however used to come here to get away from the restrictions of that world and when the opportunity came to buy it they did, and it has changed their lives.

"Since we were written about in Rolling Stone's 2009 review, the phone never stops ringing," said Karl. "We get all types here from the Hollywood set to people who just want to look around." In fact you can't just turn up; they are far too busy. You should always call for an appointment.

On August 15, there is a special event scheduled to witness the Perseid meteor shower. It is held in conjunction with the Mojave Desert Land Trust and it always attracts a wide range of people. Within the price is an opportunity for a sound bath in the Integratron.

Sound baths are a great attraction for people. You can bring your own music or accept some from the library on hand. Ideally the best place to be is in the center of the dome, but on crowded occasions, you can receive the same effect further out. Starting in September, public sound baths are to be resumed again.

Karl admits that traffic has been so continuous that they have to call a halt so that maintenance of the structure can take place to allow the wood to be oiled and other simple things attended to. Once September comes around, the public can once again attend on weekends for an hour's session.

I have to admit that I would have liked to have met George Van Tassel, who died in 1978. He must have been a very interesting man, and Karl said that she has met lots of people whose lives were affected by meeting him. Perhaps such a meeting could have cured me of my cynicism and even given me a new rejuvenated outlook on things. Nonetheless, what he left out here in the desert is well worth experiencing as a unique structure of interest.

2477 Belfield Boulevard, Landers, CA 92285
Phone: 760-364-3126
Web site: www.integratron.com

MINOR LEAGUES

I WAS RATHER shocked by my grandson's remark the other day. I was trying to arrange a visit to one of our local minor league baseball games, when he asked their ranking. When I said it was single "A", he replied: "Oh that's about the same as high school!"

Now, I'd be the first to admit that perhaps single "A" is not in the major category, but I was at pains to tell him that from a purist's point of view, minor league baseball is not to be sniffed at. In fact it has a lot to recommend it as a pure spectator sport.

I was once told that the team players of single "A" try a lot harder to impress than major leaguers who have long term and expensive contracts signed up. In the minor leagues, they go all out.

The fact remains that minor league baseball has a lot more in common with Mr. Doubleday's original game than the perfection of some of the major leagues. At the higher end the plays are almost automatic and although no doubt elegant, they lack a certain risk.

When Manny Ramirez lifts a sky high ball to the edges of the park, but not quite enough to go over the wall, there is no doubt that the outfielder is going to catch it. When a line drive is shot at Rafael Furcall at short stop, and the runner on first begins his sprint towards second base, we can leave the arm chair and go off to the fridge as we all know that a double play will ensue.

When I used to travel around the country, and found myself with a stopover in one of those out of the way towns with a minor league, and they were playing at home, I would go along. It was always very comfortable, easy to reach and a lot of fun. Usually there were a lot more runs scored and the game was over in about two hours.

We are lucky to have some good minor league teams playing in our area. In particular, I visited The Mavericks in Adelanto the other day.

This is a city not known for much more than a long line of traffic going along 395, stacks of parked planes at George airport, three prisons and a lot of dust. They do have, however, an excellent baseball stadium under the general management of Tim Altier.

It's a comfortable place to go. Constructed so that the sun is behind the building to maximize on shade, it also has easy access to all the concessions on one level – no having to go down into the bowels to buy that hot dog.

The Mavericks have done well in the first half of the season and no doubt their masters, the Seattle Mariners, are happy with the progress their men have been making.

Of course, one of the sad facts of life for minor leagues is that as soon as they are going really well, they lose their best players to the next level; some of the poorer ones face going down to an uncertain future too.

"They last about a year with us under normal circumstances," said Altier. "Then if they're good they go up to double "A," then up to triple." Of course, they all want to go to "the show," as the major league is called. But as my old headmaster once told me while reviewing my exceedingly poor scholastic results and hearing of my lofty plans: "Many are called, but few are chosen!" I can hear his sonorous tones even now!

The Mavericks Stadium holds a comfortable 3,800 seats with still others out on the grass. It's an attractive place and you can get close enough to the action to hear the grunts of scampering fielders and the comforting smack of the ball into the catcher's mitt. In other words it's exactly the way the game was designed. And as for that towering fly ball, you won't want to leave your seat, as there is chance the fielder will drop it.

High Desert Mavericks
12000 Stadium Way
Adelanto, CA 92301

(760) 246-6287
Web site: hdmavs.com

PLANES OF FAME

THE PHRASE "ONCE seen never forgotten" popped into my head at a recent visit to the Planes of Fame Museum in Chino. In fact it was more "once heard never forgotten," as what was on display I had never had close up knowledge of before.

My early experiences of the FZG 76 (V1) have been locked away for over sixty years. They were one of Hitler's secret weapons with which he hoped to turn around his fortunes as the battles of WWII went against him.

Under the control of the Luftwaffe, these flying bombs were launched from sites in Northern France and had a frightening effect on us as they flew across the English skies.

They made a curious growling noise that one would never forget. But better they made their sound as once it stopped they immediately plunged to earth as the V1 had all the gliding capabilities of a brick.

Some time when I was close to five, I asked my mother to come in to the Morrison air raid shelter which was in a corner of our living room. We lived at the time in a converted stately home divided into modest flats. The Morrison was designed to keep you safe if the building collapsed around you – or so they said.

Looking back, I have grave doubts that this small steel shell could support several stories of Georgian brick from crushing you, but at least the clean up crew had an easy task of finding the bodies. They were all conveniently together in that squashed tin can.

Yielding to my childish wish, my mother came into the Morrison with me and very soon we heard the approaching growl; perhaps my infant hearing had picked up the first slight vibrations in the air. We scrunched down and held our breath. The noise passed over and then stopped. We put our hands over our heads and sure enough after a few seconds there was a loud bang. The Doodlebug - as that was our name for them - crashed into a sports field nearby, blowing out several of our windows in the process. No one was hurt.

So it was quite an experience to come face to face with my nemesis at last, as apart from films, I had never actually seen one.

Planes of Fame has undergone quite a face lift since I first went there some time ago. As you pass through the gift shop, which is quite extensive, you enter a highly polished area and come face to face with a Sabre 6, in all its aluminum glory. It's on loan from Canada.

The Sabre 6

Bill Hamilton, who has been the new General Manager for the last year is very proud of the new facilities. "Many of our planes fly every two or three months," he said. "Our members can go up in them too."

The collection spans all the years of flight and is full of planes from the WWII era. "Sadly, many of the old vets are beginning to disappear," he said. "We have an education job to do."

To help with that there is a brand new "hands on" aviation center, which explains many of the marvels of flight and the planes that have made breakthroughs. If you fancy landing a 707 into LAX, there's a simulator here to help you learn; a friend across the room can be the control tower to help with that if you like.

While there check out the upside down plane called the Bose Double Take, it's got wheels on top of the wings as well as underneath.

In the middle of the center is a working engine from a Doodlebug. "We wheeled it out during our air show in May," Hamilton said. "I was quite a long way away when they fired it up and I was surprised at the huge noise it made. It was a very distinctive sound."

I didn't need a demonstration as that sound it made has been in my head for 60 plus years.

Planes of Fame Air Museum
7000, Merrill Ave #17
Chino Airport, Chino, CA 91710
(909) 597-3722
Planesoffame.org
Hours: Every day from 9:00 a.m. to 5:00 p.m.

FILIPPI WINERY

AN OLD FRIEND and I have a recurring image. We often say that life is like a reversed Advent calendar. You know the ones where you open a little window every day the closer you get to Christmas. Unfortunately he and I have found that in real life, you tend to have to close the windows of opportunity the longer you travel along the path.

One of the little pleasures that I have had to bid farewell to is wine; and particularly red wine. It started about fifteen years ago when I found that it caused me to wake up after a few hours and then firmly stay awake. Even a small glass of the stuff at dinner did it. Farewell Cabernet, farewell Merlot, and particularly my old European favorite Chateauneuf du Pape.

Nonetheless, in spite of my particular problem, I can still appreciate the wine grower's art and the history of this staple of life for so many people.

Within the growing urban sprawl of Rancho Cucamonga is a winery that has had its roots there since 1922. That was when Giovanni Filippi and his young son, Joseph, came to California from Northern Italy. They settled in the area and began to grow wine grapes.

Today the forth and fifth generation of wine growing is continuing with the present day Joseph and his son, Jared, and daughter-in-law Kristina producing a large variety of wines, many of them right here in the winery.

"We don't have enough wine grapes growing locally," said Joseph, the president of the firm. "But we bring it in, often from the Central Coast area."

In fact there is a lot of cooperation within the small number of local growers. "Its best that we work together like that," Filippi said.

"Sometimes we sell out and we need to bring in grapes either whole or crushed."

Filippi sells about 75% of its products out of the winery in Rancho Cucamonga and its annual yield is between 40,000 and 50,000 cases. "Our most popular wines are reds," Filippi continues. "But we have a very popular champagne, which has a slight almond essence added to it."

The facility is a most attractive and welcoming place – even for non consumers. There is an atmosphere of warmth and of course, bottles of wine are everywhere. The sampling area is laid out so that tipplers can enjoy the wide variety of tastes in an unhurried and leisurely manner

If you want to just enjoy a glass of wine and relax there is a pleasant seating area with comfortable sofas and chairs to lounge on. An example of an old still is there, but it's been cut down to size. "We used it to make port, which is fortified wine. But we don't make it anymore," said Filippi. "We also have a library of wines here, so that if anyone wants to try a particular product or vintage, we can take it out for them."

Regular tours of the winemaking process take place every Wednesday through Sunday at 1:00 p.m. If you have a large group, arrangements can be made and that can include tasting if you so wish. Filippi tries hard to make everyone welcome and to come away knowing more about the wine business than before.

Currently we are in the peak of the wine picking season, and afterwards things settle down a little before the holiday season kicks into gear. The really quiet period is after the New Year, when not too much goes on apart from consumption. But come March, it's time to start the growing process all over again. Tractors begin to move around the vines and weeding has to take place.

Although many of the acres formally given over to grapes have now fallen to urban housing, Filippi says he's still on the look out for patches of land nearby where they can put in more plants. If you know what you're doing, and provided the soil is right, you can grow them anywhere. After all it's been going on here for 84 years.

Filippi Winery: 12467 Base Line Road, Rancho Cucamonga, CA 91739, Telephone number (909) 899-9196.
Web site: www.josephfilippiwinery.com

RIVERSIDE ART MUSEUM

A VISIT TO the Riverside Art Museum is always a stimulating event. At the time I went the busy little restaurant in the middle of the museum was doing a roaring trade with lunch. The sound of the diners went well with the two galleries on either side; a sort of soft verbal Muzak.

But the enjoyment of a visit here starts with the building itself. It dates from 1929, and is the work of one of America's best architects, Julia Morgan. There is to be an 80th birthday celebration on November 12th.

Morgan obtained a degree in Civil Engineering from U.C. Berkley, when women just didn't do that sort of thing. She also was instrumental in helping William Randolph Hearst with his San Simeon castle.

The Art Museum was originally the Y.W.C.A. and the main galleries were once the swimming pool, now covered in, and the gymnasium.

These two galleries are currently showing two exhibits: Watercolor West, and a display of prints and printing techniques.

Lee Tusman, who is the adult education curator explained about the watercolors to me. "It's the most difficult medium in the world," he said. On entering the gallery there is a work by Scott Moore, who was the judge of the local competition. It is called Ice Cream Man, and the scene is at once detailed and very whimsical.

"Because it's a water color," Tusman explained, "the white parts are actually without any paint and that takes a lot of skill to make it blend in."

There were 670 entries for this competition so there is obviously a lot of art going on in the area.

The Riverside Art Museum specializes in work from living artists. "We also focus on artists from Southern California, "Tusman said. "In fact we try to get as much work as we can from the Inland Empire."

In the gallery devoted to print making, Tusman showed me how prints were made by running the plates many times through the ink process. "In fact we have an example of what we call 'suicide prints,'" he said. This is where parts of the plate are actually cut and discarded after printing each color.

The walls are covered by prints with a great variety of messages. There are advertisements, political messages and just plain art for art's sake.

Upstairs the central gallery is devoted to an exhibit called Son of Baby Tattooville. I needed help with this one as I didn't "get it" to begin with.

"It's art from such sources as pop surrealism," Tusman patiently explained. "It also has roots in science fiction and tattooing, as well as hot rods." Quite a mixture, but it was fascinating stuff. It also seemed to need a great variety of frames that the artists had painted to blend in with the subjects.

"We have two project spaces in the museum," Tusman said. "It allows us to show works from emerging artists, who are yet to become established." This of course, also lets the museum stay ahead of the curve in the world of art by seeing what is just around the corner.

The museum is a joint sponsor of the Joshua Tree Artists in Residence Program. Several fine photographs of the park are on display – work by Darcy Curwen.

After I leave an art gallery I always think back to the pieces that have stayed in my mind. In this case it is the Ice Cream Man that I remembered the most and would have liked to own.

But whatever your taste, any visit here is bound to leave you feeling that your time was well worth it, and you will come away a little richer for the experience.

Where: Riverside Art Museum
3425 Mission Inn Avenue
Riverside, CA 92501
Hours: Monday – Saturday 10 a.m. – 4 p.m.
For more information call (951) 684-7111
Web site riversideartmuseum.org

UPLAND AIRPORT

COMPARING OVERHEAD PHOTOGRAPHS of Upland's Cable Airport shows the enormous growth in the area since Dewey Cable started the place back in 1945.

"Back then it was mostly brush and lemon groves," said Bob Cable, Dewey's grandson, and the third generation to run this privately owned airfield.

Today however this well run and tidy place at the foot of the mountains, acts as an alternative to the busy commercial Ontario airport nearby.

But Cable is strictly a recreational airport serving the needs of some 320 pilots who use it as a base.

"We have around 200 hangars here," said Chuck Barett, the manager. "But we're hoping to add more as demand increases."

The strange thing is that some people who have lived in Upland all their lives don't know there is an airport here, although lots of activities take place on a regular basis.

"One of my ambitions is to be able to knock on any door and have the occupants say they have been here," said Cable. He also told me that statistically most inherited business die with the third generation. "That's not going to happen here," he emphasized.

Cable has almost built out the 100 acres that the airport covers, but he has also put in a small and very attractive business park to provide income for the future.

Some of the original hangars built by his grandfather are still in operation. "He used scrap metal and axle parts for the construction," he said. "He was not a pilot to begin with; he was a farmer out of Dysart, Iowa. But he learned to fly eventually."

Both Cable and Barett reported that there is still a great deal of interest and enthusiasm for flying and perhaps the future could be in the new Light Support Aircraft now coming into use. "It's a little easier to get an FAA license," Barrett reported. But the anticipated Very Light Jets (V.L.J's) are still a few years off. "Even though we do have the fuel for them."

The hangars have a wide variety of aircraft in them, and there are many more parked outside on the tarmac.

One prized plane is a 1985 Antonov-2. It's a bright yellow bi-plane, and was used in the Bosnian conflict as a jump plane. "It has the longest production run of any aircraft," Cable said. "It's a Russian plane originally built in 1947, but then they were built in Poland. Today, if you want one you can get it from the Chinese. It's the largest single engine aircraft in the world." It sat immaculate, glinting in the sun.

But running a private airfield is not always easy. "We always get the first of the regulations to deal with," Cable said. "For instance, putting in the new washing bay required a huge array of environmental issues, like underground waste tanks."

Events at the airfield are not always aviation related. They hold a regular electronics swap meet and the local Boy Scout troop holds is meetings there. There is a nice café and also an outside area where you can sit and watch the planes take off. "We also have the first air event of the season just after the first of the year," said Barrett.

The Ontario Police have their helicopter base there as it's less crowded than the busy commercial Ontario Airport. "We're proud to have emergency rescue services here," said Cable.

During my visit the 3,875 feet long runway was quite active with take-off and landings, as the pilots came in their view must be so different from the one that Dewey Cable's first customers had 65 years ago.

Cable Airport
1749, W. 13th Street, Upland, CA 91786
(909) 982-6021
Web site: cableairport.com

A 1985 Antonov still flying and still being made

BALDWIN LAKE

MOST PEOPLE WHO visit the Big Bear Valley confine their trip to the village and immediate nearby area. After all there is a lot to do in this small place, and particularly if you visit the slopes nearby.

But Big Bear Valley is a lot larger than casual visitors know about and there is another lake at the eastern end of the area. It is called Baldwin Lake. Now if you are expecting to see glittering water in it you'll have to wait for a very large storm to come through, as the lake is generally dry.

I have seen water there on a few occasions, but mostly it vanishes with the summer sun and wind. Baldwin has a lot of wind coming across from the west.

The area has been developed in a random way with small houses erected higgledy piggledy on smallish lots. It is sometimes called horse country as there are a number of stables next to the houses. Baldwin looks a little like it must have been throughout the valley in its early days. But it definitely has a rustic charm that is fast disappearing from the more sophisticated tourist areas to the west.

Apart from horses, there are several other domesticated animals looked after by a doting population. I've seen llamas, pigs and chickens pecking around on the dry ground. It all has a feeling of earlier days.

The lack of water doesn't detract from the beauty of the lake, as even when it's bone dry small dust devils swirl up to entertain the viewer. There are also lots of coyotes who make this place their home. Woe betide those with small dogs who let them wander off unleashed. Coyotes will steal them away and the chilling cries of a pack will often fill the night air. It's a startling and eerie sound.

Strangely, the wildlife in general is different from other parts to the west. Blue birds seem to congregate here but not at the other end. Rattlesnakes too and scorpions are seen in the summertime.

Perhaps the best way to see this underdeveloped place is from the saddle of a good walking horse. The local stables have a fine reputation and a good number of mounts to suit most riding needs.

Here, at Baldwin Lake Stables they boast of being open year round, weather permitting. They will take you up to the Pacific Crest Trail, which gives views out over the entire Valley.

If you don't have a desire to mount up, and would just prefer to talk to the animals, they have a petting zoo with some very friendly goats, chickens and other critters fond of people. It's a happy place all round. Both the petting zoo and the pony rides are available only on weekends and on holidays. Baldwin Lake Stables are located at the extreme East End of the dry lake. During busy periods visitors are often encouraged to exit the valley on Highway 18 down to Lucerne Valley. This is the emptiest of the roads to travel and if you do that you will run along the northern border of this quiet part of the Valley. Instead of continuing along the main highway try taking a small detour along Baldwin Lake Road and see how the area is coming along. You will find it to be a very different atmosphere to the rest of the more commercialized Big Bear Lake.

Baldwin Lake Stables
E. Shay Road
Big Bear City, (909) 585-6482

SAN BERNARDINO HISTORICAL SOCIETY

FOR A SHORT time when I was about 12, I was inducted into a little group of avid train spotters. Along with my colleagues we used to lean over the railings at Watford Junction – about 15 miles north of London – to watch the trains go by.

Now the true object of this pastime was to catch the number of the passing engines and then check in a small book and cross the number off. I lost interest in this activity after a very short time.

However, at the closing of the steam age there was another bonus for me; the sight and sound of these massive behemoths as they charged up and down the track. Our standpoint was at the exit of a long tunnel and you could hear the approach of a train long before it escaped from the confines of the earth.

With a blast from its whistle, it would appear with a cloud of steam and smoke; all energy and speed. It was a wonderful sight, soon to be displaced by the ubiquitous diesels and electric vehicles that had no personality at all.

With this memory tucked away, I am always interested to visit a site where trains are revered, and there is no better place than the museum at the Santa Fe Railroad Station in San Bernardino.

Here the Historical and Pioneer Societies of the city have pooled their resources and set up a fine place in what was once the old baggage hall of the local station.

"It was originally too much money to put our museum here," said Steven Shaw the president of the society. "But Amtrak needed the station to be opened once a day by volunteers and that produced some funds, which we used for the purpose."

There are not just railway things on show, and one of Shaw's favorite items is an old fire wagon in the most beautiful condition. "My father was a fire chief," he said. "So I'm particularly fond of the fire engines we have here." Although bright red and shining, it is hard to see how these devices could have done a lot to put out fires once they had begun however.

Alan Bone, of the historical society was equally enthused by a number of the exhibits, and spent some time showing me the station master's bay window they have on display. "It comes from the 1920's and you can see how the station master was able to see everything that was going on," he said.

Inside his office, messages for both the driver and the guard of trains could be written out. In those pre-cell phone days, the message was then tied onto a string and the string placed on a thin cane and held out to be grabbed. Inside this area too are the necessary levers and handles to stop trains and send them off to different lines. There was a lot to do.

San Bernardino was a serious railway town. Photos on the walls of the museum point to the importance of the tracks that went by. "There were 1500 people employed in the workshops here," Bone said. "They made a lot of stuff for the railway. In fact, my grandfather and great uncle worked there." He pointed out the relatives in photos of groups of men hanging off trains for the shot.

In its hay day, some 26 trains passed through the city. President Eisenhower used to stop here and park his specially designed carriage before journeying on down for vacations in Palm Springs by car.

The museum attracts between 80 and 140 people each Saturday which is the only day it is open, between 10 and 3. It is well worth a visit as it will take you back to the time of steam and old San Bernardino. It was an interesting phase in our transportation history.

The Museum is at San Bernardino Station
1170, W, 3rd Street,
San Bernardino, CA 92410

CALIFORNIA THEATER

WALKING ALONG WEST 4th street in San Bernardino, you would be forgiven for not paying a lot of attention to number 562. It is, after all a normal, rather old fashioned movie theater – the sort we've all lived with for years.

But the fact is that this large building is the home of the California Theater of the Performing Arts, and now the site of some of the best live acts in Southern California.

On my visit there, I was lucky to be shown round by Joe Hensen, a producer for Theatrical Arts International and one of the four managers that care for this Californian monument.

Entering the darkened theater it is a shock to see how big it is. Erected in 1928, it was designed not only for cinema, but during times when films were not well attended it regularly showed vaudeville. "So it has always been a live theater as well as a cinema," Hensen said.

To the left of the stage, there is a "Mighty Wurlitzer" which accompanied silent films. "It's in good working order," Hensen said. "We are having a silent film festival soon and it will be used then. We are showing The Thief of Bagdad on March 6th. The keyboard shows a few chips and some yellowing, but in every other respect it is an impressive instrument. Hensen showed me some buttons at the organist's feet. "It is for a range of special effects like horns and other noises. It's what gave us the expression 'all the bells and whistles.'"

The theater hosted many famous people and acts over its long history. The Three Stooges were here, Buster Crabbe, and more recently Sophia Loren and Jerry Seinfeld. But perhaps the most famous performance was from Will Rogers.

America's most famous comedian gave his last performance here in 1935. Afterwards he was killed in an aircraft accident. There are memorials of Rogers all over the theater, and in storage is one of his two curtains.

"Rogers used to perform in front of a special jeweled curtain," Hensen said. He had two of them and used to send one on to his next venue. Due to his tragic accident, he left one here and it has remained."

For years the theater was home of the Civic Light Opera, and I asked Hensen to define the term. "It's really any musical," he said. "Like Oklahoma or Cats." But there are a limited number of these shows, so today there are a number of single performers who play to packed houses.

Miss Saigon is due in late March and then acts like The Amazing Johnathan, Sounds of the Supremes and Wayne Newton are booked.

Concerts are also given here with Praise Mendelssohn being given on March 20. The ballet, Giselle, was performed in early February so there is always a wide variety of entertainment for patrons.

The architecture of the theater has been changed somewhat during its period of closure in the fifties. Before it reopened in the sixties, gold leaf was applied to the sides and edges of the stage; it gives a really opulent look.

It had been painted gray over the original dark mahogany, but it had taken away its original feel. The new décor was added with large murals of reproduced paintings by Degas.

During my visit I took the opportunity to ask Hensen what the role of producer actually entailed. It's used a lot in the entertainment industry, so what exactly do they do?

"Well, we oversee the entire operation," he said. "From the start to the finish. It means looking at the script, talking to the director and arranging all the aspects of a production."

I asked him about auditions and how aspiring actors handled the inevitable rejection. "We try to be as kind as possible," he said. "It's not that they might be untalented, it's just that they might not fit the concept the director or the producer might have for a particular role."

562 W. 4th Street, San Bernardino, CA
(909) 663-2293
Web site californiatheater.net

SAN MANUEL

I **HAVE TO** confess that a certain part of life has passed me by. More correctly I've passed by it, and I think it's because I lack a particular gene; so I can be excused. Maybe it's one of those newly diagnosed illnesses.

The fact remains that I am totally without interest in gambling. Making calculations and adjustments for inflation and currency changes, I think I must have invested about $20 in games of chance in my lifetime - $25 if I include office sweepstakes that I was forced to enter just to fit in. All of these outgoings were spent before I was 21.

By this time I had realized that gambling was not for me, and further, I couldn't for the life of me figure out why other people were so attracted to it.

At one period of my life I had to regularly visit a customer in Las Vegas. Travel arrangements meant that I often had an hour or two to kill before going to the appointment. I therefore used to call in to the big hotels for a coffee. I can report that never once was I ever induced to drop a single coin into a slot, or slide a note across some green baize table. My unblemished record still stands today.

With this in mind then I am probably the worst qualified person to report on the activities of one of our local entertainment centers, San Manuel Casino.

Traveling along route 210 I have often seen buildings to the north of the freeway and wondered what the activities were all about. So on an impulse, I made the turn the other day, and went the two miles up to the bottom of the hills to see this well advertised place.

I have to say that it is a very impressive locale. Firstly, there is a massive parking structure, which if filled would surely cater to most of the population of San Bernardino. Mid week, mid morning it was full of just space.

In order to reach the casino itself you pass along a glass sided bridge with the sort of moving sidewalks usually needed to reach the more far distant gates at big airports. Obviously the San Manuel tribe has moved a long way from tepees, if they ever used them.

Going down to the glittering hall of slot machines, there was the welcoming sound of bells and the clattering of winnings. Lights danced, fluttered and pulsed, all no doubt to excite the arriving gambler. It was everything that Las Vegas has to offer and more.

The building itself is a handsome edifice. Constructed in a warm beige color with wood everywhere and a hint of Indian design, it looks like it will last forever.

The gardens outside were extremely pretty, although hard to reach to enjoy for those not drawn immediately to the activity inside. They seemed to have been put there as a sort of throwaway, which is a shame as they were quite beautiful.

For those like myself who want a little more than gambling, there are a host of other entertainments to look forward to, with visiting artists and sports events; there is cage fighting in May and Johnny Mathis appears on June 3rd. All are well publicized on the Web site. From time to time I take along S.W.M.B.O. (She Who Must Be Obeyed) to enjoy my visits, but in this case, I did not make the offer. Many years ago, on our very first visit to Las Vegas, as I was settling the bill I noticed out of the corner of my eye, that S.W.M.B.O. was inserting a quarter into a nearby slot machine. I froze, but restrained myself until we were safely inside the car.

"I just thought I would see what happened," was her explanation. But I thought it best not to lead her further into temptation, so she stayed at home for this particular assignment. After all a quarter is a quarter!

San Manuel Casino
777, San Manuel Boulevard,
Highland, CA 92346
(800) 359-2464
Web Site: sanmanuel.com

PALM SPRINGS - LIVING DESERT

PALM SPRINGS IS at its absolute best in the early spring. But there is a touch of the surreal about it. Driving along the ten, you pass through the wind farms on both sides of the Freeway. I'm sure since my last visit about a year ago, they have been reproducing themselves like mad. But some of the windmills still refuse to budge; perhaps they need a little oil on the bearings.

There is usually a small cloud of dust hanging over the half dozen or so cities lined along the 111 main thoroughfare of the Coachella Valley, but once you get into the main urban areas the cloud disappears for some reason. All this adds to a slightly unreal aspect of a visit down there.

My target on this trip was a new one for me; the Living Desert, located in Palm Desert. Driving along between the gated communities with their red tiled roofs and brilliant emerald grass, I wondered how long the beauty would last if the sprinklers were turned off. Not long I fear, then it would turn back to the way nature intended without the sparkling bedding plants and knife edged creases of the hedges.

Arriving at the center, immediately you are in a different world. However here, the mark of man is still around you. Plants and trees are beautifully presented on a 40-minute walk around the well laid out path, which circles around the facility and allows several scenic bypasses to enjoy various fauna and flora.

Just inside the entrance, docent Bill Piggott was holding up a small owl on his gloved fist, explaining to a group how the bird lived and survived in the harsh desert surroundings. The owl kept a watchful eye on me as I passed by behind it, its head swiveling around in an unnatural way.

Desert tortoises were lying hunched against a wall enjoying the morning sunshine; not a lot of movement there. All around the plants are in the finest condition with labels telling the types and facts about the species.

I regretted that the area for wild dogs and coyotes was closed as I'm rather fond of the latter. A small display explained about these solitary creatures however, although I was disappointed not to learn much about their eerie howling at night. It was suggested that it was merely to keep in touch with each other.

Moving away from the North America section, you arrive at the Africa area. First to greet you are the bighorn sheep. They are well within view but prefer to keep to the far limits of their rocky home. I wanted to photograph one attractively marked creature but sometimes the start up of a digital camera is slow and by the time I had focused, it had decided to present its backside to me.

Across the way there was a cage with an Arabian cat in it. The cat looked normal, but its furry and sharpened ears told a different story. For those not able to read the body language there was a big note across the front of the cage: I Can Bite! I bet it can too.

Returning to the entrance I passed a model railway of enormous proportions. It had trains crossing scenes of America like the Grand Canyon and Mount Rushmore. Fathers in charge of children lit up at the sight it.

When I returned, Bill Piggott was still hard at it, but I noticed that the bird had changed. "It's an American kestrel," he said. "It's sometimes called the Sparrow Hawk but that's not its correct name." It was a wonderful creature, light and alert with glinting eyes, and quite at home on Piggott's hand.

Leaving the desert area once again I felt that this place is a wonderful haven at this time of the year, but it still feels a little unreal to me.

The Living Desert
47900 Portola Avenue
Palm Desert,
(760) 346-5694
Web site: livingdesert.org

PALM SPRINGS ART MUSEUM

NO TRIP TO Palm Springs is complete for me without a visit to the wonderful art museum there. Recently I was fortunate to be accompanied around the museum by Bob Bogard, the Director of Communications. Looking at good art is a very enjoyable pastime, but to have a knowledgeable guide makes it much better, as you learn so much more.

For instance I was attracted to a recent acquisition by the museum. It was The Village by Marc Chagall. It was an oil painting on 16 ceramic tiles; it weighed 200 pounds and needed the wall to be strengthened in order to support it.

Alongside the painting was a small black statue of an owl by Picasso. In itself it was a pretty thing, but much more so when you heard the history.

"The late President Kennedy had it in his hotel room the night before he was assassinated," Bogard explained. "He and Mrs. Kennedy often asked galleries to send round works of art when they stayed a night somewhere. And this owl might well have been the last piece Kennedy ever saw."

The Palm Springs Art Museum is full of tremendous talent by some of the finest artists – many of them household names. The upper floor now holds an exhibition that has been donated by Donna and Cargill MacMillan, Jr. It is a stunning collection of the very best of modern art.

In spacious rooms, pieces of great diversity are placed with enough area around them to allow viewers to really enjoy each one. Balancoires en Fer consists of two hanging children's swings. The artist, Palestinian, Mona Hatoum has placed these two swings closely together. Far too close for them to be able to work – unless they were to swing together.

As in fact the two warring societies need to do if they are to survive. The edges of the seats too are razor sharp, giving the piece another uncomfortable aspect.

Without the commentary of Bogard it would have been easy to have missed both these startling points, and the piece would have just been another sculpture.

It was hard to ignore the half dozen life sized black garbage bags in the middle of the room. Of course, the shock value of such pieces has long ago lost its edge, but the display was nonetheless rather odd.

"They are actually bronze statues painted black," Bogard explained. "At one time Mrs. MacMillan had this piece outside in her yard. Neighbors kept complaining that her garbage needed to be picked up."

As well as these avant garde pieces, there are some more recognizable items in the MacMillan collection. Andy Warhol is featured with a painting and a sculpture of a dress made from Brillo wrappings. Roy Lichtenstein's huge cartoon type prints are also on display. Familiarity over the years has by now taken away their shock value too.

A red chair minus its seat looks somewhat ordinary, but the pillow on the floor against it becomes more interesting once you know that it is actually wood and carved in a very artful way.

Bogard told me that his art museum is lucky to be in the center of a comparatively small area, but with a great deal of wealth around; together with a great interest in art. The generosity of the patrons makes this a definite must see on your next visit to Palm Springs.

Palm Springs Art Museum
101 Museum Drive
Palm Springs, CA 92262
(760) 322-4800
Web site: psmusuem.org

Closed Mondays, Thursdays and major holidays.

PALM SPRINGS - DATES AND TRAMS

AS PACIFIC STORMS start to bring winter weather down to the Southland, it is now that The Coachella Valley comes into its own. This near neighbor of ours has at its ends, the Palm Springs Aerial Tram, and at the other, the date farms of Coachella itself. And in between exists all the rush and bustle of the earnest retirees of Palm Springs, Palm Desert, Indian Wells and Indio.

Generally, dates do not form a major part of most people's thoughts outside the realms of their calendars. In fact, this waxy fruit quite possibly does not enter many minds at all. And yet, one Mr. Shields, originally from Iowa, made them his lifetime passion. He even made and narrated a film called "The Romance and Sex Life of the Date," which plays continuously at the Shields Date Gardens in Indio.

Within the confines of this business, located on the main drive eastwards out of the green manicured lawns and constant spring flowers of the Indian Wells area, one can learn everything you ever wanted to know about dates. You can eat them, drink them, examine them, and of course, learn about their sex lives. Mr. Shields wanted nothing held back about his little charges.

One has to wonder about such a fascination. Particularly when one realizes that it is not an easy life developing the farms necessary to raise the crop. And yet something about the date caused Mr. Shields and his wife to roll up their sleeves and create a life for themselves in the valley that eventually runs down to the Salton Sea. Date plantations still grow extensively there and from the road, you can easily see the brown paper covers to protect the fruit from rain, which ruins them.

The Shields Date Gardens have been in operation since 1924. Most of the original saplings came from Algeria, and their pollination has to be done by hand. One male plant in a crop is sufficient to provide enough pollen for 48 female plants. And it takes 20 years to produce the first crop. So this was not a case of instant gratification for the former Iowan farmer. But he persevered, and we can all enjoy the fruits of his extensive labors. The Date Shake is certainly to be recommended, and then a quiet sit down in the 108-seat theater at the end of the shop to learn all there is to know about the subject.

Perhaps after purchasing a box of one of the 119 types of dates from the counter, you may wish to drive through to the other end of this interesting valley. You can either take the 10 freeway or the more populated drive along Route 111 through the back-to-back cities of golf courses, gated communities and shopping malls all catering to this expanding desert lifestyle. At the far end of this you will find directions to the Aerial Tram, which has been a part of the list of things to do in the area since 1963. It again was the dream of one man, Francis Crocker, to construct a cable car to the top of Mount San Jacinto, 10,804 feet above sea level. The dream was soon dubbed Crocker's Folly.

The financing and building of the project was to take some thirty years to reach fruition, and its inauguration was in September of 1963. Thirty-five years later in 1998, the tramway announced plans to upgrade their facility and a year ago, the new Swiss-made cars began to whisk riders to the top of the mountain.

These new cars are designed to allow passengers the luxury of a 360- degree view during the trip. This is done by a rotating floor, which gives everyone a clear view all around during the ten-minute ride to the top. A commentary describes the scene and the size of the project. It even warns you of the slightly odd feeling as the car passes under each of the five supports.

It is a double reversible aerial tramway, also known as a Jig-Back Tramway, and although we know it is impossible, the other car passing us down, does seem to be travelling at a lot faster rate, although they are joined together on the cable, some 25,500 feet long.

The cars have a capacity for 80 people and run every ten minutes to a world completely different from that at the lower station 6,000 feet below. Up here all is cool and windswept, as large ravens swoop in the clear skies, and squawk at the visitors gazing at their effortless flight.

The upper station has plenty to offer in the way of food, drinks, souvenirs, and even conference facilities. There are hiking trails, and the opportunity to enjoy the natural world all around, while gazing down at the hot desert floor below from telescopes.

PALM SPRINGS

THINGS ARE STARTING to warm up in the Palm Springs area. With the month of May, prices seem to magically drop as the winter "snow birds" return to their native northern states. And yet the main town of Palm Springs is still a great place to visit, with its sophisticated shops and cafes. And with the approach of the heat the latter mostly have cooling mists circulating overhead to aid in the refrigerating process.

During the electricity crisis of last summer, a radical scheme was hatched by one of the more dignified of Palm Springs institutions, the Desert Museum. They offered all day tickets for people wanting to escape the heat by using the air conditioning of the museum. It remains to be seen if such an offer will be needed this year. However, even though such extremes are not exactly necessary yet, this outstanding museum is well worth a visit for the treasures inside.

The exhibits are arranged into three basic types. There is a large permanent and visiting collection of art and sculpture; a section devoted to living history, and finally the Annenberg Theatre, which shows live performances of all types.

As for the art exhibition, with the temporary closing of the Smithsonian Museum for renovations, the Desert Museum is proudly showing a number of works owned by that institution. There are pieces by American artists, and in particular Latin artists living here in the US. Numbering 66 pieces, the art is varied and interesting, from vibrant painting to a sculpture by Luis Jimeniz called "Man on Fire," which depicts the legend of the Aztecs who refused to submit to Spanish colonization.

In keeping with some of the lightheartedness of Latin American art, a number of whimsical sculptures are featured in the entrance hall. A cowboy in full outdoor regalia stands alone by the elevators, constantly waiting. A work entitled "Old Couple" sits on a bench, causing some concern as they are so lifelike, people are not convinced it is art. Upstairs a huge glass piece seems so fragile it could beak, and security keeps a watchful eye on it.

A small number of more traditional works are displayed, and there is also a permanent exhibit of Meso American early art. The ubiquitous Henry Moore is also well represented. He seems to have a place in most well ordered museums.

The natural history section is currently showing an exhibit on the Namib Desert, one of the world's ten great deserts. Here visitors can see how desert life exists in the southwest of Africa. There is even a wind machine to allow children to see how the desert sands swirl and shape the terrain and affect the life clinging to the edge of existence. The exhibit runs through September this year, before it makes way for another desert scene.

If your tastes run more to live performances, then the Annenberg Theater section of this museum will cater to you very well. It hosts a number of well-known artists from all sections of the performing arts. In the past year, the range of performances has been from Debussy string music to Broadway shows, and from big bands to ballet. For a list of upcoming concerts and shows as well as for all the news from the Palm Springs Desert Museum call (760) 325-4490 or visit the website: psmuseum.org.

Either to end the day or perhaps if you are a really early riser, you may consider flying high across the palm trees and the orchards of La Quinta, just thirty miles to the east. But not in an airplane, try a hot air balloon instead. These graceful and brightly colored globes powered by nothing more that hot air float along with occasional bursts from the burners beneath.

Balloon Above the Desert is one of several companies that offer this fun way to see views from aloft. They are located at 40373 Moonflower Court, Palm Desert, but will pick you up from most locations in the area. They will ferry you to one of four different launch sites and then it is just a question of climbing in the basket and watching the crew let go of the ropes.

Clotaire Castanier has been flying balloons for 35 years. First in his native France and then out here in the desert since 1989. He and his fellow pilots command four different balloons, which can cater for six, eight or ten passengers. The start up takes a good hour from unpacking to lift off. Fans fill the canopy and then the burners do their work, filling the great yellow shapes with the energy necessary to hoist a load aloft.

They start early in the day to avoid too much wind, and the location allows the balloons to drift out to the east away from traffic and bad landing areas. Tracker vehicles follow the path and collect everyone at the end of the flights, which usually last about an hour. Champagne is served. The season lasts from Labor Day to Memorial Day. Telephone number for reservations and details is (800) 342-8506.

YANKS AIR MUSEUM

ONE OF THE finest air museums in the world is located here in Southern California. It's in Chino, and it's called Yanks. The statement that it is one of the best comes from my brother- in-law who came along with me on a recent visit.

He is quite an aircraft enthusiast and knows all the numbers and letters that manufacturers put on their products. I think they do it to put the rest of us off and also to trap newspaper correspondents who occasionally wander off in the accuracy department.

Woe betide a writer if he should accidentally call a 536J/b12, a 546B/j12, the email box will be full the next day with correcting information.

So, the B-i-L has done a bit of world touring and being a pilot has been to a number of air museums in his time. "It's one of the very best in the world," he said. "It's amazing."

I knew it and quietly smirked. I had come here first about six years ago and was stunned at the quality of the place. The floor shone almost as much as the immaculate planes housed in the hangar.

On this last visit we met up with Frank Wright, the restoration operation manager in his huge workshop. There the planes were far from pristine as this is where they are rebuilt and restored to their original condition. "We have to get everything absolutely correct," said Wright. "We worked for five days to get the color on that one's wings completely accurate." He spoke some sort of alphanumeric code for the machine in its skeletal shape, but the references blurred before me.

The B-i-L knew about the aircraft and joined in for a few jaunty minutes quoting letters and numbers as my eyes glazed over.

There was a British Harrier jet parked out back and there was a spirited discussion as to whether it was the X or Y model. I marveled at the fact that such a huge monster could actually lift straight up before the nozzle from its engine swiveled, and it surged forward. It did need a lot of restoration work however, but having seen the result of previous efforts I have no doubt that its new gleaming shape will soon be reflected off the exhibition's hangar floor.

Passing back through the reception area it was obvious the place had grown significantly. Wright told me it was about three times the size, but it's still very manageable.

The planes are laid out chronologically, and inside the entrance, you are met with a Pigeon Flying Boat. It's quite small and wooden, and built in 1920. There is a question mark over whether it actually flew. But it is a pretty thing.

Moving along beside the gleaming lines of aircraft, the B-i-L was almost drooling. He reminisced at a Link trainer, where he had sat many years ago before he gained his license. Then he stopped to admire a Gypsy Moth and other fixed wing planes from that era.

I was drawn to the life sized bust of General H. Doolittle who was referred to on the plinth as "The Master of the Calculated Risk." An interesting title and one I'd never heard of before. He lived a long time for a warrior and died in 1993, at aged 95.

Doolittle was placed under the protective wing of a large Mitchell bomber. Built in 1940, it carried a crew of six and it was a B25J – 30NC. Now if I've made a mistake with those figures please don't email me, as my B-i-L assures me they are correct. If necessary I'll give you his email.

The Yanks Air Museum
7000, Merrill Avenue
Chino, CA 91710
(909) 597-1734
Web site: Yanksair.com

247

GILMAN RANCH

ONE DAY I was flicking around with the TV remote and came upon the 1969 movie: Tell Them Willie Boy is Here, starring Robert Redford and Katherine Ross.

I've seen it before, and it's a sad tale of love and tragedy. It was quite a coincidence that two days later I was standing next to where Willie Boy's original crime was committed.

Briefly, Willie and his cousin Carlota had fallen in love and Carlota's father William Mike had forbidden the match. In a struggle, Willie Boy killed Mike and took Carlotta off with him into the hills. He was hunted down and eventually killed by a sheriff.

The site of the murder is at the Gilman Ranch in Banning, and a number of the scenes of the movie were shot in the house that stands close by.

According to Jim Bowman, an interpreter with the Riverside County Parks and Open Spaces, "there are a lot of different stories about the entire episode." And a search of the 'Net indeed shows up a number of inconsistencies. Not the least of which is that the house burned down eight years after the film was made and has been reconstructed.

For all that a visit to the Gilman Historic Ranch and Wagon Museum is a fine opportunity to catch up with the past. "This entire place gives us a little bit of California history from the time of the Indians to the Spanish, and then the Anglo settlers," Bowman said.

The house nestles in an area where James Marshall Gilman came in 1869. He had originally come out from New Hampshire and been a bookkeeper in Oregon. However he had an interest in breeding cattle and for that he moved to S. California.

He tired of the cattle business and moved to farming, and then changed again to growing olives – the olive treatment shed is still there with its big concrete baths.

Inside the house itself you can feel the elegance of the age and also some of the new inventions Gilman and his family enjoyed. An upright piano is in the living room and also a Victrola gramophone.

I suspect that the Victrola came after Gilman died in 1916, but it is an interesting device. "The kids love it," Bowman said. "Particularly the novel volume control."

He referred to two doors underneath the turntable. The sound is taken from a steel needle through a metal tube down to the megaphone type box beneath. The two doors muffled the sound and to increase it you simply opened them.

Young people, most of whom no doubt have iPods in their pockets, must be amazed at such a big device to simply replay recorded music.

In the kitchen is a large black iron stove. It has a prominent chromed handle which allows the user to switch from wood to coal if the need arose. "Once you got used to it, people were fine with it and had problems changing to the newer gas and electric models when they came out." Bowman explained.

It was a lovely day when I visited the ranch and the roses smelled sweetly outside the main steps. "They are from the era of William Gilman and have been specially planted here." Bowman said. As I left I looked over to the creek where Willie Boy shot William Mike and wondered if the true tale will ever be known.

Gilman Historic Ranch and Wagon Museum
1901, W. Wilson Street,
Banning, CA 92220
Open Saturdays year round from 10 a.m. to 4 p.m.
(951) 922-9200

RAGING WATERS

WHEN THE REALLY hot weather hits, it's hard to work up a great deal of enthusiasm for a trip outdoors. Unless of course, it's to laze around on a white beach under a coconut leaf canopy, or perhaps to float lazily along on a big inflated tube in a meandering river. These activities and a whole lot more are available for the entire family at California's largest water park, Raging Waters.

Located close to the junction of the 10 and the 210 at Raging Waters Drive in San Dimas, the park has the greatest variety of rides in the entire United States. This, according to Terry Mackey, the facility's general manager. He explains: "Technology in this business has advanced so much that we can now provide smoother, faster rides that are much more thrilling than they used to.

"In fact," he continues, "If it has been a couple of years since you came here, you'll be surprised at the improvements we've made." One of these is the park's new attraction, Neptune's Fury, which was opened in June this year. It is a thrilled packed ride for the entire family that allows four persons to ride together in a unit. "We've had rave reviews by riders since it opened," Mackey states.

Raging Waters has been in its current form since 1983, having taken over a park and swimming hole previously managed by the State. The facility is owned by Alfa Smart Parks, out of Jacksonville, Florida. But the employees are mostly locals and there are over 900 of them. 325 are lifeguards who watch over the family's safety with great dedication. "We're extremely proud of our safety record here at Raging Waters," Mackey says. "In fact, we have won the regional championship, and we've come second in the nationals. Our lifeguards are a group of very talented and conscientious people."

It is obvious from the moment you enter the park that the water is wonderful - clear, and clean and very blue. No matter which of the more than twenty-five rides you choose, you will find the water inviting and the surroundings attractive. There is the ever-popular beach scene with a wave to send the floating tubes rocking. White sand, regularly raked, will make you feel you are on one of the best tropical islands in the Pacific or the Caribbean.

If your fancy is to make your heart miss a bit and the adrenaline rise, then climb the steps to the launching area of the Drop Out for a plunge down the slide to a water splash landing zone. A notice advises those with weak hearts and other health problems to avoid this ride. But the rafting river will allow the most fragile and tense to relax as they gently bob along under the trees and Polynesian scenery.

Raging Waters has many little nooks and crannies to sit quietly and enjoy some refreshments that the park supplies. No food or drink is allowed to be brought into the park, but patrons' coolers can be put in the lockers provided outside. Ink stamps allow re-entry once again.

The season officially ends on September 21, but Mackey explains: "For one last week after our official closure, we are holding a Taste of Southern California Expo. We'll have all the usual restaurants and merchandising events with a food fair. But this time people will be able to jump in and cool off as they enjoy the displays. It promises to be a great event and a wonderful way to end the summer."

Details on this and all other attractions can be obtained from the park at (909) 802-2200, or on the web site at www.ragingwaters.com.

QUEEN MARY

GOING TO THE Queen Mary in Long Beach is a bit like visiting an old, but very elegant aunt. In my case the visit is particularly emotive, as I have known the old lady for many years.

As a young boy I regularly visited my grandparents in Southampton, England for vacations, and as the busiest passenger port in the world, the transatlantic liners were always coming and going to the terminals there.

The journey from New York to Southampton took five days and the activity around the docks was exciting for any young person. It was the epitome of luxury and class to make the voyage, and many famous people took this route before the advent of the jet plane. The Queen Mary was one of the most famous, and my grandfather would often say "That's the Mary coming in," on hearing the ship's hooters roaring. As a boy I believed his ear was tuned to some naval wavelength that I lacked. Years later I realized he read the ships' movements in the daily paper's shipping news.

The Queen Mary was always a very important liner, although she lost her status of being the fastest to such ships as the Rotterdam, the United States and her sister ship, the Queen Elizabeth. This last great liner unfortunately now languishes at the bottom of Hong Kong harbor where, in retirement, she sank several years ago.

Today, in her permanent berth at Long Beach, the remaining queen still holds up well, and visitors can share something of her illustrious past with regular tours, and also with stays in her 365 hotel rooms. Past travelers look down from life sized photos taken during the voyages of her glory days. Famous film stars like Fred Astaire, and Noel Coward and Bob Hope. The Duke and Duchess of Windsor were wrapped in good British tweed for their portraits, reminding us that the Atlantic is a very rough, tough, cold ocean.

In fact the Queen Mary was notoriously unforgiving of any one with a propensity for sea sickness, and passengers could be confined to their cabins if their inner ears were too sensitive to motion.

During World War Two, the great queen was conscripted into service and her familiar black, white and red colors were covered over with a nondescript gray. Then known as The Grey Ghost, she ferried troops across the oceans and Hitler placed a $250,000 bounty on her, with the promise of an Iron Cross for any sailor who could sink her. But she was too fast, and too maneuverable for any U-boat.

Sadly although she herself avoided any harm, she did cause the sinking of a British cruiser, called H.M.S. Curacao, with the resultant loss of over 300 lives. The Grey Ghost was not allowed to deviate nor stop for any reason, and the cruiser crossed her path with deadly results.

It is said that the spirits of some of the dead sailors from the Curacao haunt the ship, and can be seen on the ghost tours that the ship arranges.

Today, in her retirement, The Queen Mary still offers luxury and fun to those that seek a different experience. She has several bars and restaurants and holds regular events within her spacious decks, and art deco banqueting rooms.

She is still imposing and elegant, although her age is no secret to anyone. Last month she celebrated her 70th birthday; it was a great party and one suitable for someone who has seen it all.

I left the ship at 3:00 p.m., which is the time the Queen Mary daily sounds her hooter. It is very, very loud and will make you jump. Nonetheless, it took me back to the mid-fifties and the peak of her working life, and my grandfather's voice saying: "Oh that'll be the Mary going out."

The Queen Mary
1126 Queens Highway.
Long Beach, CA 90802
(562) 435-3511
www.queenmary.com

The Queen Mary with the Russian Submarine at her bow

RUSSIAN SUBMARINE

DIFFICULT TIMES OFTEN conveniently recede into one's memory and it takes something to jolt them out again. It's been well over a decade since with the collapse of the USSR, the Cold War officially came to an end. We live in different times now, but it wasn't that long ago when we lived with the fear of M.A.D. (Mutually Assured Destruction.)

And yet under the protective bow of the Queen Mary in Long Beach rests a relic of that time, in the brooding dark shape of the Scorpion, a Russian Foxtrot-Class submarine.

It has a certain menacing appearance with its black riveted sides and bulging bow, but its fangs have been removed and now it awaits visitors who have some curiosity about what lurked beneath international waters keeping an eye on us, the good guys.

The Scorpion was built in 1972, which is not all that long ago and yet it has the appearance of being a lot older. It reminds us that Russian technology could be, well, just a little primitive. It almost looks as if it's been carved out of solid metal and it is not roomy to get around in. Nonetheless it is a very interesting experience although you will have to watch your head almost permanently.

Entering at the forward end, one is immediately in the business part of the boat – the torpedo section. At once one hears the commentary which follows one around. It is in a well accented Russian voice and has a sense of humor, considering the subjects covered.

Being in the belly of the boat, it is difficult to imagine it with its full complement of 78 men. Also these same men had to share three toilets and two showers for thee months at a stretch. Being an officer with one's own cabin may sound nice until you see the size of the cabin, but being a lowly member of the crew entailed sharing a "hot bunk" with one's colleagues.

One slept in four hour shifts and as soon as you left the bunk someone else was waiting to get in; it gives new meaning to the term basic.

To move from compartment to compartment requires passing through watertight openings – just circular holes two feet off the floor and about three feet in diameter. This requires a certain agility, so be warned. The crew perfected a technique of holding a grip above the opening, jumping up with their knees to their waists and swinging through. This is not recommended for casual visitors unless they are members of the US gymnastic team, and in training.

However, as moving rapidly from one end of the boat to the other during diving and surfacing was required by many of the crew, no doubt they became good at it. For the less strenuous it is recommended to use the more sedate manner of slowly lifting one leg through followed by the other.

The acquisition of The Scorpion, whose Russian designation was B-427, came about through the efforts of some Australian businessmen, who negotiated the sale in 1995. The boat was towed from Vladivostok to Sydney where it became a part of the Australian National Maritime Museum, until it was sold and ferried over to Long Beach in 1998.

As one continues to the rear of the boat one passes the galley where some of the best food in the Russian navy was prepared; in fact it was one of the reasons there were so many volunteers to be a submariner. The cooks must have been very creative as the galley does not inspire confidence.

On leaving the submarine, one has the chance of visiting the extensive gift shop. Here they even have Russian naval officer hats on sale; very tempting, but where would one wear it exactly?

A trip to The Scorpion is a worthwhile reminder of past days when we had an enemy with normal resources and recognizable ambitions that we could all clearly understand.

The Russian Submarine
At the Queen Mary,
Long Beach.
Hours: 10 a.m. to 6 p.m. daily
www.russiansublongbeach.com

L.A ZOO

IT CAN SOMETIMES be a little overwhelming living next door to a very big and sprawling neighbor, but the proximity of Los Angeles does give us all some amazing opportunities; museums, theaters, attractions, and a world-class zoo. Zoos are funny places. We have all visited them at some time, and most of our memories are happy ones, but we don't often make a habit of regularly taking a day to look at the one most local to us. And if that hasn't happened in a long time, then there are some pleasant surprises in store.

Los Angeles Zoo is a work in progress. Over the last couple of decades, it has improved its appearance and the general presentation of its exhibits by leaps and bounds. Strangely enough, as the management of the zoo has made every effort to house their charges in more animal friendly habitats, the atmosphere for the human visitors has gone up tremendously.

In the last two years, there have been two new developments that will appeal to all 1.5 million visitors that pass through its turnstiles every year. Last summer, it opened a new Red Ape Rain Forest Area, and this summer the new Children's zoo opened, with a contact area that has been closed for 14 years.

The Red Ape Exhibit compliments the Chimpanzee area that was opened in 1998. Orangutan means old man of the forest in its native Malay, and one look at the four current residents of the LA Zoo, confirms that they are indeed like old people. Bruno, the only male in the group, is just over twenty, and he likes to be by himself. All orangutans are naturally solitary, and the new exhibit allows them a lot more space than before. "They are a lot stronger than we are, and also they're very clever," says one of the keepers permanently assigned to their care. It seems they also get bored easily, which is not good for them.

Their old home needed a lot of clutter to keep them amused, but now in this splendid new $6.5M facility, there are more built-in distractions for them. Like a plastic durian fruit, which is a favorite of the breed. However, it has such a strong and unpleasant smell, that it is unsuitable to be near humans. So the enterprising zoo handlers fill it with an assortment of other goodies and then lower it to their charges. Everyone, young and old alike can't help enjoying the antics of these huge apes, even if it is just to see them sitting quietly eating a piece of fruit. In the case of the chimpanzees next door it might even be consuming a favorite beverage, pickle juice.

If the children need a little more stimulation during their day out, then just wander over to the new Winnick Family Children's Zoo, which opened in August this year. Here, after passing by an original work of art, a hand washing fountain, you can enter the contact area. Children can pet smooth coated goats and soft little rabbits, under the watchful, but not intrusive gaze of attendants. The hand washing procedure before and after the visit is more for the animals benefit than ours, as of course the entire accent of the zoo is to provide a safe and enjoyable environment for all.

Within the children's area, shows are held to explain the various species and also there is a small trail to show off desert animals like tortoises, lizards, and insects such as tarantulas and hissing cockroaches. In fact everything for an inquisitive little mind.

One cannot but be impressed by the lushness of the LA Zoo's setting. It is obvious that it is under the control of some very caring folk. The plants, trees and bushes that surround each exhibit show every indication of being displayed to their best advantage. There is an air of calmness over the whole place even though it is just a few miles from downtown L.A. and it houses over 1200 animals. Parking is easy and access is from the junction of the 134 and 5 freeways.

The Zoo is open at 10.00am every day. More information can be had at the website, lazoo.org and the phone number is (323) 644-4200.

THE REAGAN LIBRARY

FROM HIS BIRTH in Tampico, Illinois, until the last tragic words of his final letter to the American people, Ronald Reagan had led a full and almost perfect life. Sadly those awful words still ring loudly in the mind: I now begin the journey that will lead me into the sunset of my life. I know that for America there will always be a bright dawn ahead. However as he accepted the long suffering of Alzheimer's disease, he still showed an unbridled optimism for the country he had always loved, and led for those unforgettable eight years he was in the White house.

Even for those that did not care for him – and there were many – the final sentence that life passed on him was too cruel a price to pay for him and his family. The long decline into sadness that is the inevitable fate for those struck with the disease, is a terrible end to a man who put his permanent stamp on the greatest country in the world. And it was Ronald Reagan's unshakable belief that the USA was the greatest country in the world.

Within the Library that bears his name in Simi Valley, his farewell letter is displayed outside the replica of the Oval Office that was his inspirational home throughout his two terms. The Library is a fine establishment, whose site was chosen by the former President himself in happier days. It's location reminded him of the Californian landscape of his favorite retreat, Rancho del Cielo in Santa Barbara, where he and his devoted wife, Nancy, used to ride their horses. On November 4, 2001 it will celebrate its tenth anniversary.

The replica Oval Office is typical of the care with which the organizers of the facility have gathered together the trappings of his life, including the eight years of the Reagan Presidency. From his humble beginnings in Illinois to his fifty Hollywood films, and then his ride to the White house in 1981, his life is stretched before the visitor in a long detailed route that is full of interest. One passes by a BMG 109G missile, a forerunner of the modern day Tomahawk, one of the weapons that kept the peace during the long cold war. On display are many of the gifts from a respectful world, together with a full account of his meetings with Gorbachev.

Throughout the journey, the voice of the President, that we all knew so well, pays part time commentator. He was often criticized for being 'just an actor,' but his skills with the microphone and before the camera, helped him earn the title 'the great communicator.' As well as the commentary itself, there are many museum guides, who are only too happy to provide any details that might be needed. And their knowledge seems limitless.

One display graphically details the events on March 30, 1981, just ten weeks into the new Presidency. Film clips show the attempt on his life by John Hinckley Jnr., and the fight for his life. His off-the-cuff question to the surgeons before he was anesthetized 'I hope you're all Republicans?' was typical of his good humor and cheerful outlook. He made a rapid recovery from the .22 slug that was buried in his chest, and in under a month he was able to address a full congress to the cheers of all.

Ronald Reagan, like Nixon, was a polarizing President. And yet unlike Nixon, he was able to communicate well and effortlessly with the people. Perhaps his acting really did help. But more likely he was able to speak from the heart. Also his message was simple and direct.

The Presidential Library is quite a long way from the high desert, but with his voice all around on various commentaries, and the artifacts that made his time with us on full display, it was well worth the extra journey time.

The site is perhaps not as intimate as the Nixon Library, some seventy miles nearer, but to once again hear from the President about the things that occurred during the Cold War and his other experiences was a wonderful experience. 'Mr. Gorbachev, tear down this wall;' is perhaps the saying that I will remember the most. And I could not resist the purchase for $7.50 of a piece of that same wall which for nearly thirty years had so effected our lives. The fact that we can no longer hear that famous voice, and it's quiet inspired confidence is probably the greatest loss.

The Ronald Reagan Library is located at 40, Presidential Drive, Simi Valley, CA 93065. (A three-mile ride from the 118 Freeway, also named after the President.) Telephone number is (800) 410-8354. Web site is reaganfoundation.org. The museum is open every day from 10.00am to 5.00pm.

Web site: reagalibrary.org

MUSEUM OF TOLERANCE

THIS MUSEUM IS not for the very young or those with a nervous disposition. As a ten-year-old, my first experience of the Holocaust was a book that my father acquired called 'The Road to Bergen-Belsen.' It contained several photos of the concentration camps that have over the years become a part of the psyche of our lives. At the time I found it all bewildering, and it took several years before I understood exactly what had happened. The museum contains many similar images in a very sophisticated way via the latest in video, sound and lighting.

Divided into two parts, after a short orienting session, the museum provides every one of the visitors with the opportunity to face their own intolerance. A choice of two doors is available early on: Non-Prejudiced over one, and Prejudiced over the other. The Non-Prejudiced door does not open, thereby assuming rightly or wrongly that every one is guilty of the sin to some extent. There then follows a session sitting at oval tables with multiple choice buttons. These are to be pushed in answer to questions given over the screens located around the darkened room. This first experience is focused on the prejudice shown towards women in various parts of the world. Currently the extreme behaviors of the Taliban are very timely, and graphic.

Following the fifteen-minute presentation, visitors leave this area and are given a credit card each. They have a picture of a child taken prisoner during the Nazi regime, and forced into the death camps. By inserting the card, a history of the child is shown on a screen. After visiting several places in the facility, the fate of the child is given and a printout is available as well. Now we are ready for the Holocaust side of the museum.

The organizers have laid out this exhibit in a very clever way. Various tableaux are presented in the form of models, chest high and with lighting that follows the scene as it unfolds. Here we see families and individuals discussing the gradually enfolding net, as it begins to restrict the Jewish population of 1930's Germany. We have to consider how we would all react if we found ourselves in such a position. Every day with a little less freedom to move around, until eventually there is no chance of doing so, and no escape from the inevitable.

Models of the camps and the transportation are all on display, together with commentaries given from the letters and conversations of the millions of victims. A chilling experience is in the last room; an actual replica of a gas chamber. Here unlike for the original victims, there are some seats as one witnesses the accounts of the last moments leading up to 'the final solution.' It is a frightful reminder of man's inhumanity to man.

Obviously, the Museum of Tolerance by its very name is not going to be a joyful day out. However, it is probably a very necessary day out for those not old enough to have gone through the Nazi experience. For those over sixty, it may be just another jolt to the memory.

Situated within the Simon Wiesenthal center, the free parking starts one off with a feeling of unease, as the vehicle is given a very thorough security check. Within the building itself, security begins to bite. No possible 'weapon' can be allowed into the exhibition, and this includes nail clippers, small knives and the like.

Visitors are not allowed to roam around, but rather kept in groups, with guides to assist as one goes through the various rooms. For anyone with a specific interest in the subject, this is undoubtedly the ultimate experience, as it gives you a complete perspective of how if unchecked, raging prejudice can lead to crimes against humanity that will never be forgotten.

The exhibition does however leave one feeling a sense of guilt, which in my case is rather odd as my family were in the gunsights of several Nazi planes, one of whom did manage to blow up our house in 1940. But if the effect is to make one realize that prejudice even in a limited form can be extremely harmful to not just other's health but also one's own. The museum estimates that it takes about 2 1/2 hours to fully tour the facility.

The Museum of Tolerance is located at 1399, South Roxbury Drive, Los Angeles, CA 90035-4709. Telephone number (310) 772-2458. Web site is www.wiesenthal.com.

AUTRY MUSEUM OF WESTERN HERITAGE

GENE AUTRY AND Roy Rogers shared many things in life. They both epitomized the cowboy image and both had a tremendous love of all things "Western." And they were both hugely successful. However, the two museums that carry their names could not be more different. Whereas the Roy Rogers Dale Evans Museum in Victorville, is based around the life of one family, and more specifically, one man, the Autry Museum is totally different. Here, the entire "Western" experience is laid out for visitors.

Based in Griffith Park opposite the Los Angeles Zoo, the Autry is a substantial exhibition of the life of the western United States, from Ute Indians to Hollywood. From gold miner to settler. Roy Rogers' image and personality within the Victorville location is everywhere, but at the Autry, virtually the only reference to Gene Autry and his horse, Champion, is at the entranceway, where a splendid bronze is erected. Here the "singing cowboy" is portrayed with his faithful companion looking on.

Currently, the Autry is showing an exhibit called "How the West was Worn!" It is a collection of the clothes that were the mainstay of the era. Real Cowboys, Movie Stars and Dudes is how one scene puts it. And nothing better could encapsulate the way we view the "West." After all, the European colonization of the west only took a couple of generations before the original inhabitants were subdued. Then the image of the wild men and cowboys of the west was carried on in myths and legends, and none so effective as that perpetrated by Hollywood. It is not for nothing that the first sight that greets one is that of a huge

Stetson hat over the gate. It is a reproduction of one designed and worn by Hollywood designer Nudie Cohn.

The hat is studded with rhinestones and silver embroidery that represents the glamour and glitz to which the movie world has taken the idea of the West. The real thing was very different. And yet, the image side of our ideas has every right to exit alongside the original, and it is this synergy that the Autry handles so well. After all, the clothes worn by the cowboys of old are the basis of the western wear affected by so many today.

The Autry is also showing a collection of artifacts once owned by the Ute Indians. These people, who were among the original settlers this side of the continent, and have a long history of living within the region and coping with its many facets. The legend of our beginnings is romantically told of how the water grandmother sent out the Coyote to see if there was enough land for her people to live on. The Coyote returned to say that there was. It is obvious that the animal did not go out in search of this space during rush hour on the 5, or he would have filed a very different report.

Downstairs at the permanent exhibit, there is a closer look for children to enjoy. Here a hands on approach is encouraged for younger visitors to experience all that made up living out here in years gone by. Also, serious reference is made to the life that Chinese immigrants brought with them to the area

There is an opportunity to sit astride a saddle and appear in a cowboy movie on the permanent set. Lights, camera, action are all there for anyone that wishes. Also a life size set up of the Fight at the OK Corral is on display. At the touch of a button, a commentary will bring to life the actions that took four lives in the famous shoot-out. Like so many legends, distance lends enchantment to the view, and the disembodied voice reports that the episode is permanently distorted with the passage of time. The combatants and witnesses are now all dead - either on the spot or years later.

This distortion is no doubt a part of all cultures, but out here in the west, we live a little of it every day. Whether it's a corporate executive on her day off, sporting a cowboy hat to keep the sun out of her eyes, or the Harley Davidson rider wearing chaps on a dry, warm day, cruising

The Pacific Coast Highway. We all to some extent have a share of the image.

A visit to the Autry will clarify that image in as much detail as anyone could want. Just a walk through its substantial, modern building will allow you to understand a little more of how the immediate history of the last 150 years has impacted us all.

The Autry Museum of Western Heritage is located at 4700 Western Heritage Way, (Just off the 5 freeway) Los Angeles, CA 90027. Telephone number (323) 667-2000. Web site is autry.com. Parking is free and the museum is open from 10:00am to 5:00pm Tuesday through Sunday.

AQUARIUM

THE AQUARIUM OF the Pacific in Long Beach is truly a day out for the entire family. Its mission statement is to "celebrate the planet's largest and most diverse body of water, the Pacific." And it certainly does that within a five-acre site alongside that same body of water. Its expansive building could fit three football fields within, and yet the way the exhibits are divided up, it never gives the feeling of being too much, or promotes the danger of losing the kids. It's spacious and intimate at the same time.

Seventeen different habitats are displayed and over 12,000 ocean animals are on show in attractive areas where the height of glass windows caters for tall and short visitors alike. The sound systems cleverly compliment each general area. And inside the first hall - The Jellies - undulating, wobbly chords resonate around as you peer inside the illuminated tanks at these Jello creatures floating around in their watery homes. There are lots of things everywhere to keep little minds occupied with all the wonders of the deep. This is the beauty of the Aquarium

Due to its impressive size, a real live whale could not be kept, but there is a life-size sculpture of the beast hanging in the main hall to help us keep a perspective on our puny stature and also to compare to the other living things on show. The Northern Pacific hall shows the wave action and the life of this region. Here you can witness seals and sea-lions and spot the differences between the two. Check out the ears, and they way they swim around.

A reconstruction of the Baja Peninsular has water on both sides of the walkway to demonstrate the different life on each side of the narrow landmass below us in Mexico. Waving kelp is also displayed at the end of the main hall in a huge tank. Every half an hour, a wet-suited diver hangs behind the nineteen-inch thick glass to explain the habitat from his watery microphone. The kids loved it.

They also loved the outside exhibit too. Here, there is a non-water area where there are some brand new visitors. These are brilliantly feathered, tropical birds, called Lorikeets. Their home is a tropical rain forest where waterfalls sparkle and lush foliage envelopes visitors. For an additional $1.00 you can buy a cup of nectar, which will encourage the little parrot-like birds to settle on your arm, and feed. You can also adopt one of them, through the Aquarium's adoption program, which will bring you closer to life in this very special place.

Perhaps the greatest pull for younger visitors is the area devoted to touching our seagoing friends. Turtles waddle around behind the glass as children and adults alike lay down across a ridge watching two-foot wide Rays swimming around. One father was shocked when a ray swum up to his face in a close encounter, for which he was not prepared. But the rays are harmless, and seem to enjoy the constant stroking and caressing of the people leaning over. A guide, with microphone attached, watches over the fun and explains the lives of these graceful creatures. Everyone enjoys the experience.

So too do the people crowded around the little shallow pools where plants gently wrap their tentacles around small fingers. It's all perfectly safe, and great fun to enjoy or just watch.

The aquarium has an excellent café, where fresh food is made up on the spot. It adds to the overall family atmosphere of the Aquarium, where you must allow extra time if you bring along the kids, as they will want to linger over many of the exhibits. They, of course, will love the Sea Otters, floating on their backs and rotating to keep themselves groomed. There are chrome-like anchovies glittering in huge schools. Also, the quirky walks of lobsters and other crustaceans will make everyone chuckle. Don't forget to pay a visit to the excellent gift shop on the way out. There are lots of interesting items to buy there.

The Aquarium of the Pacific is located at 100 Aquarium Way, Long Beach, CA 90802. It is just at the end of the 710 Freeway. Parking is free. Telephone number (562) 590-3100. Web site is aquariumofpacific. org. Opening hours are 9.00am to 6.00pm, seven days a week.

THE GETTY

J. PAUL GETTY was a near neighbor of mine in Surrey, England. He bought a large country manor house in a secluded part of the county and the locals didn't quite know what to make of this remote American. Rumors of course circulated at the comings and goings to the property, and one that stuck was that although extremely rich, Mr. Getty had installed a British red telephone box in his hall for the use of visitors, who wished to make outside phone calls. An interview on BBC some time later confirmed that this was the case, and apparently Mr. Getty had no compunctions about it. It was a further testament to the strange ways of foreigners.

Many, many years later, I was to experience yet another of Mr. Getty's quirks, namely that of compulsive art buying, and the showing of his treasures. His museum just north of Santa Monica was an intimate, yet expansive collection of his favorite works, and made special reference to his interest in early sculpture dating back to the Greek and Roman eras.

He established the museum in 1953 at his Ranch House in Pacific Palisades, and apart from the sculpture he also exhibited many pieces of French 18th century furniture as well as European paintings. The facility was to expand in 1974 to a Roman-style villa overlooking the Pacific Ocean, and also now included a number of more modern works of art. Although pedestrians could always gain entry, the size of its car park limited the number of visitors, and even on busy days this helped create an atmosphere of space.

In 1997 the J. Paul Getty Trust opened its new facility, high atop the crowded 405 freeway, and the enthusiasm for it was so great that it took several months before the visiting crowds began to slacken off.

It was a wonderful monument for the people of Los Angeles to enjoy. They had watched its growth from their commuting cars for many years. It's pinkish, whitish, marble–like structure gradually rose above the crawling traffic. Not the least of their inquiries was: what was that little winding road going up to the building?

It turned out that in order to maximize the space to show off the growing number of works, this time the car park was to be located a fair distance from the museum at the bottom of the hill. The "road" was in fact a modern driverless people–mover to take visitors on a five minute journey to the top. This train is an indication of the quality of the entire organization, with its efficiency, smoothness and clean cut style. As you enter the station at the top and exit the train, you are surrounded by travertine stone. This is the limestone–like material that architect, Richard Meier selected for the buildings, even though it is not the easiest stone to work with. In fact, it took quite a lot of experimentation to find the right guillotine to cut the stone to the shapes necessary to face the interconnecting buildings that make up the museum. As one walks around one can see both sides of this stone used, rough and smooth. To compliment the travertine, off–white, enamel–coated panels are used to create a modern appearance throughout the complex.

Along with the spacious entrance hall there are five two–storied buildings grouped around the central courtyard, and they house an impressive collection of the Getty's works of art. Greek and Roman statues are still there, but also a growing number of other artifacts, together with a changing exhibition of art. In general, the paintings are located upstairs, and the heavy stuff downstairs, which must have been an enormous relief to the removal men.

The piazzas look out over the city to the east and the ocean to the west. It is a spacious place, as one would expect with 110 acres and over 160,000 square feet of glass. Also formal gardens lie beneath the terraces and welcome a short stroll to engage directly in the natural world. We are told that there are another 600 acres available to expand The Getty, although with so much to see there currently, it is hard to contemplate even more in the future.

With a bookstore, several coffee stalls and a full service restaurant, there is plenty to enjoy at this wonderful monument to the better principles of capitalism. And apart from the $5.00 parking fee (no reservations needed at weekends) The Getty's admission is completely free. It is located at 1200 Getty Center Drive, Los Angeles, CA 90049. Telephone (310) 440-7722. Web site is getty.edu. It is open every day except Mondays and major holidays. Hours are from 10.00am to 6.00pm and 10.00am to 9.00pm on Fridays and Saturdays.

THE GETTY II

THE GETTY IS such a large institution that it is impossible to see everything in a day's visit; at least if you stop to enjoy the full experience and don't blunt all your senses. The Getty is not to be rushed, it would be churlish to do so, and as it's free, you can always come back. There is bound to be something to appeal to every taste, be it just the views from the terraces, the laid out gardens or the space above the crowded city below.

If you enter one of the five interconnected buildings that house much of the collection, you can wander through the entire wealth of art from its earliest beginnings to current masters like David Hockney and Manuel Alvarez Bravo. Part of the Getty's inventory contains many photographic collections and has helped move this art form into the main stream.

Some years ago I joined a course at the earlier Getty called "How to appreciate a work of art." It was delivered by a very knowledgeable man, who started off his course by telling us that most people don't really look at a painting. Generally, they are in too much of a hurry and rush to read the title on the wall. Then they mostly move on. I immediately recognized my own lack-luster performance at galleries. The instructor then took us on a tour of several paintings with the suggestion that whatever else we did that day, we should try to remember the painting that had the most effect on us during our visit. I took away the image of two brightly colored pictures on either side of a doorway. With a cursory glance, they appeared to look very similar – just a couple of rather boring still lifes with flowers and fruit.

Our teacher told us to look more carefully and consider the details. The paintings soon took on a different view; one represented life and the other death. The former was indeed a still life with flowers and fruit, but it also had small insects and butterflies and a tremendous vitality about it. The other was in the process of decay. It had many of the same colors, but it also showed the same insects eating the flesh of the fruit, and the flowers in a stage of wilting death. I am forever grateful that our teacher made us really look.

I now try to put his lessons into practice when I visit a museum or art gallery. I try to really look at the exhibit and avoid the rush to the wall to see what it's called. For example in the west pavilion on the upper floor of the new Getty, I found a painting the image of which I took away as being of most interest to me that day. It is called Portal of Rouen Cathedral in the Morning Light, by Monet; not a particularly catchy title. At first glance, the scene is not particularly interesting either, and yet if you look at it, you begin to see that the light that comes from the scene is something other-worldly. Granted that of all the French impressionists, Monet used the magic of light most effectively, but this picture is quite different.

One of the many museum attendants was explaining to a visitor that it always amazed him how such a picture could be painted. In order to illustrate this, he took the visitor from the canvas itself right across to the other side of the room. It was only from here that one could see the detail of the picture properly. "So how could he have painted it?" was his repeated question. It is a mystery.

As well as the basic collection of the Getty, there are regular other occasional features. Currently, there is a separate exhibition running called: Devices of Wonder: From the World in a Box to Images on a Screen. It covers many of the tricks and images that amused previous generations, from a mirrored room to life sized automatons out of the mid-nineteenth century. My particular favorites were two long palettes with seemingly random paint sploges on them. If, however, you look sideways through the eyeholes provided, you will see portraits hidden. This was a technique used in earlier times when images of forbidden people were banned, and artists used their skills to find a way to break the rules.

This particular exhibit closes on February 3, 2002, but as stated earlier, the Getty is so complete, it would be impossible to cover in a day. Furthermore, it would be unwise, unless all you want to do is look at the little labels posted beside each work, which is not the way to do it. Also try to remember to take away with you the memory of a favorite and discuss it with your family.

The Getty's admission is free ($5.00 parking). It is located at 1200 Getty Center Drive, Los Angeles, CA 90049. Telephone (310) 440-7722. Web site is getty.edu. Open every day from 10.00am to 6.00pm except Mondays and major holidays. Fridays and Saturday it is open from 10.00am to 9.00pm.

SANTA ANITA

IT WAS A more than usually exciting Christmas Day in 1934. Because it was the grand opening of what was to become one of Southern California's most beloved landmarks – Santa Anita Park. Even back then it was a special place, but today, it is one of the most beautiful spots a family can visit.

Mostly people who come to this place can be divided into two types: those who like to gamble on the outcome of the 8 to 10 races that take place on racing days, and those who just enjoy being in wonderful, spacious surroundings. Santa Anita will fill your wishes in both categories.

In the 75 years since its beginning, there have been many improvements, but the San Gabriel Mountains still act as a dramatic backdrop to this championship course for thoroughbred horses, and the beautiful grounds still cater to their enthusiasts. The "season" lasts from the day after Christmas Day to late April, and there is a short autumn five-week season that starts around October. During this time 2,200 horses live in the 61 barns and when the season ends this drops to 1,600. It's a horse place. But humans love it.

One of the great open secrets of Santa Anita is the early breakfast that is served from 5.00 a.m. to 10.00 a.m. every day of the year. It's at Clockers' Corner at the West End of the massive stadium on the ground floor. There is no entry fee and all comers are welcome to appreciate the practice runs of the mounts and watch the experts and amateurs alike enjoying the morning. Outside the season, only continental breakfast is available, but when the season is up and running, everything is on sale from eggs benedict to waffles.

During these quiet times very few people are around to spoil the atmosphere, but at weekends the crowds swell to 25,000. There's plenty of room for all though as Santa Anita's record is over 85,000. Space is in plenty here and walking around is one of the great pleasures of this elegant facility.

Horses are treated with the reverence due to their bloodline and their ability to earn their keep as well as provide a lucrative income for the fortunate few that own them. As they pass from the barn to the saddling area, to the walking area where the jockeys mount up to the starting gate, they never have to walk on any hard surface. If it's not earth or grass, it's a rubber surface that protects these haughty and aristocratic feet from any possible injury as they move around.

Betting is an activity that is incorporated naturally into the workings of Santa Anita, but if you prefer to avoid this aspect, it is never too obvious, and like everything else here, it is very well organized. However the delights of the fine restaurant will be hard to ignore as whether you prefer a sandwich or a juicy steak, the Frontrunner can serve it up in surroundings that allow you to watch the races and enjoy the view.

Over 60 gardeners keep the grounds in pristine condition with a huge variety of plants, trees and flowers and the staff are all helpful. It seems like one big family where the object is to help you enjoy the delights of the place they call home. Everyone is very knowledgeable and will help a visitor to understand how it all fits together. History too is part of this. Statues of jockeys, owners and famous horses are on display.

The great champion Seabiscuit has his place in the Walking Ring: he was the world's greatest money winner of the day back in the late thirties and his life-sized statue has pride of place. Another aspect of Santa Anita's history is that it was used by the US government in 1942 as an assembly area for Japanese Americans, and then as a base for the Army.

Once hostilities ended, in 1945 racing became again and since that time the crowds have gathered here to cheer or just relax. They bring the children too - under 17 years of age there is no charge. In the center of Santa Anita there are play areas and great picnic facilities too. All surrounded by the activity and the splendor of one of the most famous courses in the world.

The Sport of Kings these days has a wider following, and most of the aristocrats are the ones galloping around, but to watch all the fun and absorb the atmosphere just take a turn off the 210 freeway to the city of Arcadia, where you'll be very welcome. Telephone number for restaurant reservations is (626) 574-1035. General information number is (626) 574-7223. Web site is santaanita.com

PASADENA

IN THE LAST decade, Pasadena has improved enormously. Areas that were once rather run down have become new and exciting places for residents and visitors alike. And yet Pasadena is still an elegant and very separate city from its large neighbor, Los Angeles, fifteen minutes drive to the south. It seems to enjoy its separateness and its very own personality.

As a day out, Pasadena has everything to offer the visitor with its shops, museums, parks and tree-lined walks. Even the city hall with its 206 feet high dome is a cool place to visit with a flowered garden in its courtyard, where people can enjoy the splashing fountain and the many shady trees. It's a popular spot for weddings on the weekend too.

In September 2001, a new center for "Pasadenans" opened with a brand new open-air shopping plaza, called Paseo Colorado. Its designers aimed to produce a large area that combined traditional elegance with urban sophistication. Judging by the numbers of office workers who congregate there for their short lunch breaks, the eight restaurants are also a draw for those in a hurry. However, Paseo Colorado also encourages the browsers and strollers who wander around the 65 shops and businesses, to spend their time in its courtyards, and main square.

To the south of the Paseo, sits the Pasadena Civic Auditorium, which has a full program of cultural events lined up to cater to very diverse tastes. As the home of the Pasadena Symphony, many fine concerts are available for those with a love for classical music in all its forms. The Distinguished Speaker Series is also running there with such guest as Bill O'Reilly, Madeleine Albright and Maya Angelou. A visit to their web site at speakersla.com will provide the details of upcoming events.

Pasadena is so full of interesting little corners that it is easy to miss one of its many pleasures. Across from the new plaza is a fascinating place you should not pass by – the Pacific Asia Museum. Once the home of benefactor Grace Nicholson, who made a living buying and selling Native American art, and then moved on to Asian art, the 1924 building with its interesting Chinese architecture has been home to the museum since 1971. Here a collection of some 14,000 works of art including paintings, prints, sculptures, ceramics, jade and textiles from all over Asia are on display.

Gathered around a central garden are a number of rooms that show the many and intricate forms that Asian art has taken – from delicate watercolors of rural scenes to a collection of Netsukes. These are 18th and 19th century small hand-carved faces of all types of people and creatures. They were used by Japanese gentlemen to counter balance possessions on their obis, or cloth sashes. Kimonos had no pockets and so tobacco pouches, purses and other small items that needed to be on hand for immediate use were suspended on strings with a netsuke to hold them in place. Each one of these little faces is a jewel of the carver's art.

Currently an exhibition is on display at the museum entitled: Where Masks Still Dance. These feature a selection of photographs by Chris Rainier taken during his many visits to New Guinea. He was once an assistant to Ansel Adams and his black and white works show scenes in this area of the world where life has not changed in thousands of years.

The Pacific Asia Museum is located at 46, N. Los Robles Avenue. Its web site is pacasiamuseum.org. The museum is open from Wednesday through Sunday 10 am to 5 pm. General admission is $5.00 with $3.00 for seniors and students.

From the Rose Parade to the Rose Bowl Game, from outdoor flea markets held on the second Sunday of every month; from the internationally renowned Rachmaninoff Piano Competition and festival to the latest in shops and restaurants, Pasadena is keeping ahead of the trend. Parking is easy and it's all just off the 210 freeway. A visitor's guide is easy to obtain from the visitors bureau at (626) 795-9311 or pasadenacal.com.

NATURAL HISTORY MUSEUM

IF YOUR DECIDE to house 33 million specimens from a time dating back 4.5 billion years, you are bound to end up with a substantial building. And the Museum of Natural History is exactly that. It's front sits on Exposition Boulevard opposite the campus of USC and greets visitors with the Museum's hallmark, the "Dueling Dinosaurs," however the entrance is around the back in Exposition Park, where the Coliseum and the Science Museum share space.

As the largest natural history museum in the Western United States, the climb up the entrance steps to the formal opening, puts one in mind of the many similarly constructed building in Washington DC, and also sets the tone for one of Los Angeles' most formal museums. It hails itself as the jewel in the crown of LA museums, and it deserves the title in many ways.

Founded in 1913, the diversity and the number of exhibits has grown exponentially as the number of species with whom we share life on earth has also burgeoned with discovery. From the air above to the waters under the earth, the visitor is encouraged to experience every facet of life in as great a detail as desired. And the development of human society is also part of that great learning experience.

A number of traveling exhibits feature within the various halls. Recently a large display relating to the Viking discovery of the northern Atlantic has delighted visitors with sagas and theories of life here 1000 years ago.

Apart from the temporary exhibits, there are many permanent displays for the whole family to experience. Children can make fossil rubbings, dig for fossils, observe live animals such as snakes, fish and lizards and touch animal pelts. It is here also that they can indulge their interest in dinosaurs. Recently, biologists and paleontologists have opined that perhaps the infamous Tyrannosaurus Rex was not such a fearsome creature as was once thought.

Their recent studies have indicated that it was not quick enough on its feet to pose a serious threat. This new information is unlikely to sway the groups of children who gaze at the models and skeletons housed in the dinosaur exhibition hall. Here they can listen in wonder to a guided tour of the animals and ask question of the skilled staff.

But man is not left out of the history of nature here. Several halls are devoted to the development, and diversity of many societies. On show is a fascinating exhibit, together with a film, of the Mayan and Aztec Ball Game. This strange game has been played for thousands of years and uses an "I" shaped court. The ball is only struck with the hips, elbows or knees – pads are employed for protection. The game has considerable religious significance and it is said that Montezuma lost a match just before the Spanish took over his kingdom. It was not unusual for other losing participants to forfeit their lives either by beheading or by being hurled from the tops of pyramids. The game is still played in remote parts but no longer with so brutal an outcome.

Much space is devoted to the various tribes of Native Americans, and the results of a 1990 census show how these tribes have dispersed in recent years. One room displays earlier life in a Mesa Verde Cliff dwelling complete with the sounds of the desert all around. You can also see the development of the Indians of the Owens Valley through their skilled basket weaving.

The museum tales pride in reaching as many people as possible with as many diverse exhibits to kindle interest in the natural world. Part of its mission statement says it hopes to "inspire the widest possible audience to enjoy, value and become stewards of the living Earth." It has made its premises ideal for this purpose.

The Natural History Museum is located at 900, Exposition Boulevard, Los Angeles, CA 90007. Telephone number is (213) 763-3515. Web site is www.nhm.org. It is open every day from 10.00am to 5.00pm.

OLVERA STREET

SHAKESPEARE ASKED, "WHAT'S in a name?" And we've been wondering ever since. Names are important as they help to shape our identities and the way others see us. People all over the world have come to refer to our biggest city in California by the rather disrespectful term of "L.A." Even residents too often refer to it that way. How different would it be then if it had always been called by its original name: El Pueblo de la Reina de los Angeles (The town of the Queen of the Angels.) Now that is a name that would command respect, while at the same time infer a gentleness that might have continued into its current day.

It is still possible to enjoy what might have been had the name not lost its Spanish glow, by visiting the Historic Monument of El Pueblo de Los Angeles. And in its heart, its bustling center, Olvera Street. Rescued from almost certain disintegration in 1926, by a bountiful Mrs. Christine Sterling, this small street is flanked by the rest of the monument to our city's Hispanic past.

Located between N. Main Street and N. Los Angeles Street and flanked by Cesar Chavez Avenue, Olvera Street is a true sample of life south of the border. Rousing music, vibrant color, beguiling smells and the sound of money changing hands allows one, in a short half-a-block enclosed street, to enjoy all that is best in Mexico.

There are 75 businesses within the small street and some very good bargains can be had from the helpful vendors of both the stalls and the shops that surround them. One can buy wonderful leather goods, and woven blankets, ornaments, furniture and antiques in an unhurried fashion. Most of these items are very well priced and yet there is still a chance of a little haggling if that's what turns you on.

It is almost impossible to visit the street without having one's appetite tempted, and there are numerous ways to satisfy that need. From stalls selling churros, to sandwich shops where one can indulge in something a little different - maybe a quick burrito or an enchilada - all the way to a first class establishment like La Golondrina. Here diners are surrounded by Latin art and the fine aromas of the best in Mexican cuisine.

In the center of the street is the oldest existing house in the city, The Avila Adobe. This was rescued along with the other parts of the area and was the home of Mrs. Sterling until her death in 1963. It has survived fires, weather and earthquakes, although it had to be closed for renovations following the Sylmar quake in 1971. Today it is a comfortable monument to the days of the nineteenth century - it was constructed in 1818. The Avila family were landowners and farmers, and Sr. Avila eventually became the mayor of the rapidly expanding city. After his first wife died, he married Maria Encarnación Sepulveda, who continued to live on in the house after his death.

Currently the Avila Adobe is a museum, with no entrance fee. Exhibits are arranged to show how life was lived and enjoyed back then. There is the main room, where most of the day-to-day activity took place, and also there is the office showing ledgers from the day and also hides which were often used as currency. The master bedroom, where the Señora spent time embroidering, praying and reading, is located between the kitchen and the children's room. For many years, the kitchen was mostly used for storage, as the meals were generally cooked outside in the courtyard. The whole villa is a quiet oasis within the activity of Olvera Street itself, and a few moments there will refresh the spirits as no doubt it did for all its occupants now spreading back over three separate centuries.

On the weekends there are many musicians who wander through the crowds, and at the top of the street there is an area for dancing or just sitting back watching the scene. There is much to see. And as you look at all the fun and energy going on you might agree that our city deserves a little more respect than just calling it, "L.A." Although "El Pueblo de la Reina de los Angeles" might be too much of a mouthful all the time.

LACMA

ECLECTIC IS A word that has been somewhat overused in recent years. It has been used to describe anything from a restaurant's menu to the inventory of car dealerships. The dictionary defines eclectic as "composed of elements drawn from many sources," and to see this in correct use, one only has to visit the Los Angeles County Museum of Art or LACMA as it is frequently called.

Situated in the miracle mile district of Wilshire Boulevard within Museum Row, LACMA is an impressive collection of buildings – six in all. The organizers of the museum have gathered some 100,000 works of cultural interest since the institution was founded in 1910. Back then it was called the Museum of History, Science and Art. However today in the building, which was opened in 1965, the atmosphere of a cultural village green has been created.

From the brooding silent statues of Rodin in the B. Gerald Cantor garden to the Japanese Art Center, this fine establishment has something literally for every one. And the changing exhibits insure that a regular visitor will never get bored. Not only Rodin's statues are on display as one enters the museum at the gate on Wilshire and Ogden, but a large Henry Moore sits in stolid silence as you make your way through to the busy courtyard.

The Japanese Art Center is built along the Guggenheim principle in New York. There the visitor is encouraged to go to the top of the building and then walk down the spiral ramp to enjoy the works. Here, a number of muted Japanese paintings are illuminated in soft light to show them off to best advantage, and in the background is the constant sound of water trickling through the area, and landing in a graceful waterfall. The soft tones of the art are complimented by the pastel greens and creams of the building itself.

In direct contrast to these disciplined and understated art forms, are the works of art on display in the Anderson Building. Some of the most avant garde art is shown here, and it is quite startling. One has to ask why an artist would think of a dark room with a large full-size movie screen backed by a mirror rotating inside. On this is reflected and shown a variety of distorted images all to the accompaniment of a voice repeating disjointed words in a monotone. Outside this exhibit, a huge set of pool balls are ready racked for a giant to play; maybe the same giant that would use the five foot tortoiseshell comb on display. Anyway, it's all interesting and fun.

In contrast, on display in the Hammer hall, is an exhibit entitled "The Kindness of Friends." Here many gifts to the museum by generous benefactors are hung, showing how necessary it is for a large establishment like this to have such friends. A huge David Hockey poster given by the artist to a former curator is at the start of this exhibit. Further priceless gifts to LACMA make way for some of the permanent exhibition. Here, the more traditional paintings are on show all the time. Some fine Monets, share space with Cezanne, and Pissaro. Traditional art from 18th century Europe is well displayed in ever increasing numbers of galleries, so that one sometimes has to think hard to remember which way the exit is.

On the weekends several students and enthusiasts are crouched beneath many of the more colorful works, as they attempt to recreate the magic of the original masters. Also if you have the time and interest, the docents to the museum will explain any work to you, or you can join more formal lectures. Once again, the entire atmosphere is devoted to enjoying all that is on show and also to teaching you something of the works of a particular artist or period.

Located off the central courtyard are coffee stalls and a fine café. A sit down restaurant is also on hand with views of Hancock Park, which is on the northern boundary. Concerts take place here, and since 1992 there has been a free live jazz series each Friday night. With three outstanding shops, and plenty of room to move around, it is not surprising that LACM is one of Los Angeles' most popular spots for leisure. Here, a visiting eclectic population can enjoy a truly eclectic experience.

LACMA is open at noon – 11.00am on the weekends. It closes at 8.00pm and all day Wednesday. For more information about upcoming exhibitions like the Ansel Adams starting on February 2, 2002, call (323) 857-6000 or visit the website lacma.org.

BREA TAR PITS

MANY OF THE fortunes made along the Miracle Mile in Los Angeles were created by what some might have called wolves in sheep's clothing. But right in the middle of the area is evidence of real wolves – and without the encumbrance of clothing at all. The George Page Museum, popularly known as the Tar Pits has so far yielded up to 1000 skeletons of Dire Wolves along with many other exciting old time residents of Wilshire Boulevard.

With the continuing interest by children of all things dinosaur, the Tar Pits are a great draw for the young. In fact there are no dinosaurs found here at all, as they became extinct some 25,000 years before the oldest relic from the site died. But that doesn't seem to thwart the imagination of the younger visitors, who are fascinated by everything on show. Immediately on entering the museum there is a hologram of a saber tooth tiger. If you move from side to side in front of the glass, the skeleton around which the hologram is constructed is exposed for all to see. It is typical of the care with which the entire museum is run. For as well as these tigers, there are re-constructions of wooly mammoths that move and shake their enormous tusks at the scenes around them. All the time the traffic hums along one of Los Angeles' busiest thoroughfares, most probably unaware of the history regularly unfolding within this sleek low building.

When George Page came to California from Nebraska in 1917, he was fascinated by the tar pits. But he was equally disappointed to find out that the fossils that the pits had yielded up were stored in the Natural History Museum several miles away. Page was a successful businessman and also a philanthropist, who among other things helped finance the

Children's Hospital. His continuing enthusiasm for the fossils from the tar pits led to the present building, which was completed in 1977.

The relics that have been preserved from the area are comparatively young, as far as antiquity is concerned. But for us twenty-first century humans, 40,000 years is quite old enough to try and imagine what life was like back then. And life was very abundant. Over one million bones have been recovered representing 231 species, and this includes the ubiquitous dire wolves, who were among the most populous.

Just inside the museum is a large vat of the asphalt from which the bones have been recovered. Positioned above this are some plungers, and people are invited to test the viscosity of the tar by pulling up on the handles provided. It is very sticky and hard to manipulate. During the summer months, the asphalt becomes quite soft and it was at that time that animals from the last Ice Age became trapped. It must have been a gruesome end for them.

Only one set of human bones has been recovered from the tar. It is a skeleton from a 4' 8" female aged between 18 and 22 years of age. She died here 9,000 years ago. Evidence suggests that she was not entrapped but instead received a formal burial at the early site.

Work still continues for the paleontologists based here, and their laboratory is a central part of the museum around which visitors circulate. The actual recovery process within what is known as Pit 91, is carried out in the July and August period, when the tar is at is most workable. Specimens are then taken to the laboratory for cleaning and identification.

Outside the museum, the tar pits visible from the street bubble and seep their gases into the atmosphere as they have done for so many eons. Statues of huge beasts struggle to escape from the clammy grasp of the asphalt, and one can only imagine the strange life of the creatures that existed here. It's a hard jump for the mind to make as the Miracle Mile goes on about its business all around.

The Page Museum at the Tar Pits is located at 5901 Wilshire Boulevard, Los Angeles, CA 90036. Telephone number (323) 934-7243. Web sit is tarpits.org. Open every day during the summer but from Labor Day to Memorial Day closed on Mondays. Hours are 9.30am (10.00am on the weekends) to 5.00pm.

LATIN AMERICAN ART

"I FIND THAT lots of people imagine Latin American to be some sort of East L.A. mural work, like graffiti." So says Susan Golden, the director of marketing at the Museum of Latin American Art (MoLAA) in Long Beach. "Part of our job here is to dispel that image, and allow visitors to experience the rich heritage of this unique art form." A stroll around this interesting building will reward anyone with its selection of the diverse art that Latin America has produced in the last fifty years.

The Museum is housed in a former vintage roller rink dating back to 1929, and its warm wooden floors and intimate galleries allow the visitor to enjoy a large collection from throughout this vast region. A map in the first hall helps people, unsure of the geographical locations of each country; to familiarize themselves before the journey begins. And it is an interesting cultural trip.

Of course, art was produced all over Central and South America for many centuries, although it was, like the history of art here in the US, often a copy of European art. "That all changed with the emergence of Diego Rivera," reports Golden. "Once he returned to Mexico, his country of origin, it began a sort of focus for all artists. And it is from that developing point that the paintings here are displayed."

Diego Rivera was a catalyst in more ways than one. He left Mexico to study in Europe in 1907, when he was 21. He worked in Spain, Paris and Italy, and his relationships with women were legendary. He was married several times and the most famous of his wives, Frida Kahlo, also produced many fine works of art. She was one of Trotsky's friends in Mexico at the time he was assassinated.

Once Rivera resettled in Mexico, he was sought out for commissions, some of which were undertaken in the US. His style is unmistakable, with its bold figures and vibrant colors. However, such hallmarks are also shared by many other Latin American artists, and at MoLAA, you will see the affinity the works share. Golden adds: "There is a vibrancy and even a lightheartedness that these artists promote. There is something about the palette and the mixes of paint that makes them unique.

"The paintings in general appeal to young viewers too. There is more figurativeness, and youngsters relate to that much more than the abstraction that is promoted by many of today's modern painters elsewhere in the world." There are some abstract pieces on show, but somehow they seem more understandable in this place than elsewhere. It is easy to get into the works and enjoy their personalities, and even smile at the whimsy often expressed.

Short term exhibits aside, there is a large permanent collection at this fine institution, and it also shares many paintings with the Smithsonian, with whom it has been affiliated since last year. These can be seen at the entrance to the main exhibit.

If your taste is more towards live art, then MoLAA has some interesting diversions on its agenda, with cabarets, flamenco dancing and an evening of salsa. All details can be obtained from their information phone number, which is (562) 437-1689.

Hours of opening are 11.30am to 7.00pm Tuesday through Friday and 11.00am to 6.00pm on the weekends. It is located at 628 Alamitos Ave, Long Beach, CA 90802. Web site: molaa.org

METROLINK TO L.A.'S OLVERA STREET

A DAY TRIP to Mexico is possibly pushing the envelope of time a little too much; particularly if you include the long lines to return back over the border. But there is a way to visit a closer Mexico as long as you don't mind a short journey, and one that maybe allows the train to take the strain.

The Metrolink takes riders on a one and a half hour trip from San Bernardino into Union Street Station, which is right in the heart of downtown Los Angeles, or to get into the swing of it El Pueblo de la Reina de los Angeles (The town of the Queen of the Angels.) This is the original name of the city that is now mostly shortened to just L. A.

To start the journey, a glimpse into the renovated station of San Bernardino shows a tiled and dated floor that looks as if it should support a rushing population of travelers in suits, smart dresses and maybe Fedora or Trilby hats. Sadly, the station is not in use today, and an open booth holds all the ticket machines needed for the modern passenger. Initially for those uninitiated in the disciplines of railway travel, the instructions look complicated but in fact it's all pretty simple to work out. And it's cheap!

For a complete list of times and fares call direct or visit the Web site: www.metrolinktrains.com

"I use the train as often as I can," said Mary Boscoe of Fontana. "I live a few miles away from the station, and it's easy to get downtown to connect with other lines." Boscoe was on her way to buy some after-Christmas bargains.

The railway coasts along in comfort, while drivers on the nearby freeway have to concentrate on the road ahead. When they share the same areas the train driver seems to step on the gas to leave the cars behind.

On entering Union Station, one is once again confronted by a scene reminiscent of an early movie; only the clothing seems to have changed. Just across the road from the station, Mexico beckons. Olvera Street is the center of town as far as our Hispanic friends are concerned. Rescued from almost certain disintegration in 1926, by a charitable Mrs. Christine Sterling, the small street is flanked by the rest of the monument to our city's Hispanic past.

Located between N. Main Street and N. Los Angeles Street and flanked by Cesar Chavez Avenue, Olvera Street is a true sample of life south of the border. Rousing music, vibrant color, beguiling smells and the sound of money changing hands allows one, in a short half-a-block enclosed street, to enjoy all that is best in Mexico.

It is almost impossible to visit the street without having one's appetite tempted, and there are numerous ways to satisfy that need. From stalls selling churros, to sandwich shops where one can indulge in something a little different – maybe a quick burrito or an enchilada – all the way to a first class establishment like La Golondrina. Here diners are surrounded by Latin art and the fine aromas of the best in Mexican cuisine.

Currently the Avila Adobe is a museum, with no entrance fee. Exhibits are arranged to show how life was lived and enjoyed back then. There is the main room, where most of the day-to-day activity took place, and also there is the office showing ledgers from the day.

If you tire of the Spanish flavor, then you can easily change your culture by visiting the Chinese American Museum located just at the top of Olvera Street. "It harks back to when China Town was a lot bigger," said Emile Turner, a guide to the institution.

Sharing the same block is Firehouse Number One. "This was operating from 1884 until 1897," said guide Tyrone (who did not want to give his last name.) "We are open seven days a week from 10 a.m. until 3 p.m." The small museum shows many exhibits of how the firehouse helped the expanding early city around it.

This historic area is a stone's throw from the famous city hall and the real center of Los Angeles. But visitors staying around Olvera Street will find themselves surrounded by an atmosphere that normally they would have to travel a lot further to enjoy.

GRIFFITH OBSERVATORY

AS YOU GO towards the entrance of the Griffith Observatory, you will see a large bust of James Dean. It has been placed in such a way as to allow visitors a wonderful view of both the ex-movie star and also the Hollywood sign beyond.

Like many others, Dean was drawn to Los Angeles to seek fame and fortune and in a short time did reap such rewards. Dean came from Indiana, but many years earlier, Griffith J. Griffith left his native Wales and made his fortune in the mining industry in Mexico, and then in S. California real estate. He loved Los Angeles and wanted to give something substantial back to it for its generosity. In 1896 he therefore bought 3015 acres of land and donated it to the city; at that time making Griffith Park the largest urban park in the US.

Having visited the Mount Wilson observatory, Griffith began to think that if everyone could look at the stars and beyond, they would become less obsessed with nationalism and feel more at one with the human race. With such altruism guiding him, he gave $100,000 to the city to build the observatory that bears his name. Sadly he was to die in 1916 before he could see his dream realized, for it was to take almost twenty more years for the Griffith Observatory to open.

The first thing a visitor notices on arrival at the top of the hill is the view of the great metropolis beneath; it is truly spectacular. In order to reach that point however, it is necessary to take a shuttle up the last few winding miles to reach the objective. Although a spacious place, parking is at a premium, and with a shuttle there is no need to worry about it.

The observatory has undergone a major renovation over the last five years, and it now looks much like Griffith intended it to look. The spacious entrance hall is built of warm hued marble, and in the center is the Foucault pendulum, whose slow swing across a plate of degrees demonstrates the turning of the earth. Check out the degree it crosses as you arrive and check again just before you leave.

But of course, the observatory is not just for the earthbound, it was designed to look upward and beyond. In every corner there are well designed displays of the planets, the stars and curiosities like white dwarfs and super giants.

One display shows how the moon dictates out tides and how the lunar gravity in concert with the sun pulls the oceans to and fro. The display, like its neighbors, is small enough to be intimate, but not so as to make it cramped. The entire observatory experience is able to cater to large numbers of visitors without there being too much crush. Also they are a plenty of volunteers around who can help with any explanations required.

The planetarium holds 300 to watch the movement of the skies from comfortable seats. The newly installed Zeiss Universarium Mark IX star projector will take you through a provocative program of scenes while a lecturer explains what is going on. Entitled Centered in the Universe, the show will take you through the ages and leave you inspired to learn more.

The Griffith Observatory was built to help us realize that we are just one small part of a universe that is so large it is impossible to fully understand. By allowing us to look outside, it also keeps us focused on where we are at present.

James Dean's famous movie, Rebel Without a Cause, starred the Observatory in its own right, even though it has been used for scenes in many other films. As you leave, you will once again pass by the actor. Sadly his life was cut short in a tragic accident; the monument behind however is expected to stand and inspire many more generations for years to come.

Where: Griffith Observatory
2800, E. Observatory Road
Los Angeles, CA 90027

Shuttle Address:

4800, W. Heritage Way (Next to the L.A. Zoo)

Los Angeles, CA 90027

To book a timed-entry pass and shuttle call 1(888) 695-0888

Web site: griffithobservatory.org

LITTLE TOKYO

Little Tokyo

DURING THE 1970'S I had the opportunity to visit Tokyo, Japan. I went there several times and found it to be a most interesting place. There is a certain fondness between the English and the Japanese – maybe it's because both live surrounded by the sea, and both are somewhat cramped on their islands. Any comparison is rather unfair in this area however, as although Britain and Japan are about the same size, fully half of Japan is uninhabitable as it is too mountainous. Also there are twice as many Japanese as Britons.

I now have a son living in Japan – he has been there for almost ten years – and I have the chance to visit him about every 18 months. I enjoy it immensely. For someone who lives in the hills in a quite rural situation, it is a big change to visit a really busy and fast moving city. And that is what Tokyo is like. It's also extremely well run, considering its size and congestion. Quite a change from a comparatively quiet and simple existence in the San Bernardino Mountains.

Although Tokyo is an old city, not much remains of its past, since the bomb damage of WWII. Occasionally one sees a small relic of what used to be, but mostly it is a city of concrete, glass and traffic. Every square inch seems to have a use and there are very few wasted lots or corners where nature can grow uncultivated. But for all that, it has moments of peace and quiet; and the Japanese are masters at finding small areas for contemplation and reflection in their very busy lives.

It didn't take long after my first visits for me to acquire a taste for Japanese food, and back in the 70's this was not easy to obtain outside Japan. Over the years however, it seems that Western taste has taken on a decided passion for sushi, tempura, Teppan-yaki and all the other things that the Japanese enjoy.

However, on my return home, it doesn't take me long to miss the atmosphere of Japan and to look forward to my next trip out there. And in Southern California I do have one place I can go to top up my need for all things Nippon. There is Little Tokyo in downtown Los Angeles. And it's really easy to get to.

Located in just one block, Big Tokyo's little brother is just off Alameda Street and 2nd Street, a couple of blocks from Union Station. It is very small, but like most of the things it shares with its older relative six thousand miles to the West, it has plenty of activity and variety in its compact area.

Once you leave the vehicle in one of the many parking lots near by, the smell of Japanese cooking hits you. It is unmistakable and if there is enough traffic swirling around, you might as well be back in the original place. Nothing here however, compares with the world's busiest pedestrian cross walk which is just outside Shibuya Station in Central Tokyo. Crossing here is a piece of cake compared to that urban madness. Here, a tall wooden structure announces that you have arrived at the start of the pedestrian precinct, and your visit begins in earnest.

It won't take you long to wander around the place. There are all sorts of businesses to look at and some of them offer goods that are quite odd. But they are from a land far away with different customs and ideas. Sadly the differences are slowly draining away as our cultures become closer with the passing of the years. But there are still some mysteries left.

Of course there are plenty of opportunities to enjoy the food on any visit, and there's a bread shop, snack stalls, and several sit down restaurants serving the full panoply of Japanese delights.

Having just returned from Japan, it's nice to know that if I suffer from withdrawal symptoms, it's a quick trip on the Metro Link to Union Station or an easy drive to downtown LA to get my necessary Japanese fix.

MARINA DEL REY

WITH THE HEAT building, at the weekend people naturally look for ways to escape from it and also get away from the steady drone of air-conditioners. Living in San Bernardino County, we always have to look at the TV weather forecasts a little longer for that all important addition of weather for the Inland Empire and valleys. L.A.'s temps are interesting but they don't compare to us.

So for a change why not go where it's cooler and have a really good day out at the beach where you can forget the heat. It's not as convenient as the local areas and water parks, but we've got freeways to help us and why not pack up the car with kids and floatation devices and face the hour and a half drive to get there.

Having lived in a beach community, I was thrilled when the 105 Freeway finally opened, as it gave a different route to the east and west other than the regularly jammed 10 and 60. Today, it's lost a lot of its novelty, but it still has the wonderful aspect of exiting directly onto the Pacific Ocean at Playa Del Rey. OK, it actually changes to Imperial Highway for the last few miles, but it's a straight run, and it even turns into a convenient parking lot at Dockweiler Beach.

If you decide that this is your spot, and you're an aircraft enthusiast, then the planes from LAX take off directly over you. Even if you think you'd prefer a place with a little less ambient noise, a stop along PCH at this point allows you unrestricted views out over the ocean and at weekends that means a profusion of boats coming out of nearby Marina Del Rey.

Surprisingly the aircraft noise doesn't carry too far, and if you settle a mile or two north towards Playa Del Rey itself, you can avoid the planes and also be closer to the main channel of the Marina. You won't avoid the crowds though as many of the bus routes terminate in this area and people tend to congregate nearby.

The village of Playa Del Rey has stayed much the same as it was when I first visited it 25 years ago. It's quaint and small and has enough shops for any of your needs should you stay at the beach nearby. When I came here all that time ago, my only experience of California beaches was through the sound of the Beach Boys, usually heard in rain and English drizzle. It all seemed a very long way off and an impossible dream to visit, let alone actually live here.

Through an accident of design, and also fate, I was to make my home in Marina Del Rey for the next fifteen years, and furthermore right opposite the central beach; known as Mother's Beach, or more correctly Basin D.

Mother's Beach is so called as the lack of surf allows small children to walk about paddling without fear of any undertow, or being swept out to sea. It does nonetheless, have a centrally placed lifeguard station, and the lifeguard on duty keeps a very watchful eye on things.

There is no safer place to sit and enjoy the beach and also the occasional boat movement from one of the many arms that are home to over 12,000 watercraft moored here.

Marina Del Rey is the largest man made marina in the world, and when it was originally built the designers left out a breakwater. The first Pacific storm that came in thundered through the docks causing serious damage.

The breakwater built soon afterwards stopped such events from happening ever since.

If this is your final beach destination, but you should become a little bored with just sitting and watching volley-ball or other sand born activities, then the Marina is an ideal place to just wander about easily and relax. A walk down any of the arms is always fun as it allows you to examine the boats up close, and the Burton Chase park at the end of Mindanao Way gives access to the main channel and lots of weekend activities like concerts, roller-blading and bar-be-que's.

If you walk in the opposite direction you will arrive within half a mile at Venice Beach, and that is a place to keep your eyes open for some of the more bizarre residents of Southern California. I remember it kept me amused for many Sunday afternoons.

With a 75-mile plus drive back to San Bernardino, you will no doubt have an eye on the return journey. But hopefully you will have that wonderful glow on you from a day in the surf and sun, and the car's A/C will at least keep you away from the heat for that bit longer.

LA OPERA

WHEN I MET the future Mrs. Summons, it did not take long to realize that one interest we were unlikely to share along life's path was that of music. Her reply to my question: Do you know what it's like to get goose bumps when you listen to music? Was met with the sort of stare I had found in most people not affected with the same passion. Furthermore, her collection of LP's contained many titles of The Best of...Not a good beginning.

This small fault however, was so inconsequential compared to the positive cornucopia of benefits she had that I largely ignored it. She too ignored my regular forays to the music machine to play loud symphonies and concerti. It was just something we didn't have in common.

One day however, we were surfing through the channels on TV when we – in fact it was I, as I had the remote at the time – came upon a production of the opera Tosca. It was the bit where the fellow is singing that as he's about to be executed the following morning everything now is suddenly so much more beautiful. It's quiet a poignant aria.

Suddenly, from the opposite sofa came the words: "I think I know what you mean by getting goose bumps!" I was amazed, and we continued watching until the heroine threw herself off the balcony to join her dead lover. There's a lot of dying in opera generally, and most of it is premature.

Now although I was obviously aware of the various pieces in the popular library of opera, it was a subset in which I had virtually no experience. But not wanting to ignore this strange effect in my otherwise tone-deaf wife, I arranged to take her to the opera in Los Angeles. It was Mozart's Cosi Fan Tutti as I remember.

This is one of those opera's that is based upon men dressing up as women in order to fool the women into thinking they are not whom they really are. All rather silly, and as it happens with so many operas of that time, the plot is not the important part. Unfortunately there didn't seem to be many good tenor arias in it either, which is what my wife was looking for.

But we progressed, and after the first poor start opera became for us a regular exciting afternoon's entertainment. We mostly used to go to the matinee performances on the weekends.

With relocation to the mountains, we allowed the habit to fall away, but could not resist a recent showing of an opera called The Rise and Fall of the City of Mahagonny, by Kurt Weil. It was the second time we had seen it. It is written by the same composer who wrote the Three Penny Opera, which has Mack the Knife in it.

I'm very glad we went again, and it is something that if you have never done you should really try to do. It is never a boring thing and it is the ultimate in the performing arts. Also they have this neat little strip across the top of the stage with subtitles in the unlikely event you're not fluent in Italian/German/French, or even English.

The costumes are fantastic, the lighting is the best in the world, and the sets are a marvelous example of what can be done with chipboard, plastic and paint. As for the music, well it's very varied and it's all a part of the unfolding scene.

Performances of each opera don't stay long, but the Web site tells you everything you need to know and if you talk to a representative they can guide you to a performance to suit you, if it's your first time. It's not expensive either with seats starting at $35, and the sound will reach you no matter where you are in the huge Dorothy Chandler Pavilion.

Approaching 25 years of marriage, I'm glad that when my initial due diligence uncovered this lack of musical appreciation, I had the fortitude to go forward; otherwise just think what I would have missed.

Web site: LAOpera.com
Phone number: (213) 972-8001

PACIFIC ASIA MUSEUM

MANY PEOPLE SAY the world is getting smaller. With the Internet and far ranging jet travel, this is becoming more and more accurate. However it doesn't take a long look to see some very big differences in the cultural aspects of east and west.

A walk round the Pacific Asia Museum in Pasadena shows up some very different works of art that have come from the east.

It's a small compact museum that was once the home of Grace Nicholson, who came to Pasadena in 1901. She contracted with a local architect to build her a "Chinese-style" house to contain a museum dedicated to a collection of Oriental and Western art.

She lived in the apartments upstairs and the collection was housed in the galleries below. She died in 1948, and the Pacific Asia Museum opened its doors in 1971.

As soon as you go past the reception desk you enter a quiet atmosphere completely different to other museums you might have visited. The Asian experience is all around you, divided into sections devoted to the East and Pacific Islands.

There are over 14,000 pieces of art in the collection, although not all of them are on display. In fact there is enough space all around to stop you feeling hemmed in.

Currently there is a display of Chinese regalia entitled: Rank and Style – Power Dressing in Imperial China. It will show you how to recognize a person of rank from hundreds of years ago, if you are lucky enough to run into one.

A circular emblem on their court robes differentiated the immediate royal family from princes of the blood and dukes, who wore square badges. Also what was in the design of the badge – whether for instance it was a five clawed dragon or a four clawed one – gave the observer instant understanding of the position the wearer had in this very structured society.

There are a huge number of details available to the visitor at the museum, with information on each exhibit as you go round. There is no hurry and it's easy to pass a substantial amount of time just looking into these details.

In the South and Southeast Asian section, there are several statues of a variety of gods. One three feet tall statue in gilded wood displays Bodhisattva Avolokiteshvara, from Vietnam. This god has six arms in order "to help all beings in a variety of ways."

Within the Japanese area is a collection of Netsukes. These are 18th and 19th century small hand-carved faces of all types of people and creatures. They were used by Japanese gentlemen to counter balance possessions on their obis, or cloth sashes. Kimonos had no pockets and so tobacco pouches, purses and other small items that needed to be on hand for immediate use were suspended on strings with a netsuke to hold them in place. Each one of these little faces is a jewel of the carver's art.

The museum is built around an enclosed garden which after a century of growth is full of rest and quietude. It's an ideal place to reflect on the big cultural differences that used to exist between the two hemispheres of the world. That is until the arrival of the ubiquitous flood of jeans and T-shirts that seem to have taken over every society today.

Pacific Asia Museum
46, N. Los Robles Avenue.
Pasadena, CA 91101
(626) 449-2742
Web site: pacasiamuseum.org.
The museum is open from Wednesday through Sunday 10 am to 5 pm.

VENICE

VISITORS TO SOUTHERN California are firstly amazed at the climate; as well they should be. It was quite a few years before I became aware that there was a seasonal change, although you could usually tell by the fact that women would alter their clothing according to the calendar rather than the temperature.

Mingling with the crowds on any weekend along Venice Boardwalk it was easy to forget whether it was winter or summer, as the same rules seemed to apply. With the sun glinting off the Pacific Ocean to the west, Santa Monica Pier's Ferris wheel to the north and the famous Venice Fishing pier stretching out to the south, it's a world of entertainment and bustle that confuses not just the sense of season, but every other sense as well.

Abbot Kinney was the man behind the dream of a duplicate of Venice, Italy when he opened the small community back in 1905. He and his partner battled the marshy land they had bought and had to bring in steam diggers to finish the job in time for its opening on July 4th that year.

Before he dug the first canal, the area was uninhabited and deserted, but those old pioneers could see things that others could not, and Kinney forged ahead.

He died in 1920 and the government of his town began to fall apart. Factions formed and eventually in 1925 the city was taken over by Los Angeles. They had, after all, provided most of the visiting population that kept Venice financially afloat during its hey-days.

Today the original canals are kept quite spruce with many famous people owning an outlook over the calm waters. It's not so attractive though at low tide with mud banks on either side of the shallow water.

Venice is not a car friendly place. Many of the houses lack a road up to them and can only be accessed by pathways. But if you manage to dump the car then take to your feet and enjoy the many businesses lining the boardwalk.

You'll almost certainly find yourself watching some of the street acts that regularly perform there. Maybe you'll even run into Harry Perry. He's the fellow dressed in white with a white turban. He was doing his thing when I first wandered there in the early eighties, and he's doing it still today.

Wearing his usual costume, and lifted up above his normal tall self on in-line skates, he'll strum a chord from his electric guitar and let out a note or two in his strong tenor voice. He always seems happy, and he's been in a lot of movies and TV programs. He's got a record label too, so there's nothing that odd about Harry.

Juggling with running chain saws is also an art form in Venice, street performer Robert Gruenberg still seems to possess all his fingers and thumbs although he's been doing this for a few decades. He always draws a big crowd.

The founder's name is given to one of the natural boundaries of Venice. Initially rather a drab little road, Abbot Kinney Street began to collect a wide selection of restaurants and bars in the nineties. It now hosts an eclectic array and locals and visitors alike come here every evening to sample the best of food in a fun environment. If you can delay your return home for just a little, then this is the ideal place to end a day in the unique atmosphere of this exciting place.

REDLANDS POST OFFICE MUSEUM

Redlands Post Office

YOU HAVE TO feel sorry for the post office. It must be galling to see one's market dropping with every year and not to be able to do anything about it. Of course, we all still use the post office and rely on the daily postal delivery of packets and mail, but how much of it is the sort of mail that we used to receive just a decade ago? When was the last time we received or sent a hand written letter? In an envelope, with a stamp?

But the post office has a long and distinguished history in the U.S. that goes back to the first license which was issued by King William and

Queen Mary in 1692. The recipient of this royal charter was Thomas Neale who used it to deliver mail between planters. The license was granted for 21 years.

About the time America was losing patience with being ruled from England, and a year before Independence, in 1775 Ben Franklin became the first Postmaster General of the United States.

Perhaps the smallest museum I have visited in the Inland Empire is the one located within the Redlands Post Office. The building itself is most attractive from the outside and the museum, devoted to all things postal, is located in what was at one time the postmaster's office.

Around the walls are many items from the day when the arrival of the mailman, or "letter carrier" in modern parlance, meant a quickening heart beat. Most of the stuff in the postman's bag was of a personal nature; so unlike today where a large percentage of it is unwelcome in the form of junk and bills and other stuff that you can't wait to throw away.

Redlands Main Post Office is designed in the Mission/Spanish Revival style and it is a wonderful example of such architecture. It was built in 1935, which was several years after the mail was delivered by more exotic methods.

If you wanted to send a letter from New York asking after Aunt Bessie's health and she had come out to California in the 1850's, your letter underwent a long and difficult journey. It would travel down the east coast by sea to somewhere in the Louisiana territory. Then it would transfer to another boat which would take it down to the Panama Isthmus to be taken across the narrowest part of the land separating both oceans. (The Panama Canal was not built until 1914.) Finally it would sail up the west coast to be landed in California. It was a journey of many weeks.

Three businessmen came up with the idea of racing across the plains and the mountains on horseback to make the journey faster, and the Pony Express was born in April 1860. It only lasted until October 1861, but was the ultimate in express mail service for the age. The original investors set up 184 stations, 400 horses and 184 riders, who would go between 80 and 100 miles, changing mounts from eight to ten times.

They averaged 10 to 15 miles per hour and could gallop up to 25 m.p.h. on occasions.

It was technology that brought the system to a halt with the opening of the transcontinental telegraph. It only took two days for the Pony Express to fold.

Today it is the same nemesis of technology that makes the Post Office face difficulties. In place of letters we now all hear about Aunt Bessie's health via email, or on Facebook, or even read her Tweets.

At the Post Office Museum in Redlands you can travel back to the early part of the last century with some interesting items. Check out the blind mailman, Mr. Roland Scott, who worked in Bernardson, Mass.

As today, weight is a most important part of charging at the Post Office and there are several examples of these calculators going back through the ages; as too are hand cranked canceling machines still in use until the 1950's.

On display is one of the original desks used by the postmaster himself. Several were found in the basement and instructions were given to "cut 'em up and get rid of 'em!" Fortunately one loyal servant managed to hold on to the one on show here as it is a real part of the past.

The Redlands Post Office Museum is the first and only one in the entire country other than the Smithsonian's Postal Museum in Washington D.C.

MISSION SAN GABRIEL

THE BASIC DIFFERENCE between English history and California history is one of size. If you became sick in class in the UK, and had to spend two weeks away, when you came back you might well have missed a couple of wars; a change of king or queen; or even a conversion of the nation from protestant to catholic. But the mixture pretty much stayed the same.

In California, although the range is smaller, the human details remain and the changes to society have been dramatic and hung on significant dates as usual.

All these thoughts went through my head as I made my first visit to the mission in San Gabriel.

The first thing you notice as you enter the church is that this place is really old. Not old in that faux way that amusement parks or Wild West places strive to effect. This is the genuine item.

The mission was begun in 1771, which in itself is a long time ago – 140 years to save you doing the math – and it generates the same atmosphere as churches in Europe that were founded much earlier.

On the day of my visit, there was a hive of activity as over 40 volunteers were hard at work cleaning, painting, gardening and generally improving the condition of the mission.

"We have Convergint Technologies here for the entire day," said Chuck Lyons, the Director of P.R. "We also have many local people lending a hand." Convergint Technologies, who are in the security camera business, spend a day every year in volunteer work, and the entire company, whose head office is based in Chicago, was engaged all over the country.

"Here in San Gabriel the work is very necessary to keep ahead of the three goals of the mission," said Lyons. "Firstly there is repair, then preservation and finally maintenance."

As the day wore on the effect of such a number at work was beginning to show. Signs were repainted, flowers dug in, and paint applied to make the place worthy of the many visitors who come here daily.

The mission is still a functioning church with six priests overseeing operations. There are 3,500 family member parishioners registered, who attend the 6 masses each Sunday. Many of the services cater for different cultures – even Vietnamese.

There is a fine museum of artifacts behind the church and I stopped to admire a pair of misereres. These are stalls placed along the chancel for ministering clergy to rest against during the long services when they were supposed to stand. You don't see them in any modern churches these days.

There are many books in original form and also religious paintings; all of the collection takes you back a very long time in Californian history.

The gardens are a refuge from modern life and also a final place of rest for the many priests who have ministered at the mission. Here the fourteen stations of the cross can be visited with explanations of each stop. It's a very dramatic process.

The annual mission fiesta on Friday, Saturday and Sunday of the Labor Day weekend includes ringing of the bells, Fiesta Royal Court crowning, children's and pet's costume contests, blessing of the animals and portrayals of early mission life. There is an international food court, rides, games, and in the evening free entertainment.

The original mission was begun on September 8, 1771 by Spaniards of the Franciscan Order. It was to be the fourth of 21 missions and one on the original De Anza Trail, the first overland route to California; a truly historic place.

Mission San Gabriel
428 South Mission Drive
San Gabriel, CA 9176-11299

(626) 457-3035
Web site: sangabrielmission.net

VINCENT PRICE ART MUSEUM

REGULAR READERS OF this column will know that there is one subject on which I admit to being a little wobbly, and that is education. Having failed to reach the shores of the Unites States until I was well into middle age, I therefore didn't make it through the US education system.

This tardiness has made me ignorant of all the little details that true natives take so much for granted. For instance, I can never figure out that Greek thing that goes on in universities – Phi Beta Kappa stuff. Also when told of a child's grade I have to add five to get close to its age.

And so a visit to the East Los Angeles Community College, in Monterey Park the other day gave me some insight into two totally different subjects; the first being the world of the community college, and also its position in today's society. I found out for instance that until the 1970's they were called junior colleges.

They offer a two-year course to gain an associates degree. After this you can go on to a four-year college to acquire a bachelor's degree. I also found out that there are 115 of these institutions around and they educate a huge number of people. ELAC for instance has 40,000 students on its books.

The principle reason for my visit to this seat of learning, however, was to find out about the other subject of my quest – the Vincent Price Art Museum located within the Performing and Fine Arts Complex. This is a new $89 million, 160,000 square feet area and it houses this fine new museum.

Back in 1951, when he was aged 40, Vincent Price was asked to give a graduation speech at the college. He and his wife, Mary, were avid collectors of art and at the time they realized that there were no art museums in this unincorporated part of Los Angeles. They began donating pieces from their private art collection and in 1957; the Vincent Price Art Gallery was opened.

Over time and until his death in 1993 at age 82, he had given away to the college some 2000 works of art.

Today under the stewardship of Karen Rapp, this collection is catalogued, and displayed to great effect along with many other works of art.

"My predecessor, Thomas Silliman, managed to acquire close to 9,000 items," she said. "The east side of Los Angeles is rather short of art facilities, and so this museum makes it a very important addition."

The museum she oversees is on four floors, and takes up 40,000 square feet. Not only are Price's works on show but also plenty of newer art from ex-students of the college.

Currently there is a gallery devoted to Mexican Modernism. One of the artists, Sonia Romero, is on display with a collection called "Politics of Consumption. You have to look carefully to understand the significance of the murals on the walls to fully understand it.

In another gallery are two works by Arnold Meskes. The first is a lifelike portrait of a woman called Twinka. Opposite hangs a fierce painting in the abstract, and it's hard to believe they are done by the same artist.

At the time of my visit they were preparing a room of Pre-Columbian pieces that dated back to the seventh century. Many of the pieces were given by Vincent Price himself. The museum opened this fine new facility on May 20th this year, which was seven days before the actor would have celebrated his 100th birthday.

East Los Angeles College
1301 Avenida Cesar Chavez
Monterey Park, CA 91754-6099
(323) 265-8841
Web site: vincentpricemuseum.org

HARVEY HOUSE/W.A.R.M.

NEXT SATURDAY, AUGUST 20th, 2011 is a big anniversary celebration for the Harvey House in Barstow. Although the building was officially opened on February 22, 1911, the 100th birthday party has been set for this coming Saturday.

The Harvey House

For many years I have visited the two museums that share the same spot alongside the railway tracks at the Casa del Desierto station, but the

Harvey House itself has always been locked up, empty and permanently closed. It always seemed such a shame.

But the other day as I went to see how the Route 66 Museum and also the Western Area railroad Museum were doing, I was told that the Barstow Chamber of Commerce had now opened up within the main building.

Granted that the new focus of this monument to rail travel of years ago is not the same as the original hustle and bustle of travelers and waitresses in their black and white uniforms, it is a great improvement on what used to be there a few years back.

Today there is a new reception area to greet visitors and on either side you can see the two huge rooms that used to cater to passengers wanting to break their journeys. A curved line on the floor of the left hand one shows the position of the counter where countless diners would enjoy some refreshment from their long travels.

Harvey Houses began under the direction of Fred Harvey in 1878, and Barstow was Number Four in a chain that peaked at 84 in number. It closed its hotel doors in 1959, and the restaurant ended in 1970.

Today the station is an unmanned stop for passengers and there are two trains a day that allow passengers on and off. The South West Chief stops at 10:30 p.m. on its way from Los Angeles to Chicago. Travelers from Chicago are allowed off on a returning train at 3:30 a.m. It's a 42-hour one-way journey.

Beth Burke, who runs the reception area and escorts visitors around the reopened building, had a grandmother who was a "Harvey Girl." "I remember her very well," she said, as she took me up to the second floor. "She died when she was 93, but she was here for years." Since opening their doors a year ago there have been 7,000 visitors to the House.

The upper floor is now home to ten local businesses, who have taken space that used to be the hotel rooms. But there are two rooms allocated to The Harvey House's history. One is the stationmaster's office, which now holds his original desk as well as a dining room set of table and four chairs just as it used to be laid out in the hay days. "My grandmother used to serve meals at such a setting," Burke said.

Across the hallway is another relic from the past, the stationmaster's bedroom and separate bathroom. "It was here in 1929, that Winston

Churchill stopped," Burke explained. "He didn't stay overnight, he just took a bath." I peeked into the bathroom and saw the tub where the leader of the free world in the dark days of life a decade further on from that event, must have soaked.

"Next door there used to be a two-lane bowling alley," Burke told me. "It's now the home of the Western Area Railroad Museum." That was my next stop, so I bid goodbye to the Harvey house and looked into the other museum.

W.A.R.M. has everything for the railway enthusiast, including a huge model railway that was donated from a man in Santa Monica. It is so huge that it had to be broken up and reassembled for its journey to Barstow.

With three sites now at the Harvey House I shall need a little extra time on my future visits, as there is a lot to see at this center of travel. The route goes back to the early tribes, and then to the first efforts of Europeans to travel west from the developing east.

Today, the Casa del Desierto has some new life in it and a trip there will allow you to capture some of the atmosphere of how travelers' lives have changed over many years of history.

Where: Harvey House
681 North First Street
Barstow, CA 92312-0703
(760) 256-8617
Web site: barstowchamber.com

LOS ANGELES MUSEUM OF CONTEMPORARY ART (M.O.C.A.)

MANY YEARS AGO I had a friend who had graduated from university with a degree in art. I had always been interested in the subject, but was still grappling with the concept of what we used to call back then "Modern Art."

Like most people I had been brought up in a world of art where you immediately recognized a painting or sculpture because it was exactly what it represented. But times changed.

My friend used to blanch when I trotted out that old question: "But, what does it mean?" Whenever we looked at or talked about yet another shock to the art world.

Mostly, the general public seems to lag behind the cutting edge of avant-garde culture by several years. And at the time of which I'm speaking artists such as Picasso and Dali had been painting for some 40 or more years.

Slowly, and no doubt with growing exposure, I was able to cross over to the stage where I could let the art "speak to me," which is what my long suffering friend wanted from me all along. It is like shifting gears in a manual vehicle. However, it soon becomes an automatic response.

Recently I visited that holy of holies for the modern art enthusiast – the Museum of Contemporary Art – M.O.C.A., in downtown Los Angeles.

The facility has two main galleries and the amount on show is so great that this is the first of two pieces on it.

The principal museum of M.O.C.A. is located on Grand Avenue in the upper part of the city. It's just down the road from the Disney Concert Hall and the Opera House, so it is ideally positioned in the center of cultural life.

The second gallery, The Geffen, is about a mile away and contains the most modern works of art. In fact the split is quite simple to understand as MOCA shows art from WWII up to 1979, when the museum was founded.

The Geffen takes us from 1980 up to the present day. As the entire collection consists of over 500 works by 200 artists, there is a lot to see.

When you arrive at MOCA to buy your ticket there is a huge sculpture that overwhelms the plaza in which it resides. It is by Nancy Rubins and it seems to be made up of a collection of airplane parts. In fact it is just that and the title of the work contains those words.

It is truly a spectacle and a good way to introduce the subject of contemporary art to the visitor.

Inside there is a huge treasure trove of modern art and it is best to try and concentrate on just a few items or artists as it can be a sensory overload. Nonetheless, if you are new to this type of thing, try to let the art speak to you and don't judge it on how close it comes to the original subject; that is if there is an original subject. Perhaps it's just a feeling of interest, color and shape, and if you enjoy it.

Within the Grand Avenue location the works have acquired a certain respectability. Over the years they have lost much of their original surprise value. Jackson Pollock's three works hang close together with his Number 1 dominating the area. "Jack the Dripper" as he was often unkindly called was a tortured man. The recent film, Pollock, with Ed Harris in the title role shows how he fought his inner demons and discovered a medium of painting that worked for him.

He said that by placing the painting on the floor and throwing, dribbling and splashing paints from above gave him a feeling of being more connected to the developing work.

Number 1, painted in 1949, shows the energy and life that he brought to his work as well as some of the internal struggles that dominated him. Hard stuff to analyze if you're looking to see what it means.

Museum of Contemporary Art,
250 South Grand Avenue,
Los Angeles, CA 90012
(213) 621-1749
Web site moca.org
Open at 11 a.m.
Closed Tuesday and Wednesday.

THE GEFFEN

ONE OF THE great joys of aging is the freedom to be judgmental. I know it's not fashionable in these liberal times, but what else is getting old for? There is an area however where such an attitude can cause you problems and that is within the world of art.

To be judgmental in that world will not get you very far, and in the contemporary art world it is pointless as most of the art is without boundaries. Trying to pigeon hole the most modern will only end in frustration and no chance of any enjoyment.

With this freedom of thought in mind you can be prepared for a visit to The Geffen, the second of the Museum of Contemporary Art's two principal galleries.

Currently MOCA is celebrating 30 years of operation and this building located on North Central Avenue close to 1st and Alameda, holds the most modern of the collection.

The building looks like an old warehouse, and it was the original home for MOCA, before the new premises were built close to the Disney Concert Hall. Today there is a split in the collection and The Geffen is showing art from 1980 to the present time.

On the day I went, there was a group of children sitting in front of a piece called The Big Wheel by Chris Burden. It consists of a motorcycle in front of a spinning wheel some five feet high. It's a fun thing and the children seemed to enjoy it.

The art here is not just of the painting and sculpture kind. Some of the works make sound, others are shown in a darkened room via a projector. All however are trying to effect the viewer in a variety of ways.

"Yes, but is it art?" Is a question many people outside the world of creativity ask? The borders of art have expanded so much in the last 100 years that virtually anything could be called art, and so the question is rather irrelevant. More to the point is "Do you enjoy it?" And at The Geffen, there is much to enjoy.

No doubt many of the artists shown have a view of the world that seems a little pessimistic. For instance on the wall outside is a huge script of the form letter sent to someone trying to come to this country. It declines the application.

Having gone through the entire process, I wonder why the artist did not portray the acceptance of a visitor visa, a green card and ultimately, citizenship. Those are letters that are not only life changing but truly positive.

There was a huge painting, some 15' by 20' called Departure from Egypt, by Anselm Kiefer that I liked. It would not fit into a modern home but here it was a colorful and interesting piece. It was painted in 1984 and there was a large shepherd's crook slanted across it.

I rather liked the huge photographic picture by Barbara Kruger. It is a 1940's style woman holding a magnifying glass which makes her eye massive. She seemed to be inspecting us all as we wandered around. It's called Untitled, but in parenthesis are the words: It's a small world but not if you have to clean it. It was done in 1990.

Another painting called Monkey Magic from 1999, by Chris Ofili was covered in glitter. It was a happy looking piece but on investigation, the nameplate explained that it used not only paint, collage and pins, but also elephant dung. Now, one is forced to ask why the artist felt the need to use that particular material. But as I say, in this area I try awfully hard not to be judgmental.

The Geffen Contemporary at MOCA
152 North Central Avenue
Los Angeles, CA 90013
Open at 11 a.m.
Closed Tuesday and Wednesday.

U.S.S. LANE VICTORY

MY FATHER WAS a sailor. He left the sea when he was in his mid-twenties; but the sea never quite left him. He would often reminisce throughout the rest of his fifty years of life although the time he spent sailing the seven seas was comparatively short.

He would tell tales of the ships he had sailed on and their many details were close to his heart. It seems that men who go down to the sea in ships forge a special relationship with the craft they go in.

It takes a great deal of enthusiasm to bring an old vessel up to the same standard it left the shipyard at it's launch, but the volunteers of the S.S. Lane Victory have managed to do that and the work goes on.

Nestled under the huge expanse of the Vincent Thomas Bridge in San Pedro, this 10,750 ton cargo ship is rather dwarfed by the huge cruise ships that berth next door at the World Cruise Center, but its heart is every bit as big as those luxury machines.

The Lane Victory was launched in June 1945 just as WWII was coming to a close. She was "mothballed" two years later but was brought back into service for the Korean War. She rescued 7,000 men, women and children during that action and there is a plaque on board thanking the crew for this work from the Korean survivors.

Basically during three runs she loaded up her holds and took civilians from the north of that troubled peninsular to the south and freedom.

Once again she was mothballed in 1953, but was recommissioned in 1966 to serve in Vietnam. Eventually retirement came in 1970, and that would have been that for the Lane, but she was to have yet another life.

She had been named after Dr. Isaac Lane, who was a free slave who founded a school and then a college in Jackson, Tennessee.

In 1988 President Ronald Reagan signed a transfer of ownership and the ship was towed to L.A. Harbor in June 1989 where it was designated a historic monument in 1991. It was then that the work really began.

Before and after photos in the on-board museum show the immense amount of work needed to bring the ship up to standard. It was corroded and it looked in very bad shape; but such is the love of seamen for their craft that today, the Lane Victory is a fine exhibit to enjoy.

As a cargo vessel it did not have much armament to defend itself, and it must have taken a lot of guts to be floating out there in the great oceans waiting for explosions to hit you. It needed a certain type of sailor to do that – ones with nerves of steel.

As you wander around the ship, you can see that it did not have much in the way of comfort. Small cramped quarters and the barest bathroom facilities were shared by a crew of 58. They used 40 tons of fuel a day to travel with their cargoes, and their top speed was 16.5 knots or about 19 miles an hour. That of course depended on sea conditions and the type of cargo they were hauling.

Today, in the main hold they have a well packed museum of items from the places the Lane has been and also from that era. It's easy to get lost among the exhibits and the history there.

One of my father's favorite programs on TV was Victory at Sea. The sound of Richard Rogers' score would alert us to the fact that it was on. For those with a passion for such times it is possible to enjoy a real Victory at Sea, as the Lane goes out with paying passengers several times a year. There are five arranged for this year. I'm sure the old man would have loved it.

S.S. Lane Victory
Berth 94, Los Angeles Harbor,
San Pedro, CA 90733
(310) 519-9545
Lanevictory.org

JUSTICE BROTHERS
MOTOR MUSEUM

I FOUND MYSELF in the city of Duarte the other day and although it had only been a couple of years since my last trip, I felt compelled to re-visit the wonderful motor museum of Justice Brothers.

The last time I was here I spent a lot of time admiring the collection of midget racing cars that they have in their head office. I had committed the faux pas of assuming that these were racing cars for extremely small people, as my UK background had omitted any knowledge of the sport that was so popular here in the 40's and 50's.

During my last visit Ed Justice Jr, the current president of the company and the son of Ed Justice Senior, one of the original founders, had shown me around and by the time he took me across the parking lot to the other part of the collection I was becoming a little "carred out." However one model did catch my attention and it was this I rather wanted to see again.

This time the president's daughter, Courtney, who looks after PR for the firm took me straight to it; an Isetta motor car that had been very popular in Europe in the mid-fifties.

It sat alone among a glittering collection of vehicles, and it still looked as quaint as when it first appeared on England's narrow road system.

The Isetta was originally built by the Italians, but soon found other manufacturers to take up licenses. It quickly adopted the term "bubble car," and by the time it had washed up on the UK's shores it had undergone some serious modifications. In order to get around the regulations, instead of having two small wheels at the back it was produced with only one. There was no reverse gear either as it was light enough to push back by hand if you needed to.

By employing these changes it was possible to register it as a motorcycle whose fees were a lot smaller than cars.

There was one problem however. In order to get in and out of the car, you had to open the entire front end of it, which swung outwards. If you were unwise enough to drive up close to a parking lot's wall, you were stuck. You could not open the door, and with no reverse you had to wait until some helpful soul came along to wheel you backwards.

Drivers only made this mistake once, I think!

The three Justice Brothers came out from Paola, Kansas to begin building Kurtis midget racing cars in Glendale. They soon became immersed in the world of racing and today they manufacture 90 different car care products in the Duarte factory as well as two others facilities.

The museum traces their world of cars and also contains some other novelty vehicles, like the "Hover-car," which was used in the film Spaceballs. "It's always very popular with visitors," said Courtney.

With so much metal on show – there are at least 100 vehicles in the collection – they need a full time cleaner and polisher to keep the dust at bay. I spotted "Jimmy" hard at work on two Mustang motorcycles here in the museum to pay tribute to the world of two-wheeled travel. As with everything else here, they were immaculate.

My only regret on both my visits was that I knew so little of American motor history as we had nothing like it across the pond.

If you find yourself in the area, it is well worth while stopping into this fascinating place, but remember it's only open during business hours Monday to Friday.

Justice Brothers Racing Museum
2734 East Huntington Drive
Duarte, CA 91010
(626) 359-9174
Hours: 8 a.m. to 5 p.m. Weekdays.
www.justicebrothers.com

Midget Racing Cars at the Justice Motor Museum

MALOOF FOUNDATION

I WAS WELL along Carnelian Street off the 210 Freeway the other day and I was beginning to wonder if I had missed my destination, when the familiar blue roofs appeared at the very top. I had arrived at the Maloof Residence and Foundation.

I was here just over three years ago for the first time, and I was extremely lucky to meet Mr. Sam Maloof in person. He sadly died in 2009 at the age of 93, but when I met him he was still working every day and earning the title of "the greatest woodworker in the world;" a description given to him by President Jimmy Carter at his 92nd birthday party.

When I met him he showed me his technique for making the curves in wood that made him famous. He used an unguarded band saw and his hands turned the wood effortlessly as he moved the piece around the flying teeth.

His house and museum are open to the public and regular guided tours are given with many explanations of the pieces on show. The house is full of things that Maloof created. Each door latch is unique and made from a piece of discarded wood that he found. The news letter that is circulated to members of the Sam and Alfreda Maloof Foundation is in fact called The Wooden Latch.

The house today has just been included in the California Register of Historical Resources. Although determined "eligible" in the 1990's, similar registration to be added to the National Register required that the building be a minimum of 50 years old and also that its creator was no longer living.

The house also stood in the way when the 210 Freeway came through, and so it had to be moved higher up Carnelian Street to its current location.

Maloof lived and worked for a very long time, and the contents of the house – by no means his only output – are many; almost too many to count. From a beautiful curved staircase going up to a higher floor, to the kitchen doors, it was all done by him. A single arm chair is set aside for visitors to try out its comfort level. Considering it is just wood with no padding it is very comfortable indeed.

A similar rocking chair is part of the current Maloof product line that still sells. It has been brought back into production as an example of mid- century modernism and is his most popular design.

These chairs sell for $25,000 each, and they are not only functional, but also individual works of art.

On my last visit, I met craftsman Mike Johnson, who works on these chairs. Today, he admits he misses his old mentor.

Martha Wolf, the Interim Executive Director showed me around on this visit and told me that there is to be a big party coming up next weekend, June 4th. "It's a celebration of his life," she said. "There will be a tent erected out in the garden, and there'll be music and talks and a full dinner." It will cost $150 a head and it's expected to attract a full house.

Sam Maloof's legacy, like the man himself, is larger than life and his work graces the White House, the Vatican and the houses of many discriminating collectors around the world. It is of great artistic importance, but can be enjoyed by anyone wishing to make the long drive up Carnelian Street in Alta Loma.

Sam and Alfreda Maloof Foundation
For Arts and Crafts
PO Box 8397,
5131 Carnelian Street, Alta Loma, CA 91701
(909) 980–0412
Web site: malooffoundation.org

ARROWHEAD SPRINGS

FOR THOSE OF us living in the Mountains, and particularly Big Bearites, our journey down to San Bernardino has been lengthened by about twenty minutes because we have to use Route 18 due to road closures. It has certainly lengthened the drive, but there are some advantages.

Firstly, the view from Rim of the World Highway close to Sky Forest is truly breathtaking. The Empire is spread out some 4,500 feet below, and on clear days there is even the tantalizing glint of the ocean far away to the west.

Lower down the drive, there are two sites that always catch the eye. The natural arrowhead that seems to be carved into the mountainside, although in fact it's a shape made from a change in the fauna. It also fascinated the Serrano Indians who were here before us; they called it "Wanhi."

The second site is definitely man made as it sits below the arrowhead, surrounded by palm tress and is a glimmering white. It is Arrowhead Springs.

The other day as I was about to make the long drive back up the hill, I decided to investigate this place, and found that the premises are not that far from the main road. You are greeted at the entrance by a ten-foot tall Indian in copper pointing the way ahead.

This splendid fellow was sculpted by Joseph Leeland Roop in 1920 and originally pointed the way to the arrowhead landmark, the hot springs and the various facilities that have been in operation since the first spa opened in 1863.

Just after the Indian, I was stopped at a gatehouse and told that I would have to call and make an appointment as the general manager was away for a few days.

I duly came back in a week and was waved through and up an elegant tree lined twisting drive towards the main building.

On arrival, I went into the reception area and it was like going through a time warp back into 1930's Art Deco time. There was no big band music playing but there might well have been as everything about the place reeked of that type of style.

Originally opening on December 16, 1939, Al Jolson and Judy Garland were among the artists performing here at the grand event. It was broadcasted throughout the nation via CBS. This was to be "The Resort" for the Hollywood elite in the days before Palm Springs and Las Vegas took over the role in the coming decades.

The view from the main reception area takes one out over what was originally an arrowhead shaped swimming pool. It's been covered over now and often acts as a setting for weddings.

The interior of the main rooms is pale, and white leather chairs offset the heavy sideboards and other cabinets that were all designed by the famous Dorothy Draper of New York. Any re-upholstering needed these days is done strictly according to that age. A couple of sofas had just returned and looked particularly authentic.

The history of the site has been mixed. It is based around the phenomena of pure water – some of it at 206°F, which makes it the hottest spring of any spa in the world. There have been several attempts to make this a profitable venture. Three earlier hotels burned down before the current one was built. There were also problems making the place viable. Even Baron Hilton had a go and failed.

Eventually in 1962 it was taken over by the Campus Crusade for Christ Inc., who have owned it ever since. Its principle purpose today is to host weddings, meetings and retreats. Sadly, it is not open to the general public, but they are working to make it more available. Which frankly it should be as it is such a gem within our area.

Arrowhead Springs
24600 Arrowhead Springs Road
San Bernardino, CA 92414
(909) 883-0660
www.weddings.arrowheadsprings.org

DEL MAR

ON THIS PAST July 20th, I was once again reminded of my old nemesis, Miss Stewart. She was a small woman with steel colored hair and piercing gray eyes. She always wore a long kilt in her clan's tartan, which was affixed with a big safety pin. As my math teacher, she tried in my second grade to instill in me her way with numbers. It was a disaster, and the subsequent humiliation caused me to try and avoid all contact with arithmetic for the next several decades.

As a result of this handicap, I steered well away from betting, as figuring out the odds was like wearing a blindfold and trying to hit a moving target with a rifle.

Therefore I never had any interest in horse racing and on the 20th of July this year it was the first time I had ever passed through the turnstiles of a grandstand horse race.

For the event I took along She Who Must Be Obeyed (S.W.M.B.O.) as she had in her previous life been something of a rider and certainly knew one end of a racehorse from the other.

July 20th happened to be opening day at the wonderful seaside racecourse of Del Mar, some 20 miles north of San Diego. It is a course that was opened in 1937 by the one and only Bing Crosby, who along with some other Hollywood buddies felt that Southern California needed a place to truly relax.

Last year there was a record crowd of 46,000 and it was hoped that the number would increase this year. "It's not just a horse race," said Craig Dado, the Senior Vice President of Marketing for the Del Mar Thoroughbred Club. "It's also a social gathering; the ladies tend to dress up."

In view of this information, S.W.M.B.O. dived into the closet and appeared with a very nice hat and accompanying dress. It was a wise choice as the event had brought out the very finest females in all their attire. There were thousands of them on show, and every one looked fantastic in hats of every type along with dresses to make the eyes pop.

Del Mar was able to cope with such numbers and even the traffic flowing into the parking lots was well directed and all the staff was incredibly patient with the crowds.

Buried deep in the excitement and the flowing colors, were some horses. It was after all a horse race, and in order to get into the full swing of things, you were supposed to choose one in each of ten races that took place every half an hour.

I had been told that the best photo opportunity was of the paddock, located closely to the rear of the large grandstand and the course itself. Here we could watch the people milling about and also the parade of horses being led out. And what horses they were too.

S.W.M.B.O. was impressed with their condition and rightly so; they gleamed and their muscular bodies showed the care that had been given to them in their training. The jockeys came out and mounted up, and at the sound of the trumpet, they were taken away on their mounts to the starting gate.

At this point we went up into the grandstand and stood along with the crowds to watch the off. Seating is hard to come by and you better wear comfortable shoes – I felt sorry for the young ladies in their four-inch high heels, but appearance is everything here.

Not having ever been to such an event I was totally unprepared for the visceral thrill of the horses coming down the final straight, and also the roar and excitement of the crowds cheering them on. It was electric, even though I didn't have, as they say, a horse in the race. I was cheering too, though for what I had no idea.

S.W.M.B.O. had picked number one which came in second, but a knowledgeable gambler would still have come out ahead and also with the next two that she picked.

As we left the grounds, crowds were still pouring in for later entertainment. I thought once more of my early experience with Miss Stewart and felt that had I never met her, I too could have been caught up in this exciting world. Not so sure it would have been such a good idea though, as the bookies always seem to win.

Del Mar Racecourse.
Racing Wednesday through Sunday.
First race on most days is 2 p.m. On Fridays it is 4 p.m.
(858) 755-1141
Web site: Delmarscene.com

MORMON MUSEUM

WHEN I CAME out to review business opportunities and the lay of the land in 1982, the first city I was taken around was San Diego. On my return from that city I stopped at a call box (do you remember those things?) to phone England and suggest that S. California was definitely where we should relocate. A year later it was San Diego that we chose to visit for our first American vacation; more accurately Mission Bay. It is a wonderful place, and I've always had a very soft spot for the entire area, although I can't bring myself to support the Padres.

Way back then the tallest building in San Diego was the Cortez Center and downtown wasn't much to write home about at all. In fact it was quite small and dingy. Things have certainly changed now with the new gaslight section and also the high rises all around.

The other area of San Diego that I've grown to enjoy over the years is the Old Town. It seems to have expanded as well, and it's possible to find a lot of things to do in this quite compact community. Of course, there are a huge number of restaurants and places to shop, but also some quite fascinating museums.

On a recent trip, I found a museum that I had never noticed before – it's a little away from the normal tracks that tourists take. It is a museum devoted to the Mormon Battalion, and it went through a complete renovation in early 2010.

I have to confess, that I knew little of the battalion although it seems to crop up in several places in San Bernardino County. There is reference to its passing through in the Mojave Narrows Regional Park in Victorville, and going down the fast road from Lake Arrowhead to San Bernardino there is also a Mormon stop. Up here in Big Bear there is a small protected flower called the checkerbloom, which is said to have originated from the feed the Mormons gave to their horses, and it originated in Utah.

So I was very interested to visit this new facility to learn a little about the Mormon Battalion.

The museum is free and it runs regular 30-minute tours through its reconstructed premises. We were shown round by two "Sisters," dressed in traditional clothes. They gave a commentary to accompany some quite effective projected visuals.

The battalion was formed in 1846 at the request of President Polk, who felt that the well disciplined men would assist greatly in the formation of the west and the war against Mexico. He was able to persuade Brigham Young to encourage 500 men and 38 women to march west from their settlement in Fort Leavenworth, Kansas to San Diego; a distance of around 2000 miles.

Carrying 60 pound muskets, which they were told they could keep after their service, the battalion set out across the plains. It was a grueling business in the summer heat and many of them suffered badly from the conditions and poor medicine. Several left the band in Santa Fe and joined the main party in Salt Lake City, but the remainder carried on until they saw the ocean for the first time in Oceanside.

On arrival in the present old town, which was then the center of activities, the Mormons found a society that badly needed help. They set about making a kiln to fire bricks and manufactured 40,000. They dug over twenty wells and used the bricks to line them. They also used the bricks to erect the first fire-bricked building in S. California, which was used as a school and also as a courthouse. On the tour, visitors pause within a replica of this building.

The Church of Jesus Christ of Latter day Saints is a proselytizing religion and there is certainly mention of the "faith" that served the battalion and current members of the church. However it is not overbearing, and after all, the tour and the museum is free.

A visit to this place is certainly worthwhile as it shows another aspect of San Diego, which still remains one of my most favorite cities in the US.

The Mormon Battalion Museum
2510 Juan Street
Old Town San Diego CA 92110
(619) 298-3317
Web site: mormonbattalion.com

WALLY PARKS NHRA MUSEUM

I TRY TO do The Sun's crossword puzzle every day, and in fact I'm not bad at it. But the other day one of the clues came up on a five letter word that had me flummoxed. It was: "famous name in motor racing."

Now this is an activity I have absolutely no involvement in and therefore I knew I was in trouble. Fortunately, I managed a lot of the words that crossed it and eventually the name Unger came up.

I was reminded of my ignorance when I crossed over the threshold of the Wally Parks NHRA museum in Pomona the other day. This is of course part of the world of racing where hot rods are involved.

Even for an ignoramus like me, this is a wonderful place to visit and it must be the Mecca for any enthusiast. It's gleaming and shining, and the amount of car wax put on the exhibits must be sold to the museum in huge quantities, as must be the effort put into applying it.

Once inside you become enmeshed in a world of great passion for those involved, and the stories of all the efforts that have gone into each vehicle is displayed for those wishing to learn. They even have the new QR codes alongside each exhibit so you can download even more information into your smart phones. What will they think of next?

I was particularly interested in a one long dragster that belonged to an Australian, called Roly Leahy. On January, 20th, 2009, he drove his car across the flats attempting to hit 200 miles per hour. It was particularly poignant as he knew he was not going to live for very long. He sadly died three and a half months later.

His attempt showed that he reached 199.70 m.p.h. narrowly missing his goal. But the car was shipped over to the museum and will take part in a second attempt with the brave Australian's ashes in a small compartment behind the crash cage so that Roly will be along for the ride.

During my visit I met up with Tony Thacker, who is the executive director. To my great surprise he suffered from the very same speech impediment as me. He's a Brit! I asked him how he came to be here in this very American place.

"I used to have a paper route in Maidstone, Kent, in England," he said. "One of my customers used to take Hot Rod magazine and I was fascinated with all the brightly colored cars under such blue skies."

We reminisced about the type of cars we used to endure back in England in those days. "Gray cars under gray skies," said Thacker. I couldn't have agreed with him more, remembering the Standard Vanguard, which was the first production car after the war. It was a big old boat, and I can't imagine one ever turning up in a wonderful museum like this.

Even with serious modifications it could never stand next to all the great machines here. I liked the several Chrisman Brothers cars on display with big changes to the original design like the maroon Ford Model A, which old Henry would scarcely recognize.

Currently on display is a special exhibition called 60 Greatest Moments in NHRA History, and at the end is a huge golden statue of Wally Parks himself, who did so much for the sport. He died in 2007, at the age of 94; still involved in all that goes on here.

Of course, now I could have added another word to that crossword puzzle that was five letters long. But in that instance the name of Parks would have been incorrect in the museum that bears his name.

Where: Wally Parks NHRA Motorsports Museum
        1101 McKinley Ave Bldg 3A
        Pomona, CA 91768
Phone: (909) 622-3389
Web site: www.musuem.nhra.com

USS MIDWAY

I SOMETIMES WONDER what life would be like if only men lived on the Earth and there were no women to influence things. This thought occurred to me again when we sailed into San Diego aboard a huge and wonderful cruise ship. It was the ultimate in luxury with a décor designed to relax you, and the services available were there to pamper you in every way. I'm sure it was not built with only females in minds but the influence was there for certain.

A few hundred yards along the wharf was the permanent museum of USS Midway. Now this was almost as large – it was the largest ship afloat when it was launched in 1945 - but what a difference it was in its design. It was a man's invention, and it looked it.

Now granted the Midway was a ship of war, but it also catered to 4,000 crew, a thousand less on board than our cruise ship. That means all the usual things that go on to allow life afloat, such as food, laundry, accommodation, as well as other additional items like guns, ammunition, and planes – lots and lots of planes.

When you enter the Midway you are firstly given a headset with a small controller. It's a very efficient device that allows you to stop and start the recording, and even dial up a particular exhibit as they are all numbered clearly in black with a bright yellow background.

Your entry point is the hangar deck which is huge; it is where the planes are stored prior to any deployment. Here planes are worked on and eventually moved to a massive lift to take them up to the flight deck above. There is also a gift shop and café if you should need some refreshment. Boy, is their coffee strong, even the decaf! If that's an indication of what the boys in blue were given on assignment, I doubt anyone ever slept.

Above the hangar deck is where all the action takes place. If you ever saw the movie Top Gun, in which the USS Midway starred, you will remember the opening where the planes were being launched; a world of steam, noise, excitement and danger. A display on the "island," which is the control tower on the starboard side of the ship, showed the colors of each position: Blue for the Tow Tractor, Red for Bullets, Green for the Catapult, etc.

The catapult is nowhere near as long as I imagined; it is at the front of the ship and only seemed a few feet in length. However it could take an aircraft from zero to 150 mph in just two seconds. The commentary said that you had to hold you head back against the restraining part, or risk losing consciousness. It must be quite a ride.

Before launching, the officer in charge had to estimate the lurch of the ship's bow to gauge the angle, or risk shooting it into the sea.

Of course, once off and going up in the wide blue yonder, pilots had to eventually return. A docent was standing in the middle of the deck in front of what was called "the trap," explaining how this was done. In the beginning of the Midway's career a "batman" stood with two huge paddles to direct the planes back onto the flight deck. Over the years as planes became larger and faster this system was modified to an array of lights to allow pilots to land and catch the arrester wires strung out across the tarmac deck. These wires always struck me as a very crude method, but it works to this day.

The self-guided tour allows you to explore below decks in "the city within a city," which is where the men, and today the women live aboard a carrier. It is complex and cramped if you are over six feet tall, and it is mostly gray. It houses the food lines, the wardrooms and the living quarters; even the chapel and the sick bay. It would be easy to get lost without the arrows to direct you.

As we left the vessel and walked back along to our cruise ship, we could look back and compare the two. There was no doubt which one had been built for men, and with very little help from the distaff side of society.

USS Midway
Broadway Pier,
Downtown San Diego.
(619) 544-9600
www.midway.org

MUSEUM OF DEATH

PERHAPS THE GREATEST advantage large cities have over smaller ones is the enormous amount of diversity they contain; diversity not just of people but of culture, museums and oddities.

I was due to go westward to our large city neighbor the other day and as I was going to take my eighteen year old grandson with me I wanted to find an assignment that might interest him.

Scanning the Web site of "things to do in Los Angeles," I found "The Museum of Death." Bingo! Like most teens he has a certain fascination with the macabre so I was sure that this would fill the bill.

After filling him up with the sort of inappropriate food of which his mother would certainly disapprove, we found the site located, naturally, in Hollywood. Not more than a few blocks from the famous Hollywood and Vine intersection.

The Museum of Death is a compact building and is designed to be walked around in an anti-clockwise direction from the entrance way. Here there is a souvenir shop to purchase items to remind you of your visit.

A small room begins the tour and it introduces you to the subject that is the entire sobering theme of the museum. Next, the first of the interconnecting rooms is devoted to the business of execution. And among the artifacts is a replica of the original "old Sparky."

It is without the electrical bits and pieces as they were attached to the prisoner at the time of his soon to be departure. For those with a special interest in the subject a video is playing showing scenes of early attempts to execute the guilty. Not always successful.

This museum is of course, not for the squeamish and during our wanderings the staff discretely came around to make sure we hadn't over done it. One attendant explained that some people are affected by the displays and become faint. I think they must be far too sensitive to suffer so. But it is a big city!

Next we passed under a banner announcing "We put the fun back in funerals." Here the mortician's art was explained in great detail including that of the embalming process. I had no idea it was so complicated. A video explained the process and on display were the many tools necessary for the job of making Grandma presentable for her final trip.

No museum devoted to the subject would be complete without several portrayals of those engaged in killing off their fellow man. George Bundy, Jeffrey Dahmer, and Charles Manson are all here – or their images at least. A life size cut out of the latter taken in his early manic days leers at you as you pass. Later on complete with his fading swastika tattoo he glares at the camera, no doubt on his way to yet another parole hearing. Fortunately, the authorities have not seen fit to release him to move among us once more.

Another display is devoted to the sects that encouraged their members to leave us prematurely. Heaven's Gate has some of the iron bedsteads with forms under their purple blankets and sneakers peeping out the bottom. Naturally Jim Jones is well represented in this area as well.

One of the greatest mass murderers in history is on show, Hitler; but I couldn't see his companions in such carnage - Stalin and Mao, who certainly did as good a job.

As you exit the final room you pass through a movie theater showing all the ways you can slip your cable and do so in some style. Let's face it none of us is going to escape from here alive so perhaps this is a good place for a little early preparation.

Some of us are a little closer to the experience than others and as we went out into the bright Hollywood sun, I checked to see if my accompanying teenager was any the worse for the experience. He was not and seemed to have enjoyed it all. It is a fascinating place.

Museum of Death
6031, Hollywood Boulevard,
Hollywood, CA 90028
(323) 466-8011
Web site museumofdeath.net

NETHERCUTT MUSEUM 1

"The Duesenberg"

IT'S NOT OFTEN these days that I get to covet something, I'm glad to say. However on a recent assignment I was rather overwhelmed by something even older than me, and in far better shape. It was a 1936 Duesenberg automobile. It was in a prime spot at the Nethercutt Museum in Sylmar.

Originally it had cost $13,750 when it was first rolled out into the world, and today it's anybody's guess what it would cost to buy.

"We're not in the car sales business," said Skip Marketti, the curator of this remarkable collection of vehicles. "We don't talk about their value, they are works of art."

Marketti looks after 260 of the world's greatest cars as well as a lot of other precious items including a private train, which we'll cover in an upcoming column.

But on entering the spacious museum, one is confronted with chrome, and deep polished paintwork that looks like it has never come close to the surface of a road.

But all these beauties run. "We take them all out once a year," Marketti explained. "We change all their fluids, run them for about 20 miles and then put back in special chemicals so that they can stand for another year without gumming up."

There was one very old machine that looked like it could do with some attention but they are going to keep it looking its years. It was a 1907 Westinghouse and its interior showed its carriage heritage; some of the stuffing was showing through. It only added to its charm.

The Nethercutt's made their money in the cosmetic business. Merle Norman was the aunt of J.B. who had lost his parents and came to live in Santa Monica from his original home in South Bend, Indiana.

At the time Merle was making cosmetics in her kitchen and providing her customers directly. Her partnership with her nephew caused the business to grow dramatically.

So too did J.B.'s love of cars, and he began collecting and refurbishing them.

J.B.'s son Jack and his daughter-in-law Helen continue the business and also the love of prestigious motor cars. They regularly win prizes at the Concours d'Elegance, often winning the best in show award.

In the collection there is a magnificent Mercedes Benz from 1938 that was ordered in Italy by an Englishman. He had it fitted for right hand drive, and then war intervened. An American soldier came upon it and had it shipped out here where today it stands in perfect condition in its gleaming black and chrome.

Its original price was $5,000. No one knows if the Englishman got a refund!

Along one wall is a line of Rolls Royce's. They're still making them, although I have to say that for all that the new ones cost, I'd rather have one of the older models. Marketti agreed with me that the ones with the double headlights were the best.

One particular Rolls Royce belonged to an Arab Sheik. It was made in the late fifties and only has 9,000 miles on the clock. Well, the sheikdom may be rich, but it isn't very large.

Rudolph Valentino had a Voisin which he bought new. He had a couple of scrapes in it, but it's all done up now and looks as good as the day he bought it back in 1923.

After spending some quality time at the museum and enjoying the wonderful commentary by Marketti, I couldn't help thinking back to what it must be like to drive that beautiful Duesenberg, or even own it. Well perhaps it's OK to dream; as long as it doesn't reach the coveting stage.

The Nethercutt Museum
15151 Bledsoe St.
Sylmar, CA 91342
(818) 364-6464 Admission Free.
Web site: nethercuttcollection.org
Open Tuesday to Saturday 9:00 a.m. to 4:30 p.m.

NETHERCUTT MUSEUM 2

THE NETHERCUTT COLLECTION encompasses not only the most beautiful cars and a huge array of mechanical instruments and clocks, but outside its halls there is a private train.

Strangely, a few weeks earlier for the very first time I had entered the quiet confines of a private train; it had been the preserve of the general manager of the Santa Fe Railroad until the mid-seventies.

It was a businessman's conveyance used to get him about his territory and to keep an eye on things, but it was pretty luxurious.

The one at the Nethercutt Museum however is pure exorbitance, and wonderful to boot!

Back in 1910 a local millionaire, Lucky Baldwin, the owner of Santa Anita, several hotels and other businesses died. He left his money to among others, his daughter Clara. She received $10 million and for the time that was an absolute fortune.

The lady liked to travel and so she bought a private railroad car and had it decked out as well as could be done back in those days. Fortunately for her there were lots of craftsman who knew how to make such a task possible and the result of their efforts is available twice a day on a guided tour of the conveyance.

Entering the carriage one is immediately surrounded by the warmth of wood. It is Cuban mahogany in fact, and where needed there is marquetry to highlight the depth of the shine. Much of this exquisite work has been refurbished to its original condition as when the museum acquired the carriage it was in a sorry state.

"The candelabras were all hanging down," said Skip Marketti, the curator of the museum. "We had to lift the ceilings too to begin the work." It took three years to complete the transformation.

When she ordered the car she used a very versatile floor plan. It has an observation and dining room combined at the entranceway. Here guests could enjoy their cocktails and watch the disappearing track, or even stand on the platform to enjoy the passing view.

The dining table is laid with a dining set, called California Poppy, in accordance with the fashion of the day of 1912, when the car was delivered.

"It took us a lot of effort to find the set as we had to go all over the country to find the pieces," said Marketti.

The car was ordered from the Pullman Palace Car Company in Chicago; it was called the "California." Every window was decorated with leaded glass throughout, to add to the luxurious feel.

The leaded work however was not continued through to the servants' quarters which were at the forward end. In true upstairs/downstairs fashion there was a distinct dividing line between those who served and those who were waited upon.

The carriage had an en suite owner's bedroom and two guest compartments, for when Ms. Clara wanted company. She was an inveterate traveler and it's believed she visited every state; most likely in this luxurious train.

At the front of the carriage is a Canadian Pacific steam locomotive with all the latest inventions, including a self-stoking mechanism. No need to shovel. It's not quite of the era of the carriage but nonetheless it sets of the entire tour beautifully.

Back in the day, it must have been an imposing sight to enter this world of mahogany, maroon furnishings, gold leaf striping and polished brass.

As with the other parts of the museum, entrance is free.

The Nethercutt Museum
15151 Bledsoe St.
Sylmar, CA 91342
(818) 364-6464
Web site: nethercuttcollection.org
Open Tuesday to Saturday
Admission Free.

THE NETHERCUTT MUSEUM 3

GUIDED TOURS CAN sometimes be a little restrictive, which is why I tend to avoid them. I prefer to wander around museums and galleries on my own and read the information cards of exhibits that interest me, or ask a nearby docent.

However on occasions a guided tour is the only sensible or possible way to go and such was the case with the Nethercutt Collection.

A couple of years ago I had visited the facility in Sylmar to look at the magnificent collection of automobiles, which is by far the finest of its kind I have ever seen. At the back of this museum is a completely restored 1937 Canadian Pacific locomotive and a 1912 private railway carriage. I wrote columns on both of these wonderful exhibits.

But there is a third part of the Nethercutt Museum and it's the one they call The Collection.

The Nethercutt family made their fortune in cosmetics with the Merle Norman brand begun in 1920. With the money earned they invested in automobiles of the highest quality and standard.

Every item in the museum works to the same standard as when it came off the production line. In fact the tour I attended was prefaced with the statement that it contains "functional fine works of art."

All 260 cars in the collection are taken out yearly; their fluids drained afterwards before they're put back on display.

The guided tour begins with a look at the lower salon. Here a 1970's bright orange Lincoln rubs shoulders with some of the earlier types of automobiles that still had the steering wheel in the middle or on the right. We were told that it was 1922 when the US government stepped in and ordered that all steering wheels be located on the left hand side.

351

This was to make passenger safety easier when exiting the vehicle on the sidewalk.

After fifteen minutes or so our guide, who was the chief engineer of the many mechanical devices owned by the foundation, led us up to the Grand Salon. This is truly breathtaking in its scope and size. It looks like a car dealership once found on Wilshire Boulevard in the 1930's. Huge pink marble columns support the gilded roof high above and spotlights bring to life the richness of the paint and chrome of the 30 cars shown here.

At the center of the display of Cadillacs, Renaults, and Packards is a 1933 Duesenberg that was made for the Chicago exhibition of that year. It was the talk of the show due to the magnificence of its silver paintwork and chrome and also its cost of $20,000. At the time an average house in Los Angeles cost $1,500.

During our stay in this opulent room we were serenaded by a performance by George Gershwin, via a piano roll made by him. This was on a full size grand piano halfway up the curved stair case which eventually led us to the other part of the Nethercutt Collection; that of mechanical musical instruments.

The highlight of this section is in the music room, where the Nethercutt's used to entertain guests of a Friday evening.

The large room is lined with European orchestrions and nickelodeons from a hundred years ago. But the true high spot of this closing of the tour is a performance of the Mighty Wurlitzer, which comes up out of the floor and booms out Phantom of the Opera. It is the third largest such organ in the world and its 5,000 pipes will truly amaze you.

As I said earlier I'm not a big fan of guided tours, but this was not only the best I've ever attended, but it's all free!

The Nethercutt Museum and Collection
15151 Bledsoe Street, Sylmar, CA91342
(818) 364–6464
info@nethercuttmsuem.org
Museum self guided tours Tuesday through Saturday 9 to 4:30.

Collection guided tours:

Thursday, Friday & Saturday

10:00am or 1:30pm (only 1 tour available on Thursday & Friday)

ADVANCED RESERVATIONS ONLY

MARITIME MUSEUM

ALONG WHERE THE big cruise ships berth in San Diego is a wonderful place to visit if you have an interest in old ships – furthermore if those old ships still venture out into the ocean.

The Maritime Museum has grown a lot since it began back a decade or so ago.

Then there was just the Star of India to look at, and this is still a wonderful example of a Tall Ship.

It was built on the Isle of Man in 1863 and sailed around the world 21 times before it was sold to the Alaskan Packers Association to help in the transportation of salmon.

Today it still ventures out at least once a year, but tied up along the dockside it looks ready to go at any time with its sails unfurled and moving gently in the wind. It is listed as the oldest three-masted iron hulled ship afloat.

Of the collection of ten ships, perhaps my favourite is the HMS Surprise. Originally called the Rose when it was constructed in 1970, this full scale replica was used in the movie Master and Commander - The Far Side of the World.

It shows what a fighting ship was like in Nelson's Royal Navy at the time of the Napoleonic wars. Below decks is the area where the big guns blasted across the water to attack the enemy. One can only imagine the noise and confusion in these cramped and dangerous conditions. The gun teams slept with their iron weapons and kept them in fighting trim at all times.

The differences in the classes is easily seen within the captain's grand salon at the stern of the ship. Here, the officers in their finery were expected to keep a dignified appearance at all times. Nonetheless hidden in benches and closets, guns were stored waiting to be wheeled out when action was necessary.

Further below is closed off to the public, but that is where the majority of the crew slept in their swinging hammocks.

Out on deck there is a bewildering array of ropes and knots and all the necessary equipment to gain a few extra knots from the sails. Speed was of the greatest necessity when up against "Boney's" fleet.

The Berkeley ferry boat acts as a permanent museum of seafaring things. She was the first steel hulled double ended propeller driven ferryboat to operate on San Francisco Bay and helped to evacuate people from the burning city after the 1906 earthquake.

Sitting quietly alongside the Berkeley is a small launch named the Medea. It was built as a gentleman's luxury boat for a wealthy Scottish landowner, who used it to entertain his friends and to cruise many of the inlets and lochs of the west coast of Scotland.

It was used in WWI by the French as an escort boat, and in the second it was tied up at the mouth of the Thames to become an anchor for a barrage balloon to help protect London from the Luftwaffe.

Having changed ownership several times, it was eventually purchased in 1973 by Paul Whittier an oilman. It was renovated and donated to the Maritime Museum, where it is on permanent display. It is an elegant little boat and on my visit, it was being spruced up for a private sail that evening at sunset. No doubt it appreciated the purpose for which it was originally designed.

Maritime Museum of San Diego
1306 N. Harbor Drive
San Diego, CA 92101
(619) 234-9153
Fax: (619) 234-8345
Web site: sdmaritime.org

UNION STATION

UNION STATION AND I celebrated the same milestone birthdays this year. There has in fairness over the years been a great deal of maintenance on the Grande Dame of Los Angeles architecture. However I expect she'll also last a fair bit longer than me.

I traveled into Los Angeles via the Metrolink the other day and I took the opportunity of looking around this wonderful piece of L.A. history.

It's hard not to imagine what it was like for all those visitors arriving here to this vibrant city over the past decades; people with hopes and dreams of a new life "out west."

Today, the foot traffic is still pretty active and as usual with such places everyone knows where they're going, and trying to get there in a hurry.

The station was designed by a father and son team John and Donald B. Parkinson, and it can't have been easy. The name "union" was intended to show the union of three different railroad companies who were to use the building as a terminus.

These three companies were Southern Railway, Union Pacific and the Atchison, Topeka and the Santa Fe. It was they who wanted a building to reflect the Mission Revival style that would attract visitors to the Spanish heritage of the city.

The architects and the city wanted a building that would fit in with the other styles that were present in the downtown area. The railroad firms won.

It can't have been easy. The magnificent booking hall for instance has a 110 foot long counter and each company oversaw one third of it. The same went for the rest of the building.

The booking hall these days is closed off to the public behind a rope, but its polished floor and unique design are often used in films and adverts.

All the ticket clerks have been replaced with machines that have been designed for ease of use. It would be a great idea however if they devoted one for practice as these things are never that easy on the first go.

The waiting room is one of the most famous of Union's features with a high wooden ceiling; except it isn't wooden. It's actually steel that has been painted and surfaced to look like wood. The chandeliers above weigh some 3000 pounds each so it's comforting to know that the building is seismically safe. The furniture is also the original and its appearance fits in perfectly.

I took a stroll outside into the gardens that are landscaped well, and give a different perspective to the design of the tower. It all has that look of adobe, but it's far too large to allow such a material.

In 2011 the station was bought for $75 million by the Los Angeles County Metropolitan Transportation Authority (Metro) and the new owners have opened up the floor area to a number of new restaurants and retail businesses. No doubt it has increased the flow of people, whose count each day is estimated at 60,000.

People who don't know Los Angeles very well are often fond of saying that the city doesn't have much of a center. Well, anyone who has gone through Union Station and stepped outside and looked around will no doubt argue with that. It's quite a scene of activity; suitable for any major metropolis.

Amtrak/Metrolink
800 North Alameda Street
Los Angeles, California 90012

Metro
801 Vignes Street
Los Angeles, California 90012

VICTORVILLE'S ROUTE 66 MUSEUM

ONE OF THE true joys of returning to the museums and galleries in our area is the revisiting of old friends. Of course, many of the docents and volunteer workers of these small jewels, as well as the management fall into this category, but it's also the inanimate objects that they protect and promote.

Over the years I have become very friendly with many of these works of art and artefacts and I look forward to catching up with them whenever I walk through the doors.

This was the case when I went along to the Route 66 Museum in Victorville the other day. As soon as I crossed the threshold there was one of these items I was so pleased to see again. It was a bright blue and white "Teardrop" camper that had been at the museum on the last couple of times I had been there.

It is in immaculate condition and opened up so that visitors can see the neat inside which can sleep two people comfortably as well as hold clothes and the other things necessary for a successful camping trip. Also the galley area at the back was on full display with blue and white matching dinnerware laid out ready to receive whatever the campers were to serve. There is a small stove inset into the body of the trailer at the narrow end.

I asked Chick Kirk a past president of the organisation if it was still on loan. "Well, we managed to raise enough money to actually buy it," she said. I was very pleased as that way I can revisit it at any time in the future if I might want.

There has been a lot more put on show at this small but crowded piece of history since I was there last. It has a lot of stuff for any enthusiast to enjoy as well as the casual visitor. You won't be disappointed.

As I made my way over to the second room which holds another old friend I stopped at a new display featuring the exploits of a George Air Force base officer, called Mark Ward, who lived locally.

His helmet was on show together with several articles about the base. "Tennessee Ernie Ford was a bombardier there," Kirk told me.

Although it's not strictly a Route 66 place, the museum seems to have spread out its interests to include local history, which maks it all the more fascinating.

On our short tour, we passed a couple of high tech items – well high tech in the 40's! Washing machines were in their infant days back then and these two do look their age.

Nothing seems to age as quickly as technology, but at the time I am sure some housewife must have been thrilled to welcome either of these labor saving devices into her home. It was the late fifties before my own mother got her hands on one.

Finally I went to see the other item I wanted to revisit. It is a 1917 Model T truck. It is on loan from the La Barge family and has not been "done up." It is in the same condition in which it arrived from the mid-west back in the early days of the Mother Road.

It is very basic, but once again at the time, I am sure it was the proud possession of the people who bought it.

One can only imagine the discomfort of travelling the 2,500 odd miles to a new life here in the west.

Wandering around such thoughts are bound to occur, and that of course, is one of the many happy moments you can enjoy in such wonderful places.

California Route 66 Museum
Between 5th and 6th Streets
On South D Street (16825)
Victorville CA 92395
(760) 951-0436
cart66musm@gmail.com
route66merchandise.com
Open Thursday – Monday 10 to 4 p.m.
Sunday 11 to 3 p.m.

PEGGY SUE'S DINER

EVERY SUMMER MY son and I take a road trip on motorcycles. We've been up to the Canadian border, into Oregon and explored the High Sierras on a couple of occasions.

We consider ourselves quite the road warriors and have learned some of the tricks of the trade on our travels.

One of these is to gas up early, and gas up often! We learned this once we got out onto the wide open spaces where we found that America is changing a great deal.

To begin with we would often look at our map and decide that the next small town would make an ideal stop for gas and perhaps a sandwich, only to find that there was no gas station, no small café and in a lot of cases no town at all.

With the urbanisation of the country, people no longer can make a living in these small out of the way places and so for the traveller on the empty highways who would prefer not to use the Interstates, you can go a long time with little human contact.

Location of a business is therefore all the more important and if you can set it down near to a busy Interstate and not on one of the empty highways you have a chance to be successful.

Such has been the story of Peggy Sue's Diner, just off the 15 Freeway to the north of Barstow.

Technically it doesn't sit on the freeway, just a few blocks to the south of it, but everyone knows it's there and it's always busy. It's the sort of place my son and I dream of on our travels; but we rarely find.

Another secret to the success of this place is that it seems a lot more intimate than its actual size shows. As you enter the front door a large

Betty Boop mannequin welcomes you, then there is the counter and a smallish dining room with about twenty tables.

I've been coming here for years and until the other day, I had always managed to sit in this area, and believed that was all there was; but there is another bigger dining room further in to the establishment and then another and yet another still.

"We can sit about 300," said Sarah Loehr, the manager who kindly gave me some time on my last visit. And it was eye-opening. "We have a park outside too," she added.

Peggy Sue's was a diner from 1957, but the current owners, Champ and Peggy Sue Gabler bought the original place in 1987 and brought with them their large collection of fifties movie and music memorabilia.

The menu reflects the theme with sandwiches named after the stars of the day – check out the Frankie Avalon Philadelphia cheese steak.

The background music is carefully chosen so that if the 50's isn't your favorite, it's not intrusive but if you hear something that sets your toe tapping, then you can hear it quite easily.

Loehr took me outside to the dinosaur park, and on the way we passed through a full size pizza parlor in full swing. "We make all our dough freshly," she said. "And we also cook and cut all our own meats for the sandwiches. We bread our chicken breasts too."

The park is the ideal place to stretch your legs if you want a break from the long drive from Las Vegas. And if you fancy some fifties candy to help you on your way, then a call into the shop will certainly provide whatever you need.

America used to have so many of these types of places – although perhaps not a large as Peggy Sue's but they seem to be fast disappearing. So next time you get the urge for a look back in time to a different era, then make the stop here in Yermo.

Peggy Sue's 50's Diner and Dinosaur Park.
35654 West Yermo Road, Yermo, CA 92398
Phone:(760) 254-3370
Hours: 6:00 am – 10:00 pm

THE GAMBLE HOUSE

The Gamble House in Pasadena

THERE ARE TWO rumors that have to be put right about the Gamble House in Pasadena. Firstly in spite of what you may hear, nails and screws were used in its construction, although you will be at pains to spot any; and secondly, you can't play poker or blackjack there – it's not a gambling house.

The house's name refers to the original owners, the Gamble's of Proctor and Gamble fame.

It was built as a winter home for the family who lived full time in Cincinnati where the climate was not so benign. Mrs. Gamble had weak lungs and so Pasadena's weather was ideal for her.

The house is a wonderful example of what is known as the Arts and Crafts movement. It uses 16 different types of wood in its construction and also has touches of Japanese styling. However the overall effect is one of opulence and luxury although it's not overbearing.

Entering the main hallway which is extremely spacious, you are struck by the rather subdued lighting. I was shown around by Dorena Kneppler, the director of the building and she explained that they only use 40 watt lighting which is in keeping with the bulbs of the day.

Even though the effect is of dimness it is not a depressing feeling, but rather adds to the overall warmth of the building.

The two architects, Charles and Henry Greene paid great attention to detail and the wood panels that line the rooms are rich and inviting. All the wooden furniture was also designed by them. Therefore you feel as if there is a general systematic flow to the house.

Domestic comfort has changed quite a lot since the house was finished in 1909, but it reminded me of many well-to-do houses back in the UK that I visited in my childhood in the fifties.

The kitchen is full of windows, and although Mrs. Gamble didn't cook she oversaw a design that many today would be comfortable in.

In the pantry the bottom draws were constructed to take table clothes on rollers. The idea was to dry them after laundering so there would be no creases. Apparently it was unacceptable to have such lines across a finely laid table.

The architects were from out of town as well as the owners. They had started with degrees from MIT, and then moved to Chicago where they experienced the effects of a financial depression in 1893. They decided to move on and ended up in California.

Construction began in 1908, which was two years after the great San Francisco earthquake, so it has been safely built from that standpoint.

The house eventually became a full time dwelling for David and Mary Gamble until their deaths in 1923 and 1929, respectively. A sister then lived in the house until her death in 1943.

A grandson, Cecil Huggins Gamble and his wife lived in the house beginning in 1946. They considered selling it until they found out that some potential new owners were considering painting the unique wooden exterior white.

In 1966, Cecil and Louise Gamble turned the house over to the city of Pasadena in a joint agreement with the University of Southern California School of Architecture.

The City is responsible for the outside and USC cares for the interior. The system seems to work very well and it has preserved this remarkable home.

The Gamble House was declared a National Historic Landmark in 1977.

4 Westmoreland Place,
Pasadena CA 91103 Phone: 626-793-3334
Westmoreland Place is a short, private street that runs parallel to the 300 N. block of Orange Grove between Walnut and Rosemont.

Web site: gamblehs@usc.edu

POMONA MEDICAL MUSEUM

LIKE MOST PEOPLE I get emails that often complain that life is not as good as it used to be. These types of circulars are often amusing and remind us of life back a few decades ago. They imply that we're not as well off today as we think we are.

Whereas these memories prompt fond feelings for the past there is one area that never gets the rose colored application and that is medicine.

Even a short walk around the Southern California Medical Museum newly located in downtown Pomona will remind you that when it came to treating illnesses, things were not that much fun back in the old days.

The museum is under the direction of Dr. Hans Davidson, who has taken many of the exhibits that used to be on show in its original home in Riverside. I recognised immediately the office that belonged to Dr. Julius Simon, once in Beverly Hills. It has gone from there to Riverside and now resides in Pomona complete with equipment from the time he practiced in the 1930's. It looks very antiquated, as does the dentist's chair complete with the pulley system drill.

I remember being under the care of such dentistry before the high speed drills came in. It was rather unpleasant.

Dr. Davidson took me around the museum and pointed out some of his favourite artefacts – he has added many of his own to the collection. "I'm an unashamed collector of all types of things," he said. He also runs a museum devoted to plastic in the Dutch town of Zwolle.

We stopped by a case devoted to hearing aids. There were the very first types which were animal horns that amplified sound when the narrow end of the horn was inserted into the ear. The technology progressed through large battery types up to the microscopic ones that are worn today.

One cabinet displays a selection of medicine bottles. "The poisonous medicines were originally produced in blue or green bottles," Davison explained. "But they also had ridges on them to help in dark conditions or for the blind." He then explained that children were attracted to the colors and so eventually plain glass was use, but the ridges remained. "They're really works of art," he continued. "Especially if you compare them to a modern plastic container."

One unique bottle on display is for "Prescription Kentucky Whiskey," which could be prescribed by a doctor during prohibition days.

Perhaps Davidson's favourite exhibit is the one showing off a variety of feeding spoons for the sick. Many of them are Sterling silver and the dates range from the 1700's to the early 20th century.

We spent some time looking at the display of what can only be described as "quackery." Inventions that were designed to fool people into thinking they could cure them of whatever ailed them.

Such a device was a form of horse collar that went around the waist. It had copper wires in it and an electrical current lit up various lights. "It was marketed by a firm called Ionaco, which means I own a company," Davidson said with a smile.

One other machine was a series of switches that were turned in order to read the radio waves that you transmitted. Then other switches were rotated in order to correct your radio emissions; very elaborate and of course, quite useless.

One is bound to wonder in this interesting place how many of today's medical practices will end up here for future generations to consider.

The Medical Museum is located in the Western University of Health Sciences
350, South Gary Avenue,
Pomona, CA 91766
(909) 273-6000
Web site: socalmedicalmuseum.org
Hours: Friday and Saturday 1 p.m. to 5 p.m.
Second Saturday in the month 1 p.m. to 9 p.m.

SAN BERNARDINO 66ERS

IT'S BEEN A few years since I went along to see the Inland Empire 66ers play minor league baseball. It was an evening game – most of them are – and as usual it was a lot of fun. On my recent visit however, it was during the day, the stadium was empty and I was there to meet Adam Franey, who looks after the marketing for the team.

To compensate for the lack of action, Franey set up the interview in the best sky box they had. I'd never been in one of those before and I was interested to see what it was like.

Located over the top of home plate the view was spectacular and the accommodation was luxurious. It costs $885 to rent this box during a game, which might seem expensive, but it does cater for 21 people. At just over $42 each, and considering the luxury, it's no doubt a very good value if you want to entertain a large group of people. Servers are on hand and there's a fine bar just outside the door if you don't want to wait.

Minor league baseball is a different experience to the majors. I was told some years ago that not having to guard expensive contracts, the players tend to go all out for every play that they can make. Perhaps they are also hungry for attention too as the next stage up the competitive ladder is just another statistic away.

The San Manuel Stadium is a fine place to enjoy a game. It seats 5,000 people and with grassy areas and other spaces, it can reach 8,000 for full capacity. That happens every July 4th for the game and the firework show.

"It's all about entertainment," Franey said. "It's fun for the entire family." It's also wonderful value. On Tuesday and Friday it costs $2.50 to get in and a hot dog will only set you back $0.50.

They also have theme evenings. A recent Zombie Apocalypse brought in a full crowd and there was a lively auction for the team's jerseys with all the proceeds going to charity. On the night of the interview they were preparing for a Big Labowski theme night which promised to be a lot of fun.

The season officially ends on September 7th, but the last home game is on September 4th so there's not a lot of time left. The 66ers are doing pretty well however and they might well extend the season with post season play. There are ten teams in the southern California League, which reaches up to the Stockton area. Three from the north and three from the south will battle it out for the championship.

Since 2011, the 66ers have been an Angel team. The last time I went they were Dodgers, I think. Franey told me that the major teams contract with the facility, and the Angels are very happy with the current arrangement and have already extended their current agreement.

As was explained to me all teams look for excellent facilities and the 66ers certainly have those. The ground is fresh and green, the seats first rate, and there's plenty of parking. It's a fine place to spend a couple of hours watching the national pastime, even if it's not in the sky box high above.

Inland Empire 66ers
280 South E Street
San Bernardino, CA 92401
909-888-9922

Web site: IE66ers.com

PATTON STATE HOSPITAL MUSEUM

A READER WROTE to me the other day that he had been to visit a small museum in the Patton State Hospital and had found the experience very interesting. He recommended that I should go along myself.

I duly tracked the place down and after some coordination joined the 1:00 p.m. Sunday tour of the small facility.

Patton State Hospital Museum

When it opened in 1893, the hospital was termed the California State Asylum for the Insane and Inebriates. A rather formidable title, and one that has slowly changed over the last hundred years, in keeping with the improvements in the treatment of mental illnesses.

At its peak and just before the deinstitutionalization of such facilities in the 1970's, Patton, as everyone knows it, had 5600 patients in its care. Today the number is close to 1500 with 2000 staff to look after them.

The museum opened in April this year and is an all volunteer site; the guide for my tour worked in the hospital and was very knowledgeable and enthusiastic about his work.

The tour began with a look at the history of Patton with an interesting fact that it is its own city with its own zip code. It was originally 668 acres although it is about half that area today.

It was set up by Quakers and many of those principals helped in its early establishment. For instance, it was believed that beautiful surroundings and gardens would assist those in mental distress with a faster return to normality.

As a result in those early days, people would flock to the grounds with their families to enjoy the views – Patton was erected on a high part of the county. Often they would picnic there, and a small collection of picture postcards is on display to show the scenes that were sent off via the mail service.

Being a large employer of San Bernardino labor, several generations of families have worked at the facility and there is an atmosphere of genuine care and understanding.

Patton is one of seven state hospitals that care for those suffering from a variety of mental disorders. Ninety-two percent of the patients are there because of forensic reasons. In other words they have been sent there by the courts for a variety of offences. They might be deemed to be incompetent to stand trial, or crimes were committed while in a state of mental illness.

The original building by the architect Kirkbride has long been torn down, but it was constructed specifically for the purpose of housing people with mental conditions. A series of tunnels ran underneath it and a small train was used to deliver all the food necessary to provide three meals a day.

The tour of the half dozen rooms eventually entered one that dealt with the difficult subject of treatments used over the ages. Psychiatry is a very modern science and some of the cures today may seem excessively harsh. But times have changed and no longer is the straightjacket used at Patton, and electrical convulsive treatment (ECT) and lobotomies are no longer a part of their syllabus.

When Patton was opened there was a great deal of curiosity about those labeled "insane." Much of the fear and guilt associated with such conditions have disappeared, but for any remaining, this is an excellent place to see how such problems are dealt with today.

To arrange a visit it is necessary to go to the Web site which will appear if you enter Patton State Hospital in the message box, then select the "contact us" label and request a time and date. They will return your request in about a week.

Patton State Hospital
3102 E. Highland Ave.
Patton, CA 92369

INDEX

Printed in the United States
By Bookmasters